NEW IMAGES OF THE NATURAL
IN FRANCE

NEW IMAGES OF THE NATURAL IN FRANCE

A Study in European Cultural History
1750–1800

D. G. CHARLTON

Professor of French in the University of Warwick

THE GIFFORD LECTURES
IN THE UNIVERSITY OF ST ANDREWS
1982–1983

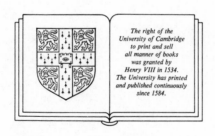

The right of the
University of Cambridge
to print and sell
all manner of books
was granted by
Henry VIII in 1534.
The University has printed
and published continuously
since 1584.

CAMBRIDGE UNIVERSITY PRESS
Cambridge
London   New York   New Rochelle
Melbourne   Sydney

Published by the Press Syndicate of the University of Cambridge
The Pitt Building, Trumpington Street, Cambridge CB2 1RP
32 East 57th Street, New York, NY 10022, USA
296 Beaconsfield Parade, Middle Park, Melbourne 3206, Australia

First published 1984

Printed in Great Britain by the University Press, Cambridge

Library of Congress catalogue card number: 84-45441

British Library Cataloguing in Publication Data
Charlton, D. G.
New images of the natural in France.
1. France – Civilization – 17th–18th centuries
I. Title
944'.03   DC33.4
ISBN 0 521 24940 6 hard covers
ISBN 0 521 27090 1 paperback

CONTENTS

PREFACE

The original intention of this study was to provide a survey and an evaluation of a particularly distinctive movement of sensibility and outlook in the later-eighteenth century for students and other readers with a specific interest in French culture and thought. I hope it still serves that purpose and will help them to situate particular works of literature, art, ideas and history within a context that gives them added significance over and beyond their intrinsic interest and qualities. My early work quickly led me, however, to realise that developments in France could only be adequately appreciated within a far broader European setting, that national cultural history is forced, finally, to become international and comparative, if only for reasons mentioned in chapter 10. It was at that stage that I was honoured by the invitation of the University of St Andrews to deliver the Gifford Lectures for 1982–3, and this led me even more firmly and of necessity towards an aim which I already believed the subject required: to treat of the particular case of France as one instance of something far more general (whence my sub-title). Anyone who feels in danger of what is too often castigated as 'narrow' specialisation will find it a helpful exercise to talk, each week over a period, to an audience ranging from historians, philosophers, theologians, geographers and natural scientists to specialists in the history of literature, art, music and landscape-architecture in several different countries – and, at the same time, to respect Lord Gifford's wish that the Lectures should be 'public and popular'. Happily, it suited my book, in both senses, and I am most grateful to my listeners in St Andrews for the collective stimulus and individual responses which so much helped me towards completion.

The outcome, all the same, as I am all too conscious, is an

attempt at cultural history viewed through a telescope and not, which may often be the more rewarding, through a microscope, by means of close commentary upon individual cultural phenomena or artefacts. Here that awareness is reflected in only one respect, which should be mentioned: a deliberate limiting of my illustrations even as regards France but especially so for England and Germany. In a work that has so much else to describe, it was only by recurring reference to the same few works that I could hope briefly to suggest how far even a single poem or short novel – or a garden or a painting – may speak to us of a whole culture, as may also attitudes to particular elements in our lives such as to children or to death. I am confident, however, that readers will easily supply their own further examples and substitutions: Goethe for Rousseau, Haller for Gray, Reynolds for Greuze, English or German gardens for those at Ermenonville and Versailles, and many others.

I have contracted numerous debts which I am glad to be able to acknowledge here. I am grateful to the University of St Andrews for its invitation – and all the more so since it was made (thanks, finally, to the admirably eclectic definition of natural theology given by Lord Gifford himself when establishing his Lectures in 1885) to one who, unlike almost all his predecessors, is neither philosopher nor theologian – and for its kindly arrangements for my periods there, and I am especially grateful to numerous of its members for their most friendly and generous welcome. I am thankful too to my own University for its grant of leave to allow me to prepare the lectures and then to revise and somewhat expand them for this book. I am particularly happy to express my warm thanks for the direct, personal help I have received: to Professor A. H. T. Levi for his timely encouragement; to Mr Roland M. Renyi, formerly of Warwick's Graduate School of European Cultural History, to whose own work, under but transcending my supervision, parts of chapter 9 are indebted; and, most especially, to Dr A. M. C. Brown (of the Cambridge University Press), Professor Garnet Rees and Professor S. S. B. Taylor, all of whom have most usefully read and commented on my manuscript at various stages. Above all I am greatly indebted, in what is explicitly attempting to be a work of synthesis, to the many scholars whose own studies I have drawn upon (and not, I very much hope, mis-represented). The bibliographical essays I have added are designed for readers wishing to pursue specific subjects further, but they, and the notes also, may serve to make some acknowledgement of all that this book owes to the researches of others. The faults that no doubt remain, despite all those debts, are my own work, as are any contentious interpretations – though as to those one may draw courage from words of Lord Gifford himself: 'I am persuaded that nothing but good can result from free discussion.'

This book is dedicated, with most affectionate gratitude, to my wife and the three other members of our version of 'the happy family' as discussed in chapters 7 and 8. Without Kate, Nicholas and Jane it might never have been started, for it was their respect for 'the natural' in several of its present-day expressions and commitments that renewed my interest in some of their eighteenth-century predecessors. Without Thelma and her constant encouragement, help and forbearance it would – even more importantly – never have been finished.

D. G. CHARLTON

University of Warwick
December 1983

CONTRASTS

Men in all ages have been preoccupied and challenged by nature, obviously enough – living in it, part of it, dependent on it for basic survival, pleased and threatened alike by it. In all ages, therefore, men have expressed their understanding and attitudes about it, most notably in their religions and philosophies but in many other ways as well. Primitive worship of natural elements like fire, water and the sun; polytheistic ideas that particular gods lie behind and direct the vital phenomena of nature; the belief of many of the Ancients (in marked contrast to the Christian view) that nature was uncreated, had permanently existed in the past and would persist eternally in the future; the pantheistic reverence for a world felt to be in some sense 'divine'; the claim of others that nature is wholly material and determined only by blind chance: these are just a few instances of men's responses over the centuries and from culture to culture. Partly these responses relate to what is believed to *be* natural, though that is certainly not just a matter of new knowledge. Partly they relate to people's sense of their relationship to the natural, whether they feel affinity and approval or separation and distrust. Nature itself may have remained relatively the same within the life-time of mankind, but mankind's views about nature have often changed distinctively. Confirmation of that fact, if one needs it, is readily found in such major general studies as Clarence Glacken's *Traces on the Rhodian Shore*, with its sub-title, 'Nature and Culture in Western Thought from ancient times to the end of the eighteenth century', or Robert Lenoble's *Histoire de l'idée de nature*.

This book relates to one particularly striking European example of such a change, especially relevant to us, moreover, since one could well argue that it is still in process today. Over the past two to three centuries, in Europe at least, many people have gradually come to think about and react towards the natural world around them in a much modified way compared with their ancestors, and similarly in relation to 'the natural' in general, within man himself as well as outside him. The fresh perceptions and sympathies have in part been expressed in new intellectual theories – in philosophy, theology, political theory, aesthetics, and so on – but they have also markedly affected our responses regarding many other elements of our lives – on matters as diverse as the scenery and the gardens we like, our attitudes towards animals and even towards death and burial, our views on women, children, family life and good reasons for marriage, and numerous others. This study will try to evoke the first clear emergence, over 200 years ago, of the revised vision and evaluation of nature that have been involved – the beginnings, amongst only a minority, of what would become a major element in nineteenth-century 'Romanticism' and has now become a much more widely-shared re-appraisal of the natural, not least amongst today's younger generation, even compared (say) with their grandparents in *their* youth.

The eighteenth century was at many intellectual cross-roads, but never more so than in its controversies and uncertainties as to what nature is 'really like', what is 'really natural', what answers to it all are most appropriate on questions both general and detailed. The subject is vast and complex; this examination can only make representative 'soundings' in a veritable ocean of cross-currents, and even so will be drawing on a wealth of scholarship by others. One considerable delimitation has been consciously adopted, however, to make the topic manageable: a concentration mainly on France as one representative country and culture. Even so reference will fairly often be made to evidence from other countries, England and Germany in particular, partly to stress the undoubted European dimension of the whole subject, partly to clarify French developments, partly for comparative reasons.

Before coming to the eighteenth century one obviously needs to consider what preceded it, and the essential starting-point is found in the traditional Christian teaching over the previous centuries. That teaching involved a quite explicit ambivalence of view. On the one hand, for the Christian 'the Heavens declare the glory of the Lord'; Nature reveals God's goodness and His caring love. He has set our Earth at the centre of His Creation and fashioned it for man, the crown and true purpose of His creative act: the stars shine in their spheres for man's delectation; the plants and animals are for man's food, service and pleasure. Yet, on the other hand, the Christian doctrine interprets the world as a 'fallen creation', itself fallen into corruption as a consequence of the 'Fall' of man himself. To give one minor example of this amongst many – one that still preoccupied earlier-eighteenth-century writers like Louis Racine and the Abbé Pluche – why do we suffer a tiresome climatic alternation between summer heat and winter cold? A common answer to this puzzle was that the Flood, sent by God as punishment for human sin, caused the polar axis to tilt from its original vertical alignment to the oblique – whence followed the present alternation of the seasons in contrast to the permanent spring-like climate of the pre-diluvian period. (It is perhaps ungenerous to this ingenious explanation to note that the climate was only spring-like for the temperate zones these writers knew, as opposed to the tropics sweltering in endless heat and the polar regions in endless cold and night of which they knew little and possibly cared less.)

The natural world is not only 'fallen' in this long-standing Christian view, however. Above all it is irrelevant to man in the long run. It may even come to its total end at any time. Predictions of an imminent Day of Judgement were commonplace for centuries, and what they reflected was the assumption that man's essential destiny lies in a life-to-come. Salvation to eternal life, not happiness within this natural world, is man's final end; nature is a mere background, a transitory setting for an essentially spiritual quest. The world is little more than a vale of tears, whose sufferings may help to purge us of our sins and may even be recompensed in the heavenly life; it is, finally, dispensable. Whereas for many Ancients man was *a part of* nature, for Christians he is *apart from* nature. It is true that the

New images of the natural

Christian faith retains a belief that, with the Apocalypse, the world of nature will be redeemed – like man himself – and the lion will lie down with the lamb, but by then man himself will be elsewhere, before the judgement-seat of God.

This is inevitably to simplify the Christian teaching. Theologians have constantly differed as to just how deeply the corruption of man and the world has gone. For Aquinas, for instance, grace completes the natural and can work through it rather than conflicting with it, and to this day the Roman Church in particular retains the notion of 'sins against nature' – against, that is, nature uncorrupted by the Fall. All the same, for all Christians man himself was under the blight of 'original sin' and the world around him was not only 'fallen' – to whatever extent – but was in the last resort spiritually irrelevant. The predominant outlook of these earlier centuries can be well captured by a quotation from the *Book of Common Prayer*, and this illustration is not chosen randomly. One may well think that hymn-books and (where church services were in the vernacular) works of prayers and offices may offer especially valuable evidence to the intellectual and cultural historian. Whereas the literature, art, and so on of so-called 'high culture' speak only of the preferences of a limited class, these religious works not only tell us of the theological and moral understanding of the educated men who wrote them but have also exerted an immense influence on the humbler church-goer, repeated by or to him from week to week and year to year. Here, therefore, to sum up the long-prevailing assumptions, are words from the *Order for the Burial of the Dead*:

Man that is born of a woman hath but a short time to live, and is full of misery. He cometh up, and is cut down, like a flower; he fleeth as it were a shadow...[And after the committal] We give thee hearty thanks, for that it hath pleased thee to deliver this our brother out of the miseries of this sinful world...

This stress upon 'the miseries of this sinful world' was particularly strong in the Protestant Reformers and Puritans of the sixteenth and seventeenth centuries and in some of the Counter-Reformation Catholic theologians (notably, the Jansenists) also: the natural is so corrupt that grace comes direct

4

from God, by-passing the natural. The Middle Ages had perhaps achieved in some ways a more relaxed attitude – reflected, one could argue, in that element of earthy gusto found in some medieval literature and art. Certain writers of the period of the Renaissance and beyond (especially those affected by the Ancients) affirmed even more the joys of living in this world and the potentialities of human nature. One thinks of Petrarch, as early as the fourteenth century, living and loving by the wooded gorge of the Fontaine de Vaucluse and enjoying climbing the Mont Ventoux; of Ronsard's feeling for 'Nature, bonne mère'; of Montaigne in his garden amidst 'notre mère Nature'; of Théophile de Viau's nature poetry a little later; and of La Fontaine still later – all of them responding to nature with sympathy and pleasure. Nor do they in general accept the view of Calvin or Luther that natural man is 'depraved' and without personal merit. Erasmus; Rabelais, claiming that men who are well-born and well-bred 'have by nature an instinct and spur that impels them to virtuous acts'; and Montaigne, at least when he writes on cannibals or the rearing of children: these are especially noteworthy examples of the Renaissance's anticipation of the new attitudes towards natural man which we shall observe in the eighteenth century, and at that time they would even be invoked as precursors. Yet these humanists were exceptional in their time – and also, one could argue, not always wholly orthodox in relation to the Christianity of their age. The far more pervasive view of man even in seventeenth-century France – despite exceptions like the 'libertins' or Molière, who were likewise not orthodox – is that expressed by Jansenists such as Arnauld, Nicole and Pascal, by Bossuet as he thundered against the sins of the Versailles court, by Racine depictin3 his Phèdre in the grip of irresistible sin, even – at the very end of the century – by a doubter like Pierre Bayle as he stressed the evil in man. For all of them – and for Corneille, Mme de La Fayette, La Rochefoucauld and others too – natural human impulses were to be distrusted, controlled if possible, even defeated; only a few heterodox writers like Molière appealed to such 'natural' instincts as love between the young as opposed to arranged marriage. As to the world of external nature, Frenchmen by the seventeenth century were rather more responsive than previously – both in liking, if upper-class, to withdraw occasionally to a country retreat and also in some of their aesthetic preferences: for the nature descriptions of *L'Astrée*, for instance, or of various poets, for the new landscape paintings of Claude and Poussin, for enlarged gardens around their properties. Yet such sympathies appear to have been limited and conditional. Even in the *later*-seventeenth century the gardens were ordered and controlled in the manner of Le Nôtre's Versailles, and the painted landscapes were 'ideal' and were always peopled. In the greatest of Classicist literature, moreover, outside nature had little place; the attention of Corneille, Racine or Mme de La Fayette was concentrated on man, living out an essentially mental drama against a largely featureless backcloth, with little or no place even for physical action.

Such is the contrasting background for the new appreciations, but lest so rapid a sketch may mislead, a further point of some importance should be added. The whole transformation under discussion has often – even usually – been interpreted as a replacement of a supernaturalist by a naturalistic view, as a manifestation and a product of the decline of Christian belief in modern Europe. Jean Ehrard, for example – the most authoritative of scholars of the eighteenth-century 'idea of nature' – describes it as 'a pagan idea' on various grounds: its determinism excludes belief in Providence; its claim that nature is good ignores the doctrine of the Fall; it has served from the days of early Christianity as 'a ferment of irreligion and heterodoxy'.[1] Similarly, Simone Goyard-Fabre, in her study of *La Philosophie des lumières en France*, concludes – as have numerous other students of the Enlightenment – that this idea was a 'powerful catalyst' in an age that was 'fundamentally anti-Christian'.[2] A far less clear-cut alignment will be suggested by this present study. Such claims as theirs may be true in regard to much of the century's abstract theorising. Undoubtedly, thinkers like Diderot, d'Holbach and Helvétius embraced 'the natural' in reaction against Christianity, and one can readily agree with Ehrard that for them the idea of nature was 'the favoured instrument for the secularisation of morality'.[3] But far more people in the eighteenth century retained their religious faith and absorbed many of the new attitudes into their ultimately supernaturalist beliefs – and that is true whether one thinks they were right or wrong in doing so. The changes of view ran more deeply than even the contrasts of atheism and Christian conviction, surprising though that may seem. The new perceptions modified alike the philosophy of the un-believers and the interpretations of Christian teaching that were developed by some at least of the believers, as will become evident from time to time in later chapters.

However that may be, eighteenth-century thought was obviously dominated – some would say bedevilled – by, in the first place, the *idea* of nature in many theoretical forms. It was undoubtedly 'the governing idea of the age of the Enlighten-ment', as Ehrard says,[4] and for England it was no less justifiable for Basil Willey, for example, to give his survey of *The Eighteenth-Century Background* the sub-title 'Studies on the Idea of Nature'. Notions of natural religion, natural morality, natural man, natural society, and natural law – the first Chair of Natural Law in Paris was established in 1771 in the Collège de France – were endlessly elaborated and discussed. Yet there is certainly no need to add to the many studies of the Enlightenment which deal with such ideas of the natural in these more abstract, generalised meanings. Little will thus be said about a mass of theoretical works in the eighteenth century – Morelly's *Code de la nature*, Diderot's *Pensées sur l'interprétation de la nature*, Delisle de Sales's *Philosophie de la nature*, d'Holbach's *Système de la nature*, and numerous others in France alone. Interest here lies elsewhere – and somewhat closer to another feature of the eighteenth-century scene, especially, as regards France, in its later half: namely, the rise of a new 'feeling for nature', as it has often been called. For France the great work by Daniel Mornet on *Le Sentiment de la nature en France de J.-J. Rousseau à Bernardin de Saint-Pierre* remains basic after over seventy years, and other books – by Charlier, Van Tieghem, Dédéyan, and others – have filled out the picture. Some have

seen this 'sentiment de la nature' as complementing in the later
part of the century the 'idée de nature' earlier; others have seen
them as antithetical and interpreted the new 'feeling' as a
reaction against the abstractness of the 'idea' – as, in Lenoble's
words, 'a violent reaction of affectivity'.[5] But, whatever the
truth as to that, this whole late-eighteenth-century movement
seems to call for further examination, notwithstanding the
studies by Mornet and others. It is not only that all of them
(unlike the books by Ehrard and others on the idea of nature)
are now inevitably somewhat dated, despite their continuing
helpfulness. In the first place they concentrated almost wholly
on new appreciations of *external* nature alone, and secondly and
above all their stress on 'feeling' for nature seems to be
somewhat restrictive, if not even to rest on a mistaken
polarisation of 'reason' and 'emotion'. And thirdly, a great deal
of scholarship over the past twenty years and more has opened
up or re-examined aspects of the whole subject to an extent that
calls now for fresh assessment.

   It must shortly be said what is intended by the term 'images'
in this book's title. One need not define 'the natural', however.
This is, clearly enough, a word that is notoriously confusing:
Littré's dictionary of the French language lists some twenty-nine
meanings of 'la nature'; Lovejoy in a well-known article on
'"Nature" as aesthetic norm', noted even more meanings
merely in regard to theories about art and nature;[6] we can all
agree with the *Encyclopédie* when it dismisses 'Nature' as a
'terme vague'. Many an age has tried to invoke 'the natural'
to win support for its own ideas, whether by praising or
castigating it. One could write a history of thought largely by
describing each period's notions of 'the natural' and their
differences from other periods – and that is partly what is being
attempted here for late-eighteenth-century France. For such an
attempt any present-day definition would be irrelevant; what
matters is how the people of that period themselves understood
'nature' and the 'natural'. All one needs to say is that our
concern will be with their views of the world of nature around
them and, as an extension from that, with their views of nature
as illustrated by certain sorts of human beings whom they

thought 'natural', as opposed to 'civilised' or as in some way conditioned to be other than they 'naturally' are. There is certainly a theoretical separation here between the natural outside us and the natural within us. To respond favourably to the world of nature does not require us to respond similarly to 'natural man'. Yet in practice the two tend to be inter-related by the eighteenth-century writers and others to be discussed. We shall see how often some newly-appreciated natural scene is felt by them to be completed – to be reinforced in its impact upon us – by the presence of an appropriate 'natural man'. The pastoral landscape is thus linked with the figure of the good and usually happy peasant, the wild Ossianic mountains with the wild bard, the bountiful Pacific islands with their no less bountiful and sexually 'natural' young women, and so on. Moreover, we shall note how often it is argued that 'natural man' can only achieve full happiness or morality if he lives within the appropriate context in the world of external nature – for example, in the countryside as opposed to the corrupting town. Indeed, such linkings reflect a primary aspect of the whole change of view: namely, the assertion that between the world of nature and man in his natural state there exists a profound and wide-ranging *harmony*. The only outstanding question – for the late-eighteenth century and perhaps for us today – is how far that harmony goes or should be taken. Granted there exists some degree of affinity, does it extend to natural phenomena like earthquakes and volcanic eruptions and – even more – to the natural phenomenon of death? Further-more, is the harmony really so deep that we would all be happier and better if we became 'as little children', or imitated the 'noble savage', or withdrew from society to rural communes, or followed our natural impulses and emotions rather than reason or external dogmas? It is the eighteenth century, more than any previous period of at least Christian civilisation, that began to perceive and to explore such questions.

But if the century may be left to define 'the natural' for itself, the concentration upon 'images' demands explanation. Its use and the contrast with 'ideas' are certainly being adopted primarily for reasons of practical convenience and would be readily abandoned if more suitable substitutes were offered, yet at the same time they do rest on particular suppositions which, right or wrong, help to explain the approach later chapters will illustrate.

It might be better if we lived solely by reference to those 'clear and distinct ideas' recommended by Descartes and our more austere professors of philosophy or, alternatively, by reference only to those 'reasons of the heart' so misleadingly praised by Pascal. But in practice people are usually impelled – do we not constantly observe? – by wider, more confused forces than pure reason or pure emotion – by 'attitudes', by 'clusters', as it were, of ideas, emotions, partial knowledge, opinions and beliefs, all mixed up together. We normally judge and react, in short – and whether we like it or not – under the influence of complex 'ways of seeing things', of multi-caused 'perceptions'. This is the first meaning one can give to the word 'images', and the analogy is with 'photographic images' – which, though of the same scene or person, will differ according to the equipment we use, the angle of the shot, and many other factors as well as 'what is actually out there'. 'Images' in this sense are certainly not in the first place a matter of our emotional responses. Nor are they only or even primarily derived from reason and knowledge, even though those normally enter into their formation. The history of philosophy is far more tidy than the history of actual human thinking – which (alas, no doubt) is made up less of 'clear and distinct ideas' than of 'images' in this sense of 'how it seemed', 'how people saw it at the time'. That, surely, is what largely underlies people's responses to most of the aspects of their lives, so that at times one is inclined to say that we think less with 'ideas' than with 'images'.

This may be true in a second way also, deriving from a different dictionary meaning of 'image': as a 'type, simile, metaphor'. We all adopt or form for ourselves stereotypes, 'images' in that sense, of groups as widespread as 'bureaucrats', 'immigrants', and so on – and we all know that in reality we are often much affected in our responses by such stereotypes, even when they are largely at odds with our theoretical ideas

– say, about human equality – or even with our knowledge of the actual facts. In the same way the eighteenth century developed (or renewed) various 'images' representing, 'embodying', as it were, the newer notions about 'the natural', especially in human form. The child; the primitive bard; the loving mother; the good peasant; the noble savage: these are some instances for later consideration, and one can mention as well the portrait of the artist or poet or the great leader as inspired genius, or even the figure of the basically good pirate or bandit. Animals add further 'images'. The horse is the clearest case, serving – as in many paintings by Stubbs – to illustrate pastoral contentment, but also, in the guise of the *wild* horse – in David, for instance, depicting Napoleon crossing the Alps – to typify dynamic natural energy. Dogs, cows and birds were likewise utilised in our period as 'carriers' of more than the mere facts of their physical reality, as symbols for (say) animal love of man and dependence on him, or rural tranquillity, or the joys of the natural world – much as Blake invoked as an 'image' of wild nature his 'Tiger, tiger, burning bright/In the forests of the night' – an instance where three other indicators of threatening danger reinforce the savage predator: 'burning', 'forests' and 'night'.

It is perhaps superfluous to note that the 'photographic' and the 'metaphorical' usages are frequently confused in human thinking – so that, for example, what we may believe to be our 'objective' perception of a given person or animal is in fact much affected by our 'stereotypes' about the class they belong to. But a different feature of 'images' by comparison with 'ideas' should be stressed because of its particular relevance. Whereas 'clear and distinct ideas' seek to avoid mutual contradictions, 'images' commonly include inconsistencies and ambiguities – as was examined most famously in regard to literature by Empson. 'Images' are not 'simple', as Descartes wished 'ideas' to be, but tend, almost by their very nature and purpose, to be 'complex'. And if that distinction has validity, a conclusion perhaps follows for the intellectual and cultural historian; to regain – as fully as one ever can – how, in some past time and place, it 'really felt', how it 'really seemed', in all its inevitable multi-sidedness, we shall be helped not only by studying people's reasoned 'ideas' and their science – essential evidence though those are for a complete under-standing – but also and at least as much by seeking to get ourselves back into their 'images'. The historian of mentalities cannot enjoy Proust-like 'involuntary memories' – but he would be much helped if he could.

It may be that this notion of 'images' has affinities with certain well-discussed notions as defined by others: with 'models', 'structures', 'paradigms' as with Kuhn, 'symbols' as with Jung, 'sources of metaphor' as with Gombrich.[7] It may also be that an age's 'ideas' and its science are themselves profoundly affected by such factors and give evidence about its 'images' as much as about what it fondly believed, often enough, to be its pure intellection or its 'purely scientific' observations. It may be, furthermore, that the language of religious discourse is closest of all to the language spoken by an age's 'images'. Christ's use of parables is perhaps the supreme illustration: His story of the Good Samaritan gives not the 'idea' of neighbourliness but an 'image' of the good neighbour, and thereby it affects the listener far more deeply than any definition.

Yet to discuss such affinities here would be an unnecessary distraction and go well beyond describing what are being adopted for present purposes, and as untheoretically as possible, as no more than 'working assumptions': their usefulness can be judged only by their consequences in practice. One con-sequence is nevertheless plain: to seek for a past period's 'lost images' requires recourse to many areas of evidence, to a range of subjects beyond the specialist competence of most of us and certainly of this author. It may be small wonder if, in Britain at least, cultural (and even intellectual) history has a doubtful reputation with specialists in accepted academic disciplines. Few can command the sheer range of knowledge of a Burckhardt or a Braudel – and even they have not been without their critics. Because of his very aims the cultural historian is perhaps fated to wander too widely, to be 'everything by starts and nothing long'. This present enquiry is explicitly restricted to a small educated minority, in late-eighteenth-century France alone for the most part, whose outlook is reflected in the books, paintings and other cultural artefacts which it created or appreciated. These still endure for us to consult – whereas what Gray, who perhaps deserves to be the patron-saint of social history, termed 'the short and simple annals of the Poor' remain largely unrecorded and can only be re-read by such approaches to the history of 'popular culture' as are practised by (say) the learned journal *Annales* (Gray's very word). Yet, though by comparison one is here more fortunate, it is nevertheless daunting to find how much 'evidence' crowds in, all relevant, to a greater or lesser extent, to what even the minority believed about 'the natural' – and not least when it must be contrasted with previous periods and their beliefs.

Some contrasts are obvious, and the more compelling for that, and the wider the time-gap involved, the more unmistakeable is the contrast. Greater problems arise with shorter time-gaps, and when vacillations of attitude, even or especially in the most original minds, can so easily cloud the comparisons. To contrast Poussin's landscapes with those of Turner – or even, rather earlier, of Vernet and Loutherbourg – is easy; it is harder to show the difference between Poussin and, only a few decades later, Watteau, Pater or Lancret. Again, the view of children at Port-Royal in the mid-seventeenth century is not so far from the educational prescriptions of Fénelon at its close; only by the time of Rousseau's *Emile* in 1762 has the gap become fundamental. Yet again, the contrast between the formal gardens at the Château de Richelieu, at Versailles and elsewhere and the very first gardens of the Petit Trianon could be discounted as a difference of scale and tone. The discrepancy becomes unavoidable only when one walks from the age of geometry, physics and rationality represented by Le Nôtre's 'grandes terrasses' at Versailles to the new age of sensibility and awareness of nature that is reflected, however artificially, in 'le hameau de Marie-Antoinette', 100 years later but only half-a-mile away, and in a plethora of 'English gardens', in one of which, at Ermenonville, Rousseau himself died and was aptly first buried. Such longer-term contrasts are found in literature, art, music, science and other cultural artefacts and no less in successive attitudes in everyday life towards so many of its elements. Some of these will be considered later – attitudes to wild storms, children, marriage, country life, for example. Others will be omitted for lack of space, yet they too would serve as cultural indicators, faithfully reflecting broader changes, as an example may briefly show.

Are mental deficiency and illness signs of divine displeasure, justifying incarceration in places like 'Bedlam' as depicted by Hogarth, with week-end visitors paying to taunt the inmates? Or are these unhappy people affected by the moon, are they 'lunatics'? Or is mental handicap a 'natural' affliction and thus treatable, as argued by an enlightened mid-eighteenth-century reformer like Dr Battie (whose name, unfairly to him, has given us a pejorative adjective) and as concretely expressed in the London hospital for mental patients he founded, close to 'Bedlam'. (In France, the equivalent to Battie is Philippe Pinel in the 1790s.) Or, finally, are mental afflictions, as some contended many decades before Dr Laing and others today, the outcome of social pressures which depart, precisely, from 'the natural'; are they, as Esquirol claimed at that time, 'the sickness of civilisation'?[8]

Even more minor cultural phenomena may be no less illustrative. For example, not only is the 'content' of literary works of great relevance; so also may be even particular techniques. Why, to take one instance, are apostrophes to nature or to natural creatures like skylarks or cuckoos so popular in the late-eighteenth and early-nineteenth centuries in comparison with earlier poetry? ('O wild West Wind'; 'O blithe new-comer'; 'Ethereal minstrel! pilgrim of the sky'; 'O lac! rochers muets! grottes, forêt obscure!' – and many, many more.) The answer is surely – in part at least – that this device presupposes the sense of an 'I–thou' ('Hail to thee, blithe Spirit!') as opposed to an 'I–it', relationship between man and the world. The new feeling of affinity between them is reflected even in so apparently technical a matter as the increased usage of apostrophe.

Dictionaries (and encyclopedias also) are a rich and sometimes neglected source. The very word 'culture' gives a good illustration. In the French *Encyclopédie* the only entry comprises a lengthy article, written by Diderot himself, that is totally devoted to *agriculture*. That was the original meaning of 'la culture', the only one given in the first edition of the *Dictionnaire de l'Académie Française* in 1694. Only in 1777 is a second meaning inserted: the sense of 'cultivation of the mind or the arts', and only in the eighth edition of 1932 does one finally find the kind of definition – given even so under 'Culture générale' – that would meet our present usage. In Germany a similar shift occurred. 'Kultur' (now so laden with memories of 'Kulturgeschichte') originally denoted agriculture; 'Landwirtschaft', now the term for agriculture, was apparently created in the eighteenth century, precisely, leaving 'Kultur' free, as it were, for Hegelian exploitation. And there is more; the deeper significance of these linguistic innovations lies in the area from which the word is stolen – the area of growth, development, biological-type process. A later chapter will observe the old 'mechanist' notion of nature being replaced by a new 'organicism'; the point here is that this change and its application to human affairs are illustrated even by entries in French and German dictionaries.

A variety of other areas of human culture in the wider sense may often be relevant. The origins of seaside resorts in the later-eighteenth century and even the ways they sought publicity offer an instance for later mention. Changing dress-fashions often reflect more than the whims of their wearers or the calculations of their designers. Mme de Pompadour depicted in her elaborate, bejewelled gown; then Marie-Antoinette dressed as a shepherdess; Mme Récamier painted later still in a simple Grecian shift, with bare feet exposed: such a progression over less than fifty years is not accidental but mirrors larger cultural developments, the neo-classical revival not excluded.

The problems of this study are obvious, in short: a vast topic; the need to draw contrasts over lengthy periods; above all, not too little evidence or too few illustrations but a plethora; evidence, moreover, of very varying weight and reliability, evidence too which it is all too easy to misinterpret. And finally one has to note just how many and what complex factors were at work in the eighteenth century which operated to affect men's views of nature and the natural.

To some degree, first, there was a certain 'secularisation' of thought. Though it has already been doubted if Christianity was consciously rejected by more than a handful, it can certainly be thought that many others were less positively pre-occupied by its supernaturalism than previously. Economic and class developments clearly constituted a second factor of great significance, whether one thinks them all-decisive or not. Agrarian 'reforms', urbanisation and the beginnings of industrialisation profoundly affected views on town and country and other matters, and the continuing rise of the bourgeoisie and the needs of capitalism have both been invoked to explain the changes involved. Thirdly, the eighteenth century was the time when the 'sciences of nature' were established and first expanded: botany, biology, zoology, geology. Collectively they vastly increased people's awareness of the workings, variety and beauty of the world of plants, animals and even rocks, and they also furnished matter for fresh arguments that overturned a variety of prevailing views. A fourth and major factor was the much extended exploration of nature across the oceans – deeper into North and South America and into Africa and above all into the Pacific Ocean, leading finally to the confirmation that an unknown continent existed and numerous Pacific islands also. When, later, we look at the 'transoceanic perspectives' revealed by such discoveries as that of Tahiti – an island quite unknown until the late-1760s, except to its happily unsuspecting natives – it will be obvious how strikingly these voyages both enriched men's appreciation of the external world and also modified in many instances their thoughts about human nature. Other factors were also operative, needless to add – including the long-standing tension in 'civilised' societies between the 'exploitive' and the 'collaborative' attitudes to nature. Even in the minds of the 'collaborators', with whom we shall mainly be concerned, 'tension' will be apparent again and again and will be manifest in a range of polarities: culture and nature; the civilised and the primitive; town and country; man and woman;

adult corruption and childhood innocence. Contrasts with attitudes that preceded are replicated in contrasts within the attitudes that replaced them – and beyond that lie even more sobering contrasts between attitudes and action.

2

PASTORAL LANDSCAPES

In this chapter our concern will be with external nature in its more tranquil, immediately attractive forms, not with wild, threatening nature as seen in savage mountains, stormy oceans and the like. The pastoral tradition in European literature had been age-long, going back to Theocritus, Horace and, above all for the eighteenth century, Virgil, a tradition renewed more recently, during the Renaissance and the seventeenth century, by Petrarch, Marot, Ronsard, Spenser, Shakespeare, Milton and numerous others. Many of these writers, and the 'ideal landscapes' of painters like Poussin and Claude also, were explicitly cherished in the eighteenth century and imitated by poets, artists and even landscape-gardeners. There is thus an undeniable element of the conventional, even artificial, in the age's liking for the pastoral scene. At first sight, at any rate, it was at its least original in this respect.

Yet this survey must start here for at least three reasons. First, the eighteenth-century observers themselves started here, and many, indeed, went no further in their appreciation. This is 'the feeling for nature' that was most widespread, was most often expressed and that has thus, understandably, been most fully described by scholars since. Daniel Mornet's basic study as regards France is devoted, apart from one chapter on mountains and a mere four pages out of 450 on storms at sea, entirely to such themes as 'les maisons des champs', 'l'idylle champêtre', 'plaisirs rustiques', 'les jardins', 'voyages pittoresques' and so on, to a literature of 'poèmes champêtres', 'pastorales', 'idylles' and 'églogues naïves' – increasingly preferred in the later century to 'églogues galantes'. Much the same is true of later studies of the subject, like Van Tieghem's and Dédéyan's, and this accurately reflects the centrality in so many eighteenth-

18

century minds of the pastoral response. We must start here, secondly, because this provided the basis, as it were, for going further. To be able eventually to find beauty in barren mountains you need first to appreciate hills and lower mountain-slopes; to enjoy the scenery of Lake Geneva prepares the way for elation amid storms at sea; to feel sympathy for horses or dogs may be a starting-point for thrilling at the savage energy of the lion or tiger. It is hardly surprising that the liking for gentle as opposed to wild nature came earlier in the century and was very markedly more common. There was in fact – and this is a third reason for beginning here – a very striking expansion at this time in men's appreciation of pastoral nature. The age-old reactions were significantly refreshed and became more broadly popular than previously, and if with some they seem banal (as with a deal of French poetry of nature), with many others they appear to have been genuine and closely-felt. Nor was this true only, or even primarily, of writers, artists and other intellectuals. In France at least *they* seem to have been providing for an existing taste: one of Mornet's major conclusions is that they were in part capitalising on already developed attitudes amongst their public.[1] Thus, for example, the early-eighteenth century saw growing enthusiasm amongst those who could afford them for 'maisons de campagne', retreats from urban life. They achieved, as Mornet fully illustrates, rising popularity all over France – near Boulogne and Rouen, along the Seine and the Loire, and, for the citizens of Lyon, in the Rhône valley. Further south too these country properties began to multiply, around Montpellier and Toulouse, near Aix-en-Provence and Toulon, and even along what had been the largely empty area of the Côte d'Azur – at Nice and Villefranche on the coast itself, more often a little inland, notably at Hyères, leaving the dangerous, brigand-infested stretches of the Estérels still largely deserted, and also the coast east of Nice, whence to reach Italy one had to take ship to Genoa for lack of a safe road. There was a novel liking too for day outings from the town into the rural neighbourhood. Sceaux, outside Paris, was (we are told) 'much frequented on Sundays', and so were Saint-Cloud, Passy and Montmartre, then a tiny community around its abbey, engaged mainly in agriculture and wholly separate from Paris. Voltaire's friend and disciple, Marmontel, for instance – though this is by the mid-century – recounts that his group liked to take 'philosophical walks' and to picnic in the outskirts of Paris and on the banks of the Seine.[2] Even royalty eventually imitated the new cult of the rural, well before the milk-maid queen, Marie-Antoinette. The great success of Rousseau's pastoral operetta, *Le Devin du village*, from 1751 – with Mme de Pompadour herself acting the male lead, Colin, in a later performance at her own 'château de Bellevue' – offers one minor instance out of many others, as does the court love for 'fêtes champêtres' – as at Bagatelle in 1757, where a 'fête' for the King of Poland included a village fair and peasants playing on rustic instruments.

During the earlier part of the century only a few writers in France seem to have shared such new sympathies: Mme de Tencin, for example, and Prévost. In his *Manon Lescaut* (1734) Des Grieux, after his first adventure with Manon, withdraws to his father's country home, to lead a 'peaceful and solitary' life in a secluded house with 'a small wood and a stream of gentle water' at the end of the garden. All the same, as one reads on, it is to discover he has arranged for a collection of books, some friends, and an exchange of letters with a friend staying in Paris. Even when resting from his escapades with Manon, solitude and tranquil nature are not quite enough.

In England, by contrast, which has a clear chronological priority over France, writers and others were already expressing the new preferences. Myra Reynolds, in her classic work on *The Treatment of Nature in English Poetry*, concludes that poetry and gardening were ahead of painting and fiction in this respect.[3] The poets in particular would be translated into French, sooner or later, and be invoked as major models: James Thomson and *The Seasons* (1726–30) especially; Shenstone; Young with his *Night Thoughts* (1742–5); Thomas Gray, notably his *Elegy*; and Joseph Warton, above all for *The Enthusiast* (1744):

> Happy the first of men, ere yet confined
> To smoaky city; who in sheltering groves,
> Warm caves, and deep-sunk vallies liv'd and loved.

Pastoral landscapes

Yet why should man mistaken deem it nobler
To dwell in palaces and high-roof'd halls,
Than in God's forests, architect supreme!

All these English poets were writing well before Rousseau, Saint-Lambert, the Abbé Delille and other French writers of the second half of the century. Likewise, the new informal landscape gardens were developed much earlier in England than in France – those at Stourhead, Stowe, and many others created by Kent, Bridgeman and 'Capability' Brown – so much so that it would even be termed 'le jardin anglais' or 'le jardin anglo-chinois' (as opposed to the formal 'jardin français') when eventually imitated by the French at Ermenonville, Méréville, and elsewhere from the late-1760s on. Swiss and Germans too preceded the French, notably Haller in *Die Alpen* (1732), also one of the very first works to include mountains within its wider appreciation of nature, Gessner in his *Idyllen* (1756), and Klopstock with *Die Frühlingsfeier* (1759). They too were much admired in France after being translated, and especially Gessner. Rousseau was sent a French translation of his *Idyllen* in 1761 and received it on a day he felt severely ill. 'Mechanically I opened the book [Rousseau wrote to a friend], thinking to close it again at once; but I only closed it after reading it all and I have put it to one side to read it again...I feel that your friend Gessner is a man after my own heart.'[4] Indeed, the admiration persisted until at least the 1780s, when it influenced André Chénier in writing his idylls and eclogues – works that, when published more than two decades later, would win him praise as 'the French Theocritus'.

More slowly than with the English and the Germans, and amongst a smaller minority perhaps, in France also the old perceptions were refreshed. A single chapter cannot and need not repeat the full accounts given by Mornet and others but may better concentrate on a few characteristic illustrations and on some principal features of the renewal of pastoralism.

A first and clearly relevant indicator is found in changes in theories of pastoral poetry, changes that reveal a distinctive progression and that were markedly to affect English theorists also. In the later-seventeenth century the leading French

New images of the natural

neo-classicist theorist of the pastoral, Père Rapin, reacting
against the extravagant artificialities of the so-called 'baroque
pastoral', had re-affirmed the tradition of the Ancients, as he
interpreted it, in line with classicist respect for 'rules' derived
from Greek and Latin practice. The Preface to a collection of
his own pastoral poems (1659; printed in English translation
1684), a 'Dissertatio de Carmine Pastorali', asserts that the
pastoral is the oldest poetic form and 'a product of the Golden
Age'. It is 'the imitation of the action of a shepherd, or of one
taken under that character' and should show to us 'the most
innocent manners of the most ancient simplicity', the characters
being 'represented according to the genius of the Golden Age'
and its matter providing 'a perfect image' of that Age. Such
was the view re-affirmed in England also by Pope in his
Discourse on Pastoral Poetry (1717) and other neo-classicists; in
Pope's words, the pastoral is 'an image of what they call the
Golden Age'. In Rapin and Pope alike, in short, it is a
long-established conventional form referring to a long-distant
and Arcadian past, with no relationship with present-day
realities.

In opposition to that appeal to the old pastoral tradition
Fontenelle, in his *Discours sur la nature de l'églogue* (1688), sides
with 'the moderns' against 'the Ancients' (as in his better-known
Digression added to the *Discours* as an appendix), and he rejects
Rapin's 'rules' in favour of 'the natural light of reason'. If
pastoral poetry is to please, it should be based on our knowledge
of human psychology and present 'a concurrence of the two
strongest passions, laziness and love'. We enjoy thereby the
'quietness and leisure' of the shepherd's life, and also a love
that for him compared with us today was 'more innocent',
'more assiduous', 'more faithful'. The pastoral work should
thus convey the idea of 'a quiet life, with no other business than
love'; it offers an 'illusion', he affirms, and, as Rapin had said
but on different premises, not realities. 'The pleasingness of
pastoral therefore consists in exposing to the eye only the
tranquillity of a shepherd's life, and in dissembling or concealing
its meanness, as also in showing only its innocence and hiding
its miseries.' This is the view that would be re-expressed in

22

England by so-called 'rationalist' theorists like Addison, Dr Johnson and others: it does not depict the Golden Age of the past but a fiction compounded of indolence and romance – though Johnson and a few others do also stress the need for 'probability' and 'truth' and, to that extent, bring the form closer to (in Johnson's words) 'whatsoever may...happen in the country'.

A third group of theorists would press this Johnsonian view further – to an attitude that had already been expressed by Allan Ramsey in his 'Preface' to *The Ever Green* (1724) and exemplified in *The Gentle Shepherd*, which, at long last, 're-connects' the pastoral with 'real' life, it has been said.[5] Most of them were writing after 1750: in Britain, the Wartons, Blair and others; in Europe, Gessner, Rousseau, and Saint-Lambert. Similar claims are made by them all. Joseph Warton's *Essay* of 1756 rejects portrayal of 'the undisturbed felicity of the golden age' as 'an empty notion' and claims that Theocritus, whom he favours over Virgil, had been realistically depicting Sicilian life and external nature, as we ought today. Gessner too would be praised for truthfulness to present-day rural life and for expressing emotion at the sight of it and of the 'enchanting scenes of nature' – by British admirers like Coxe and by Rousseau and many others on the continent, including Saint-Lambert, who provides us with a major document in his 'Discours préliminaire' to *Les Saisons* (1769), pastoral poetry inspired by Thomson's *Seasons*.[6]

Thomson was so fortunate, Saint-Lambert claims, as to be 'singing of nature amongst a people who knew and loved it'; in France the task is to convert 'a nation that is ignorant of nature and looks at it with indifference'. He rapidly rejects the views of Racan, Segrais and Fontenelle, 'authors who imitated the Ancients and the Italians and not nature' and praises Thomson, Haller, Gessner and others for avoiding 'affectation' and 'preciosity' and for a poetry which 'depicts nature and manners that are true', albeit 'embellished' in a way he approves. 'The Ancients liked and sang of the countryside; we admire and sing of nature.' This goal leads him to his principal assertions. First the poet should 'move' his readers – an aim itself illustrative of the wider movement of 'sensibility' – and he will achieve that above all by presenting external nature in such ways as to show the different emotions it may arouse in the human observer, emotions ranging from 'sublime' and 'great and beautiful' to 'agreeable and cheerful' and 'sad and melancholy', and each linked for him with a particular season of the year. His basic concern is with man's reaction and relation to the natural world: to make us 'love' it, to paint it always 'in its relationship to persons of sensitivity', to 'engrave on men's hearts and memories useful or pleasing truths and feelings'. And to that end the poet must, secondly, base himself on observation of present realities. He claims to describe the rural scenes he has lived amongst in his youth and also alleges a significant connection with modern science. Just as Thomson had greatly admired Newton and included in *The Seasons* many references to contemporary discoveries, so too Saint-Lambert asserts that 'the progress of sciences' like physics, astronomy, chemistry and botany has made 'the palace of the world and its human inhabitants' better known, has 'enlarged and embellished the universe'. We shall later note that scientists at this time were observing the world far more and far more closely than their predecessors; analogously, poets like Thomson and Saint-Lambert seek to 'look more', to perceive more sharply the real world, than those whose wish had been to evoke the Golden Age or agreeable fictions. Saint-Lambert declares a third major aim: to make propaganda in various ways for country ways and agricultural reform. We must return to that in a later chapter in order to discuss claims that representations of the peasant at this time sought to conceal, rather than truthfully reveal, that they were – however unwittingly – agents of exploitive capitalism. Here one may just remark, in relation to his 'realism', one assertion by Saint-Lambert that might seem to give support to such interpretations. The poet should certainly depict 'the manners, work, sufferings and pleasure' of rural man, he says – but not '*unhappy* peasants, who are interesting only for their misfortunes'. Nor was Saint-Lambert alone in this apparently damning assertion amongst the theorists whose views were similar to his – Tytler, Aikin and others in

Britain, for example. Thus Blair's major essay on 'Pastoral poetry' in 1783 rejects likewise the depiction of 'mean, servile and laborious' shepherds and wishes the poet to present to us 'the pastoral life somewhat embellished and beautified, at least seen on its fairest side only'. Pope, much earlier, had said the same, but that was from within a tradition unconcerned with the present and with empirical fact. Crabbe's complaint in *The Village* related to a current as well as an age-old suppression of rural 'pain':

> But when amid such pleasing scenes I trace
> The poor laborious natives of the place,...
> Then shall I dare these real ills to hide
> In tinsel trappings of poetic pride?

All the theorising was hardly matched by actual pastoral literature of quality – in France at any rate, though one authority implies this was largely true of Britain also: 'perhaps never has such mediocre poetry received so much critical attention'.[7] The best-known French works appeared in the later part of the century: from Rousseau with *La Nouvelle Héloïse* (1761) and later writings and Saint-Lambert onwards, to which may be added Roucher's *Les Mois* (1779), Delille's *Les Jardins* (1782) and *L'Homme des champs* (1800), Rétif de la Bretonne's *La Vie de mon père* (1779) and other novels, Florian's pastoral works *Galatée* (1783) and *Estelle* (1787), and, portraying tropical nature, Saint-Pierre's *Paul et Virginie* (1788), which the novelist himself terms a 'pastorale'. It is noteworthy how much later these writings are than comparable English and German works, and even so some of them seem derivative and second-hand, distinctly straining for effect and employing a tired, conventional language.

The new pastoral perceptions were more quickly and strikingly expressed by French landscape-painters than in literature and at an earlier date even than in Britain where Gainsborough and Richard Wilson belong to the later half of the century. That is so even though, despite the impression popularised by the Goncourts many years ago, landscape-painting remained in reality a minor and officially despised genre in eighteenth-century France. There was little official encouragement for it by

comparison with historical and religious painting and por-
traiture, and it was not until 1816 that a special Prix de Rome
was at last created for landscapes.[8] This coolness of the
establishment perhaps reflects the old attitudes to external
nature, but however that may be, parallel with enthusiasm for
'maisons de campagne' and the like by some of the well-to-do
went private commissions for landscapes. Painters finding it
hard to make a living in face of academic disdain were largely
launched by private sponsors and collectors – by such patrons
as the Abbé de Saint-Non, who encouraged Fragonard and
Hubert Robert and who later helped, along with others, like
Benjamin de Laborde, to create a vogue for illustrated travel-
books such as the latter's *Tableau de la Suisse* and Saint-Non's
Voyage pittoresque de Naples et de Sicile.

    Clark notes in his *Landscape into Art* that 'landscape painting
marks the stages in our conception of nature'.[9] If so, how and
how far did such eighteenth-century French painters contribute
to and reflect developments of the kind just noted in theories
of pastoral poetry? They almost all admired Poussin and Claude
and invoked them as models, along with Salvator Rosa, and that
despite two fairly evident facts about the French painters at
least. First, nature for them had often been merely background
for historical or legendary action. Poussin claimed to feel
'disconsolate' amidst nature, denied it was of central interest
for art, and asserted that 'painting is nothing other than the
imitation of *human* actions'. It should, moreover, present the
general, not the particular. Just as the classical dramatists prized
the psychological and the universal, so also did these artists,
and the commentators of the age as well, from such critics as
Félibien in the 1660s to even an innovator like Dubos in 1719,
who declared the finest landscape to be of little interest if devoid
of human beings. And secondly, if not primarily background,
nature was represented – most notably by Claude – as 'ideal
landscape'. Certainly it was no longer treated, as in much
medieval art, as symbolical, yet his scenes are 'well-bred',
affected as much as classicist plays by a sense of 'les bienséances',
of what is fitting and unshocking, and with Claude as well as
Poussin the human presence is almost always in the foreground.

With their landscapes as a reference-point one turns to the first generation of eighteenth-century painters – to Watteau and others like Pater and Lancret. Watteau in particular may seem to have remained interested in human nature above all – in the peasants around his native Valenciennes, the world of the theatre (notably the clown), and especially young men and women falling in love, as in his most famous paintings, his 'fêtes galantes'. Yet here external nature has a distinctive place as well. It may still be decorative background, a pleasing setting for the flirtations of young aristocrats, and to the next, more earnest generation Watteau would seem somewhat frivolous and artificial. But though nature is not emotionally moving, it is surely closer to reality, and his trees and grassy banks are far less stylised than the people set against them; they 'live', as it were, independently of the lovers. As to his depiction of rural living, the humans are mainly upper-class, engaged in idyllic merry-making, occupied as Fontenelle wished for pastoral poetry in 'laziness and love'. Yet two comparisons may serve to illustrate his intermediate position. To juxtapose Poussin's *Les Bergers d'Arcadie* – classical, allegorical, 'Arcadian' – and Watteau's *Les Bergers* is to note, despite the fact that his are still very pleasure-loving shepherds, with no mud on their boots, that Watteau has moved towards distinctly greater realism. All the same, to contrast Watteau's *L'Accordée de village*, depicting an allegedly rural marriage-contract, with the painting of 1761 by Greuze that has the same title is to see at once that the latter is both much truer to the actualities of rustic existence than Watteau and also far more movingly dramatic. To compare Watteau's peasants with those of Chardin also is to verify the same movement towards empiricism as that found in Greuze. Watteau – and much the same is true of contemporaries like Pater, with his *Fête galante*, *Fête dans un parc* and others, and Lancret, with his *Fête dans un bois* or his *Fête galante* – has moved away from the 'neo-classicism' of Rapin and Poussin but has only partially transcended the escapist fictions of Fontenelle.

We connect Boucher above all with depictions of buxom young women, but his first Salon paintings in 1737 were 'sujets champêtres', and his interest and outstanding ability in depicting the external world persisted throughout his career. Even though his *Triumph of Venus* is centred on the female figures, it also captures the reality of sea, cloud and sky, and he executed many completer landscapes such as his *Landscape with Watermill*. This painting reflects a somewhat conventional and artificial dream of rural tranquillity, yet it also illustrates a certain naturalism, a basis in accurate observation, as one can see again in his *Evening Landscape*, if one overlooks the implausible ruined classical temple in the background. Like Watteau, Boucher remains in part firmly within the old, conventional pastoral *tradition* – as one is reminded by his succession of paintings of shepherds and shepherdesses (*Shepherd watching a sleeping shepherdess*, *Shepherd piping to a shepherdess*, and *Shepherd and shepherdess reposing*). Yet, as such works as his *Autumn* and *Summer Pastorals* well show, there are at the same time frequent signs of a more genuine, pastoral *vision* – 'vision' in the basic sense of 'looking' – something comparable to what one observes, to give an Italian instance, in those landscapes of Francesco Zuccarelli (1702–88) that were so admired by Richard Wilson. We are not yet (to continue the Italian analogy) at the wilder nature of Antonio Diziani (1737–97) and his *Paesaggio con la Maddalena*, with its savage mountains and only a single human figure; we are certainly not at 'nature in the raw', but we are – one should claim no more – 'closer to nature'.

Watteau and Boucher were far from alone in their sharper observation of the natural world, and increasingly so after the middle of the century, with a host of minor landscapists as well as the more famous. Louis Gabriel Moreau was especially sensitive, though less successful in his own day. One can instance his *View of Vincennes*, which gives an especially remarkable rendering of the clouds, and his *Landscape* is a simple, unpretentious but vivid expression of the atmosphere and particularly the light of natural scenes. More celebrated in his own day was Hubert Robert, who had a particular liking for picturesque scenery and irregular gardens and parks – like the Parc d'Ermenonville which he helped to create, or the gardens of the famous Villa d'Este at Tivoli, which he painted. His paintings of *Les Quatre Saisons*, and especially *Le Printemps*, offer further examples, and *Le Pont du Gard* shows his liking for landscape as much as for ruins. And in his early years Hubert Robert worked in Italy alongside another, more famous painter who is not primarily associated with landscapes: Fragonard, sometimes considered (especially by Diderot) as the last, rather frivolous, even licentious illustration of the Watteau–Boucher tradition of the 'fête galante'. Yet in numerous paintings he shows a remarkable ability to convey the vitality of the natural world. For example, his vigorous, almost impressionist *Gardens of the Villa d'Este* is no doubt sylvan and 'Romantic' but also certainly *alive*. His *Fête at Saint-Cloud* is similar in quality – surely a masterpiece – and those most 'frivolous' of his paintings, *The Swing* and *The Bathers*, illustrate the same awareness of nature's superabundant, dynamic energy. Though also a picturesque background for love, the former work's trees are living to the point of wildness and engulfing fertility; there is nothing fanciful in comparing such a depiction with the new scientific 'organicist' view of the world we shall survey later or with the awareness expressed by Goethe's Werther, amongst others, of 'the swarming life of the little world between the grass-blades'.

Certain painters, greatly admired by Diderot in particular in his *Salon* reviews, will be passed by here. Joseph Vernet began with the ambition to rejuvenate the tradition of Claude; much of his early work showed Roman scenes and the countryside nearby at Tivoli, the Lake of Nemi, and so on, and it was his fame for accurate observation of gentler nature that led to the official commission for him to execute his famous series of views of French ports. But for us his interest will lie far more in his paintings of wild, 'sublime' nature, and the same is true of Louterbourg, notwithstanding such earlier works as his *Pastoral Landscape* (1763). Chardin and Greuze, above all others praised by Diderot, rarely painted external nature, and no landscapes by the latter survive. 'Realism' in them relates to the *human* inhabitants of the rural scene (as, indeed, do some of Fragonard's less often mentioned works, showing 'lower-class' country life). They are less relevant here, consequently, than for discussing later the age's 'image' of the good and happy peasant in particular.

In tracing eighteenth-century developments in pastoral

theories and in landscape paintings alike one observes three broad changes from what in general had gone before: first, closer, more detailed observation of external nature, leading to a greater, though still selective realism; secondly, a rising enthusiasm for nature, based on heightened appreciation of its beauties and abundance; thirdly, a growing sense of emotional affinity between nature and man himself, of the interpenetration of nature's life and the life of man.

Parallel illustrations are seen in other cultural phenomena of the time, and especially clearly in the case of landscape-gardening. Gardens are, perhaps, philosophies expressed in vegetation; at any rate, they obviously reflect men's attitudes to nature. Christopher Hussey remarks in his classic study of *The Picturesque* that 'an appreciation of scenery is a very late acquisition in the development of the western mind',[10] and that is well seen in relation to gardens. Originally they were mainly for herbs and medicines – in medieval times and later, as with the Paris Jardin des Plantes. It was founded in 1626 by two of Louis XIII's doctors as the 'Royal Garden of medicinal herbs', but in the eighteenth century it too was to be transformed by Buffon, its 'Superintendant' from 1739 to 1788, in ways that reflect the far wider changes, both scientific and other, in attitudes to nature. Those changes were perhaps consummated, it can be noted in passing, when the Superintendant's post was briefly held in the 1790s – ineffectively so, it appears – by none other than Bernardin de Saint-Pierre, whose statue, complete with Paul, Virginie and their faithful dog, still stands in the Jardin beneath some shady trees, close to Buffon's 'labyrinth'.[11]

The contrast between the attitudes to landscape of the seventeenth and the eighteenth centuries is nowhere clearer than at Versailles. Stretching from the great palace extended by Louis XIV run Le Nôtre's vast gardens, with their straight, mathematically-precise avenues and alleys, their sculptured trees and flower-beds, their long ordered perspectives. These are public gardens, displaying the magnificence and wealth of a royal court, a splendid setting for state occasions and official 'fêtes' – complete with elaborate water-displays which, as early as 1668, well before the 1,400 fountains of the final complex, were using more water than the entire population of Paris. Man has here imposed himself upon nature, regulated it by his own wishes as strictly as was ordered the court routine around 'le Roi Soleil', and indeed Saint-Simon said of Louis XIV that he had chosen to 'tyrannise over nature' as much as over his subjects. This is not a marriage of the human and the natural but a dominance by one over the other. Nor is there a role here for the individual; these gardens are for people in the mass, not for the contemplative solitary.

Yet after only a brief walk away from these inhuman acres one passes to a totally different philosophy of gardens and nature alike. One skirts the garden of the Petit Trianon, one of the first more irregular, English-type gardens in France, created under Louis XV, with a botanical garden as well that was much enjoyed by Mme Du Barry. Louis XVI's queen was bored even by that and gave the plant specimens to the Jardin des Plantes, thereby liberating space for the most famous – though not the first – of all the age's 'picturesque' 'hamlets'. It was completed in 1786 and comprises a group of rustic buildings at the edge of a curving lake, some of them then occupied by a farmer, a gardener and a keeper and their families. A fine herd of Swiss cows was kept and sheep, goats, pigs and rabbits, and there was a dairy, where the Queen apparently enjoyed making butter and cheese, and a water-mill – whose wheel first turned in 1789 and by which she is said to have been sitting when told that the Paris mob was advancing on the palace. She loved to live here for a month at a time, with the king obliged to come down for supper in the special dwelling created for the family, complete with library and billiard house. There was obvious contrivance and artificiality, an atmosphere of playing at milk-maids and shepherdesses, and yet all the same one can feel that here man and nature are partners and in harmony.

Between the two extremes of that contrast lies a century of French garden-history and the whole, well-documented evolution from formal to increasingly informal. A variety of influences have been discerned: the Italian garden as at Tivoli; the landscape paintings of Claude and Poussin, reinforced by Watteau, Boucher and others a little later; Dutch and Flemish artists; Alberti; Chinese examples, as mediated by William Chambers and others; and above all English writers from Addison and Pope to Thomson and Gray, English architects from Kent and Bridgeman to Brown, and English gardens from Stourhead, Rousham and Stowe to Hagley Park and Kew. Yet the English gardens proliferated in England from distinctly earlier than in France; all the influences became effective, it seems, only when enough of the French themselves had moved towards those heightened pastoral appreciations we have already seen in poetic theory and in painting. Within the French tradition itself there had been a few anticipations: even in Le Nôtre's small 'bosquet' at the Trianon as early as 1680.[12] Fénelon in his *Télémaque* describes the un-geometric 'parc de Calypso' and links it with the innocent pleasures of pastoral life. Voltaire – an admirer of Pope and English ways – attacks symmetrically-planted gardens in 1738 in his *Epître au Prince Royal de Prusse*. Above all Rousseau intervened in due course, and decisively so. *La Nouvelle Héloïse* included a rapidly acclaimed letter (IV, 11) in which Saint-Preux describes the garden created by Julie where she loved to meditate, her *Elysée*. A present-day scholar has argued that the *Elysée* is 'not a real landscape, but the symbolic description of Julie's sexual organs'[13] – a theme, if so, as old as *The Song of Songs* – but Rousseau's contemporaries, naïvely no doubt, believed that it was in garden-planning that he was attacking formality and praising naturalness:

I was struck by a pleasing sensation of freshness, created by dark shade, lively, vivid greenery, flowers scattered on every side, the babbling of running water, and the songs of a thousand birds, and all of which affected my imagination as much as my senses, and yet at the same time I thought I was viewing the wildest of places, the most solitary in nature, and I seemed to myself the first mortal who had ever penetrated into this deserted spot.[14]

Saint-Preux even adds a comparison with the scenes on the Pacific islands he had visited during Anson's expedition; the link implied is with a wild nature that transcends the pastoral and picturesque or the merely Arcadian.

Saint-Preux's letter was to inspire the creation of numerous actual gardens, alongside the impact of both foreign and native theorists – treatises on gardening from Walpole, Watelet, and others – and of the other influences mentioned already. In or not far from Paris can be named Méréville, Moulin-Joli, Rambouillet, Roissy, Chantaloup, Bellevue, the Parc Monceau (absurdest of them all), and several more, of which one of the earliest and most celebrated was the Parc d'Ermenonville, created under the explicit influence of Rousseau by the Marquis de Girardin and the place where Rousseau spent the final weeks of his life and was first buried on the 'île des peupliers' in its lake. As to the provinces one authority notes over thirty 'jardins anglais' during the late-eighteenth century.[15] The Versailles contrast is replicated elsewhere, moreover. At Chantilly the Prince de Condé ordered during the 1770s not only an English garden five minutes from the elevated terraces of the 'château' but a whole hamlet with mill, well, barn, dairy and thatched cottages, where the princesses would dress as working villagers. At Fontainebleau later a new garden was created away from the old formal gardens, and the Jardin du Luxembourg later still had an area of winding pathways and scattered trees added at the far end of the formal avenues.

It is obvious enough that the astonishing proliferation of these new gardens and estates reflected the sharpened pastoral attitudes – the love for quiet reverie amidst bosky groves and by streams or waterfalls, for tranquil vistas over banked, disordered trees, for pleasing walks along winding pathways. The aim, as the Marquis de Girardin would put it in his treatise of 1777, was 'a sort of Elysian garden' made for 'peaceful happiness and the true pleasures of the soul'; the mood he emphasises is that of 'contentment' and 'tranquillity', and the setting is for the quiet delectation of an aristocrat and his well-bred friends. Much more could be said about his Parc, one of the most revealing of the late-eighteenth century's cultural artefacts and the more interesting because so many visitors, distinguished and unknown, came to admire it. The pursuit of 'la philosophie', the cult of 'la rêverie', the liking for the primitive and 'pre-historic', the taste for the nearby 'Désert' (on whose sands Rousseau liked to walk), the addition later of ruins, tombs and monuments: all these could be studied in a 'cultural commentary' upon Ermenonville. Here, however, only one general conclusion needs to be stressed regarding this and the other examples of the informal garden in France: there is little movement beyond the pastoral limits. Wildness is present, but it is contrived and in no way threatening. Nature is allowed, even encouraged, to be disordered, but it is a 'sweet disorder' and in the last resort still under control. Withdrawal from society is a principal delight, but the hamlet still provides, as on Chantilly's charming wooded island, its 'salon de musique' and its building for billiards.

It is this wish to have the best of both worlds, of the natural and the cultivated at the same time, that is so well symbolised by what has been claimed to be one of the most indicative innovations of eighteenth-century England, alongside the invention of the corridor and the dumb-waiter: the garden 'ha-ha'. The notion came early in the century – and perhaps even from France, oddly enough, where it was termed 'une claire-voie' – but its popularity increased greatly later.[16] The outlook from the stately home is no longer limited by a wall or railings, and yet the concealed dry ditch is there at the end of the lawns to prevent intrusion by such forms of nature as the cows in the far meadow. The eye can rest, with no barrier intervening, upon the pleasing perspectives of woods, of fields and, indeed, of cows – but cows unobtrusively kept at a distance.

We have seen Rousseau's impact upon even the design of landscape-gardens. For a final illustration of the renewed pastoral vision of the later-eighteenth century his immensely wider significance demands attention. Indeed in regard to this book's total subject Rousseau is the undeniably outstanding figure, certainly in France and arguably in Europe, for probably only Goethe could challenge his stature. He invokes 'the natural' in numerous ways, as later chapters will have to consider: in attacking urban society and 'civilised' standards, in advocating a new view of children, their family upbringing and their education, in developing a new 'ideal' of the 'natural

woman', in defending the 'noble savage', in linking religion
with the cult of nature, and in other respects as well. For this
chapter, however, it is only his reactions to external nature that
are relevant – in *La Nouvelle Héloïse*, his *Lettres à M. de
Malesherbes*, his *Rêveries d'un promeneur solitaire*, and elsewhere.
Here too he was of high importance. The new appreciations
of nature were developing before him and independently of
him; none the less, he, more than any other single writer, stated
them as a wide-ranging and greatly influential synthesis.

His responses to the natural world were complex and
multi-sided, and it has been well said that they 'varied from that
of the scientific botaniser, to that of the creator of literary
myths, to that of the semi-mystic'.[17] They have been frequently
and fully studied and with entirely justified appreciation. Here,
therefore, three points only that are of especial relevance will
be suggested. The first and last may seem to point to limitations
in his literary rendering of nature but are not made as criticism,
only to characterise it. The second, however, indicates a
supreme aspect of his achievement.

First, Rousseau is concerned less to present the details, the
'picturesque' interest, of the natural world than to convey its
psychological impact on himself or his characters. It has often been
repeated that whilst Saint-Pierre in his writings was to describe
'les *sensations* de la nature' – external, physical, exotic –
Rousseau evoked 'les *sentiments* de la nature'. Some concrete
description is certainly found, and he himself loved to look at
and examine plants and flowers in particular – 'herborisant',
as he termed it, in the manner he evokes in his *Cinquième Rêverie*,
wandering with 'a magnifying glass in my hand and my *Systema
naturae* [Linnaeus's great botanical work] under my arm'. He
knew the details, but he only spasmodically chose to give them.
More often one finds that abstract nouns indicating a mental
impression replace any particulars, and there is a constant stress
on the inner reaction of the author or the character to what he
is observing. This short passage from his third *Lettre à
Malesherbes* (1762) is typical; from a couple of rather vague
specifics he rapidly moves to himself and, as regards the natural
scene, from concrete details to abstract nouns:

The golden colour of the broom and the purple of the heather struck my eyes
with a luxuriousness that moved my heart; the majesty of the trees covering
me with their shadow, the delicacy of the bushes around me, and the
surprising variety of grasses and flowers that I trod beneath my feet kept my
mind in a state of continual alternation between observation and admiration.[18]

Many of his nature-descriptions were similar in their
emphasis. The description of Julie's 'Elysian garden' conveys
an enchanting impression of freshness, flowers, streams and
birds, but it rests on details which (we read) 'spoke to my
imagination at least as much as to my senses'. The final purpose,
as Saint-Preux makes plain, was to inspire 'reverie' in the
human observer rather than to achieve a sensory or purely
aesthetic effect. Moreover, despite its appearance of irregular,
rather wild naturalness, the new garden was in fact to be
carefully designed by its human creator – something Rousseau
particularly stressed. Traces of man's intervention have been
concealed, we are told, but essentially this garden resulted from
a collaboration between man and nature, illustrative, Rousseau
believed, of what can be achieved if only they will act in
harmony with each other. 'It is true [says Julie] that nature has
created everything, but under my direction and there is nothing
there which I have not ordered.' (Nature, one feels, confronted
by Julie, would not have dared to step out of line!)

Another example is offered by the scene of the 'promenade
du lac Léman' (IV, 17). This is, once again, above all about
Saint-Preux's feelings for Julie, and even the evocation of
Alpine scenery is related to the inner responses of the sensitive
person. The mountain wilderness is in reality a background;
what actually matters occurs within those who observe it.
Indeed, the feature which Rousseau valued even about
mountains was what he called, in a celebrated description of the
Valais (I, 23), 'a surprising mingling of wild nature and
cultivated nature which everywhere showed the hand of men
in places one might have believed they had never penetrated'.
Centrally, in short, though fully aware of all the detailed
beauties of nature, Rousseau constantly stressed the human and
inward far more than the sensory and external. In his seventh
Rêverie there is a most significant sentence that captures his

predominant approach. Of the sensitive observer of the natural world he writes: 'All individual objects escape him; he sees and feels nothing but the unity of all things.'

That emphasis on 'unity' points to a second and major point. More than any other French writer of the century Rousseau discerned and expressed a sense of the potential harmony between man and nature. In the course of the eighteenth century – in the new 'sciences of nature', as we shall see later, but also in broader ways – the notion of nature as a mechanism, as a divinely-designed 'order', perfect in its essentially passive regularity, gradually yielded, in some minds at least, to a notion of a no less divinely-intended 'harmony' between two creative, developing 'organisms' – man and the natural world. No-one in France prior to the Romantic movement illustrates that change more clearly than Rousseau.

The harmony is, first, psychological. Man's moods are matched, as it were, by nature, which is in sympathy with him. Rousseau does not get to the point reached later in Lamartine's *Le Lac* of asking the lake and rocks to preserve the memory of his dead beloved, though at one moment Saint-Preux draws Julie's attention to a rock on the shore of Lake Geneva that is 'a place so filled with you' (IV, 17). All the same, the sensitive soul – unlike corrupted urban man – readily feels the affinities. 'This solitary spot formed a wild and deserted retreat, but filled with those kinds of beauty which please only sensitive souls and appear horrifying to others' (IV, 17). The harmony, secondly, is aesthetic: we respond at once to 'those kinds of beauty' offered by nature in both its gentler and its wilder expressions, and that are so much preferable to the artificial, painted 'beauty' seen in the arts (as his first *Discours* had argued) or in the dresses and rouged faces of the ladies of the court. Thirdly, the harmony is moral, in the sense that man is not only happier but also lives more ethically amidst nature than in towns and cities. This theme of corrupt town versus good countryside is one we shall return to; enough here to note a few examples. In his *Lettres à Malesherbes* the village of Montmorency, from which he wrote them, is in his view the ideal setting for 'a charming company' of people 'worthy to inhabit' such 'retreats of nature'. *La*

Nouvelle Héloïse abounds likewise with virtuous country-dwellers, unconcerned about money, bountifully generous – like the peasants of the Valais refusing payment for their hospitality to Saint-Preux (1, 23). In such Alpine heights man becomes calmer, purer; his meditations take on a quality that is 'great and sublime'. 'It seems that in rising above human habitations one leaves behind all base and worldly feelings' (1, 23). The novel's description of a rural wine-harvest (v, 7) is perhaps the apotheosis of this whole emphasis on the good moral impact of living amidst Nature; at the end of the feast, everyone (save one man who misbehaves and is dismissed the next morning) goes to his bed 'happy with a day spent in working, cheerfulness and innocence'. This letter also illustrates, moreover, a fourth area of harmony between man and nature: economic. In the very year the novel was published, the French government set up a Department of Agriculture to promote the new ideas of Physiocratic economics, as propounded by Quesnay and others. A later chapter will need to consider these ideas further, but, briefly, the claim is that 'economic value' lies above all in 'the good earth'; a nation's basic wealth derives from the effective cultivation of its land. Soon Adam Smith would advance the different 'labour theory of value', but meanwhile a variety of reforms were introduced – some of which, alas, rendered the peasantry worse off than before. Rousseau clearly has a Physiocrat type of view. The wine-harvest scene has criticism of peasant-exploitation – of 'the grasping greed of a miserly "fermier", the inflexible harshness of an unfeeling master'; of the conditions suffered by 'unhappy peasants emaciated by fasting, worn out by weariness and dressed in rags'. In contrast, the good owner, collaborating with nature, ensures a fruitful harvest and the general well-being: 'how attractive to see good and wise stewards making of the cultivation of their land the means to ensure blessings, recreation and pleasure' (v, 7). A further illustration of economic harmony is in the letter (v, 2) where Saint-Preux describes Wolmar's running of his estate in some detail and affirms that 'the condition natural to man is to cultivate the earth and live upon its fruits'. And along with economic harmony there also seems to go a social harmony, a reconciliation of the classes.

In some instances there is even a further element in this harmony with nature: as well as psychological, aesthetic, moral, economic, and even social elements, it may include a religious reaction, as the *Profession de foi du Vicaire savoyard* in *Emile* especially suggests. Rousseau is a deist, not a pantheist, and yet at times nature not only gives evidence of its Creator's goodness and provides a major foundation for belief in God; it almost, in itself, inspires the kind of religious elevation that Wordsworth, Lamartine, and others would suggest later, the reaction of a 'semi-mystic'.

Several of these illustrations may have suggested, however, a final characteristic of his portrayal of nature: it remains predominantly pastoral. To suggest this is in no way to doubt Rousseau's deep love of the unspoilt natural world; this persists from his earlier years in Haute-Savoie, especially with Mme de Warens at Les Charmettes, to his last few happy weeks at the Parc d'Ermenonville. Nor is it to question the outstanding emotional and stylistic intensity of Rousseau as painter of nature or the extent to which he anticipated and influenced the nature poetry of the Romantic generation. It is merely to note – but not in criticism – that what he loved and described was in general a gentle, rural world that charms us into peaceful reflection and emotion, that is the setting for good and contented peasants, grateful, moreover, for their paternalistic squire.

It is true that Rousseau was one of the very first French writers to describe wild mountain scenery – in *La Nouvelle Héloïse* – but in reality (we shall shortly note) that remains in the background and is largely viewed at a distance. One may differ as to how far he shared the sense of 'wild sublimity' found in others in the late-eighteenth century, but there is some substance at least in C. E. Engel's rather hard accusation in her study of *La Littérature alpestre* that what he did was to 'embellish with idylls' the mountain-slopes alone.[19]

Yet more than any of his French contemporaries Rousseau, whilst remaining within the pastoral world, transformed 'tradition' into 'vision'. As a boy he loved d'Urfé's *Astrée*, an archetypal example of the old Arcadian tradition, and he (and many of his contemporaries) retained an affection for it. But in him there is little or nothing – after *Le Devin du village* at least – that is second-hand, artificial, conventional. He *sees* external nature; if he describes it less than others, that is because he above all *responds* to it, emotionally and intellectually as well. For with him 'vision' is not only (or primarily) 'looking'; *his* 'pastoral vision' also involves those other meanings of the word that imply imagination, insight, even dreaming of a prophetic kind. His concern is not with a 'return to nature', to a past in 'the Golden Age', but with the pastoral world as an 'image' of a possible, hoped-for future.

This chapter has concerned the external world of 'pastoral landscapes'. But it would be wholly false to leave the landscapes empty of all save vegetation and earth, for they were almost invariably presented in ways that showed the natural scene *completed* by the presence of humans and also of animals, living contentedly within it. What 'fits' with the 'pastoral landscape' is, of course, the good peasant and, secondly, the 'happy beast' – as works of literature and paintings in their scores attest. We must return to them both later but, meanwhile, may illustrate the harmony of nature, man and beast with a single, early, English example, the very first stanza of Gray's *Elegy*:

> The Curfew tolls the knell of parting day,
> The lowing herd wind slowly o'er the lea,
> The plowman homeward plods his weary way,
> And leaves the world to darkness and to me.

3

WILD SUBLIMITY

It is one thing to appreciate the gentle pastoral landscape, to feel a sense of harmony with the sunny, contented world of nature represented by the country retreat, the 'English garden', the tranquil rural scene. It is a more difficult thing to appreciate and feel harmony with nature in its wilder, more threatening expressions – to respond to high, barren mountains, dangerous oceans, savage storms on land or sea, black and perilous night-time. In the eighteenth century, however, for almost the first time in European thinking, a minority achieved these more difficult responses and thereby very significantly helped to enlarge men's imaginative and aesthetic reactions to nature. And if that seems too large a claim, one need only read a study like Marjorie Hope Nicolson's *Mountain Gloom and Mountain Glory* to be persuaded:

Theology, philosophy, geology, astronomy – basic and radical changes in all these occurred [she writes] before the 'Mountain Gloom' gave way to 'Mountain Glory'...It was a result of one of the most profound revolutions in thought that has ever occurred.[1]

A preliminary point is necessary here, however. This book centrally concerns France and how far in France appraisals of nature and the natural were modified during the later-eighteenth century. Yet in this chapter the French will be largely absent as compared with the British, the Germans and the French-speaking Swiss. That fact does not imply irrelevance, however: what did *not* happen in France whilst occurring elsewhere may be highly significant. The point was well made by Sherlock Holmes in the Silver Blaze case, when he drew the Inspector's attention to 'the curious incident of the dog in the night-time'. 'The dog did nothing in the night-time', replies the Inspector. 'That [Holmes answers], that was the curious incident.' So, likewise, is the comparative absence in France prior to the Romantics of the nineteenth century of a full appreciation of wild nature.

For us today it is hard to recapture the sense of repulsion, displeasing irregularity or, at best, disinterested boredom felt by most people prior to the eighteenth century (and still during it) at the sight of mountains (or of the sea). John Evelyn, to give a mid-seventeenth century example, crossed the Simplon Pass in 1646 and was, incidentally, set upon by brigands as an additional suffering. He tells that the way – said to have been 'covered with Snow since the Creation' – was 'through very steepe, craggy, and dangerous passages,...through strange, horrid and firefull Craggs and tracts', and he concludes: 'Nature has swept up the rubbish of the earth in the Alps.' Dryden was only a little more sympathetic: 'High objects, it is true, attract the sight, but it looks up with pain on Craggy Rocks and Barren Mountains.' And still later, in 1730, another Englishman, John Spence, could declare: 'I should like the Alps very much, if it was not for the hills.' Even English hills – in Derbyshire or the Lake District, for instance – could inspire similar distaste, as when Daniel Defoe describes Westmorland as 'a country eminent only for being the wildest, most barren and frightful of any that I have passed over'.

What could account for such excrescences on the face of God's world? How had our earth ceased to be smooth and round – to be 'the mundane egg', as Abelard and others had long described it in its original state, fresh from the hand of the Creator? The overwhelming answer was that, thanks to the sin of man, the Creation too is fallen; the Flood, sent by God as punishment for human wickedness, produced the seas and threw up the mountains. Calvin might argue that mountains are not blemishes – since moving to Geneva he had lived near them – and that external nature is not fallen, but even he conceded that the Flood had destroyed some of the earth's beauties. Luther, by contrast, was clear that the Flood had wholly wiped out those beauties: 'even the earth, which is innocent in itself and committed no sin, is nevertheless compelled to bear sin's curse'. And a prime example for him was provided by mountains, which 'exist where fields and fruitful plains before flourished'. This was still the dominant view at the start of the eighteenth century. John Ray was quite unusual when, in his *Wisdom of God* of 1691, he listed no fewer than twenty ways in which mountains are useful. Thomas Burnet's *The Sacred Theory of the Earth* (in Latin in 1681, in English in 1684, and later expanded) was far more influential in the shorter term and was taken seriously even by Diderot and other French 'philosophes'. For Burnet mountains – along with other irregularities like indented coastlines and caves – were the 'Ruins of a broken World'.[2]

The Face of the Earth before the Deluge was smooth, regular, and uniform, without Mountains, and without a Sea...And the Smoothness of the Earth made the Face of the Heavens so too; the Air was calm and serene; none of those tumultuary Motions and Conflicts of Vapours, which the Mountains and the Winds cause in ours: 'Twas suited to a golden Age, and to the first innocency of Nature.

Storms, one notes, are as much the product of human sin as mountains and the sea: the whole world is degenerate – and some had added, since Galileo's discovery of spots on the sun and moon, interpreted as blemishes, that the whole cosmos is degenerate. It is against this background in particular that one has to measure the originality of the new reactions which emerged in the eighteenth century – tentatively in its first half, more firmly in its second – and which became more widespread still with the nineteenth century.

Why the change occurred seems difficult and perhaps impossible to say. Some, as regards new English responses to mountains, have pointed to the increasing prevalence of the Grand Tour to Italy, across the Alps, which thus familiarised at least the travellers with them. Certainly it is worth recalling how few people earlier had actually seen high mountains; the seventeenth-century Christian 'defender' of mountains, Henry More, never had, for example (nor, come to that, had Kant even in the late-eighteenth century). Yet crossing the Alps could provoke very antipathetic responses, as with Evelyn, and going on the Grand Tour in 1671 created in Burnet the major religious crisis of his life. The Tour's dangers did not significantly lessen

– and although by 1686 Shaftesbury went on it and returned eventually to write the mountain rhapsody found in *The Moralists*, praising the diversity and superabundance of God's creation, and to invoke mountain scenery as a major source of man's sense of 'the sublime', and though Addison in 1701 and Gray in 1739 were both impressed, we lack enough accounts from those who were not and who did not extol Alpine sublimity to assume such views as theirs were characteristic. Others have invoked intellectual and theoretical influences to explain the novel reactions: for example, in England, the contentions against Burnet's arguments of John Ray, William Derham, and others, or the theoretical development of an 'aesthetics of the sublime' by Shaftesbury, Hume, Burke and others, not forgetting French variations earlier on the notion of the sublime in Longinus. Certainly some people were helped by such theories to express the nature of their own reactions – Diderot by his reading of Shaftesbury, for example. But just as one can breathe without having a prior theory of breathing, so one can respond to a wild landscape without having first read in Burke's *Enquiry into ... the Sublime and Beautiful* that: 'Whatever is fitted in any sort to excite the ideas of pain, and danger, that is to say, whatever is in any sort terrible, or is conversant about terrible objects... is a source of the sublime.'[3] Nicolson argues persuasively that in England at least what she terms the 'natural Sublime' was earlier than the 'rhetorical Sublime' and was 'far from being merely a "debased" Longinianism'; she even suggests that the experience of the sublime itself may have been positively inhibited in France by the dominance there of Boileau's version of Longinus in his *Traité du Sublime* (1674).[4] If she is correct on either count, one has good reason (over and beyond any bias towards empiricism) to doubt whether the actual responses of individual men derived from pre-existing theories. It seems rather to have been the other way round: the responses experienced initially by a few and described by them encouraged both similar experiences in others and also theorising about the experiences.

Addison offers a good example of the initial, ambivalent response. He is writing to a friend in December 1701:

I am just now arriv'd at Geneva by a very troublesome Journey over the Alpes, where I have bin for some days together shivering among the Eternal Snows. My head is still Giddy with mountains and precipices, and you can't imagine how much I am pleas'd with the sight of a Plain.

The Alps, he says, 'form one of the most irregular, mis-shapen scenes in the world'. Yet he also declared that 'they fill the mind with an agreeable kind of horror', and he would later express the same reaction to storms at sea in almost the same words:

I cannot see the heavings of this prodigious bulk of waters, even in a calm, without a very pleasing astonishment; but when it is worked up in a tempest...it is impossible to describe the agreeable horror that arises from such a prospect...A troubled ocean, to a man who sails upon it,...gives his imagination one of the highest kinds of pleasure that can arise from greatness.[5]

Very gradually such feelings became more common. In 1739, for example, Horace Walpole and Gray set out together on the Grand Tour. Both gave graphic descriptions of the dangers and difficulties of their travels amongst the mountains, but there was a small difference in their personal evaluations. Gray felt the same horror and fright as Walpole, not least among the Grande Chartreuse, but at the same time he found its 'rudeness' to be 'magnificent'. It forms 'one of the most poetical scenes imaginable', and he adds, in often-quoted words: 'Not a precipice, not a torrent, not a cliff, but is pregnant with religion and poetry. There are certain scenes that would awe an atheist into belief without the help of other argument.'[6]

Even the French had not been wholly unresponsive. There are very isolated and uncharacteristic instances in the seventeenth century in paintings like *Mountain Landscape with Lightning* by Francisque Millet (1642–79), and even some from Poussin, notably *L'Hiver ou Le Déluge*, albeit with biblical or mythological characters present in a minor way. Some eighteenth-century theorists like Roger, Piles, Lacombe and Pernety had praised 'le paysage héroïque' – with rocks, torrents and mountains – as well as 'le paysage pastoral'. More strikingly, as early as 1735 one finds Mme de Tencin in her *Mémoires du comte de Comminges* relishing the wild Pyrenees: 'This abode of such wildness pleased me by the very fact that it added further to my

melancholy.' All the same, reactions like hers, Addison's and
Gray's seem to have been isolated cases during the first thirty
or forty years of the century. As regards England there were
minor poets like Richard Blackmore and there was Thomson
– defended by Nicolson as 'the finest English mountain poet
before Wordsworth'[7] – and by the middle of the eighteenth
century there was the landscape-painter Richard Wilson,
adapting the Claude tradition of ideal landscape in his paintings
of Wales and the Lake District, to be followed a little later by
George Barret and Joseph Wright (who especially enjoyed
depicting Vesuvius). As regards continental Europe also the
new appreciation was initially restricted – largely to a few
Germans (mainly from the south, near the Alps, not surprisingly)
and Swiss, of whom the most notable was the celebrated
scientist Haller. In fact it was Haller's work as a botanist that
first took him into the Alps, as it had earlier taken the geologist
Scheuchzer to look for fossils and would later lead the Swiss
scientist Saussure to study the rocks of Mont Blanc. Haller went
to collect plant specimens, but the outcome was the first major
work of mountain literature, his long poem *Die Alpen* (1732).
Yet even this appears to have had few immediate admirers; for
example, it was not translated into French until 1750 –
whereafter it became widely valued, with four editions in
translation by 1773.

Those dates perhaps reflect a wider pattern. Van Tieghem,
writing of European literature as a whole, distinguishes three
phases: from about 1730 a gradual rise of interest in mountains;
from about 1762 a more emphatic liking for the lower, more
pastoral slopes of mountains; from about 1773 an extension of
that liking to include the high, deserted mountain peaks.[8] His
dates may seem unduly precise, but the same broad progression
is found in the detailed study by Claude Edmonde Engel of *La
Littérature alpestre*. It is also confirmed if one looks (as we now
briefly shall) at developing responses to a single Alpine area,
the Valais, and, not far away from it, a single mountain – the
highest in Europe – Mont Blanc, and especially as illustrated
by two French-speaking Swiss observers, Rousseau and
Saussure.

Rousseau's novel *La Nouvelle Héloïse* (1761) was an important landmark in the history of mountain appreciation. Born in Geneva, he had later spent several years living in the Savoy Alps, near Annecy, then outside Chambéry (the novel itself is set 'in a little town at the foot of the Alps'), and had visited the High Alps in 1744 and returned to the lower Valais area in 1754. He evokes them in particular in the letter (I, 23) where Saint-Preux describes to Julie his visit to the Valais and also in the letter (IV, 17) about an outing on Lake Geneva:

Sometimes immense crags were hanging in ruins over my head. Sometimes high and resounding waterfalls soaked me with their dense mists. Sometimes a ceaseless torrent revealed at my side an abyss whose depths my eyes dared not fathom. Now and then I was lost in the darkness of a thick wood...

This solitary place formed a wild, deserted retreat; but filled with those kinds of beauty which please only sensitive souls and appear horrifying to others...[9]

Such passages became admired throughout Europe, and yet the characteristics of Rousseau's landscape-descriptions as a whole, noted in the previous chapter, apply also to these mountain views, even though one may think Engel is over-harsh to claim that Rousseau hardly knew and barely liked the High Alps and that he had at the same time 'determined and falsified' the literary representation of mountains.[10] First, the view is usually at a certain distance, and the details are general and even vague: 'immenses rochers', 'hautes cascades', a 'torrent éternel', 'un bois touffu'. Secondly, his view is focussed far less on mountain-peaks than on mountain-slopes, on precisely where nature and human beings meet. In both letters he quickly descends from the heights. Within a few lines of the passages quoted we read (I, 23) of a pleasing meadow or (IV, 17) of 'the charms of a pleasing, rural sojourn' discovered 'amidst these great and splendid objects' (a noun in itself implying a certain distancing). Thirdly, and linked with that, the view is valued less for any external beauties than for its impact upon Saint-Preux's inner life. What he prizes above all in these mountains is that they offer an effective setting, first, for a tranquil life far from urban stress; secondly, for a virtuous life far from urban corruption; and, thirdly, for a rich mental life far from urban superficialities and fashions. 'One's meditations take on inde-scribable qualities of greatness and sublimity' (I, 23). And likewise what distinguishes for him his 'promenade du lac Léman' (IV, 17) is that it was the day 'when, without exception, I experienced the keenest emotions'.

In short, what one finds in Rousseau's depiction of the Alps is an outstanding illustration of Van Tieghem's second phase: the liking for mountain-slopes. There is an undoubted and sincere affection for mountain *scenery*, a sense of affinity, of psychological harmony, between a rather generalised wild nature and some of man's more elevated or 'sublime' inner experiences, and an affirmation of the morally beneficent context for human life provided by the 'unfailing purity' of these 'ethereal regions'. 'Ethérées', ethereal, is perhaps a significant choice of word, however: for Rousseau mountains are still not quite part of this real world; they are built of reveries more than of hard rocks.

A professional interest in hard rocks was precisely what first led to Mont Blanc Horace Bénédict de Saussure, a Geneva professor of geology whose statue now stands in a square in Chamonix with a hand pointing to the heights. As early as 1760 he had offered a reward to anyone taking him to the summit, but it was August 1786 before the mountain was first climbed and August 1787 before Saussure himself reached its summit. He spent his 4½ hours there not, as we might, in viewing the scenery, but in taking readings on his barometers, thermometers, and electrometers, in testing magnetic variations, finding the temperature of boiling water, taking the pulse-rates of others in his party, and so on. But his reactions were not only scientific, any more than Haller's had been, and his work in four volumes from 1779 to 1796, *Voyages dans les Alpes*, makes him a major figure in the rise of 'la littérature alpestre'. First, his work gives numerous descriptions of the mountains he had observed and actually climbed, and these are detailed and first-hand whereas Rousseau's had been general and vague. Secondly, they concern the mountains' peaks, the regions of bare rock, even more than their slopes, again in contrast to Rousseau, and the human presence is often missing – and is irrelevant to Saussure. For, thirdly, his strong emotional reaction to the mountains is far from Rousseau's pastoralism; he feels and expresses, perhaps for the first time in French literature, a sense of their wild sublimity. A single passage must serve here to illustrate his exceptional responsiveness; he is describing a night he spent on the Tête-Rousse, high in the Mont Blanc range:

The sky was pure to perfection and without clouds; the mists were no longer to be seen except in the depths of the valleys; the stars glittered but were not twinkling in any way, and they diffused an extremely weak and pale light over the summits of the mountains, sufficient, however, for one to make out the masses and the distances. The tranquillity and the deep silence ruling over this vast expanse, and further increased by my imagination, inspired in me a kind of terror; it seemed to me that I alone had outlived the universe and that I saw its dead body stretched out at my feet. However sad may be ideas of this kind, they have a sort of attractiveness which is difficult to resist.[11]

One may fairly conclude that Saussure, along with Ramond in his two *Lettres sur le Valais* (1780) and his *Observations dans les Pyrénées* (1798) and a few minor writers, exemplifies Van Tieghem's third phase, as Rousseau had the second. In French literature, however, they remain isolated in general, and such French mountain poetry as one finds is marked, Engel concludes, by 'banal elegance'.[12] It was English poets yet again who, following Thomson earlier, would establish mountain sublimity as a major literary theme. In the Long Vacation of 1790 a Cambridge undergraduate crossed the pass leading up from Martigny in the Valais where Saint-Preux had earlier mused and first beheld Mont Blanc:

> That very day [wrote young Wordsworth]
> From a bare ridge we also first beheld
> Unveiled the summit of Mont Blanc...
>   The wondrous Vale
> Of Chamouny stretched far below, and soon
> With its dumb cataracts and streams of ice,
> A motionless array of mighty waves,
> Five rivers broad and vast, made rich amends.

Amongst others Shelley would soon follow, and express a similar feeling in his *Mont Blanc*, 'Written in the Vale of Chamouni':

> Far, far above, piercing the infinite sky,
> Mont Blanc appears, – still, snowy, and serene –

Its subject mountains their unearthly forms
Pile around it, ice and rock; broad vales between
Of frozen floods, unfathomable deeps,
Blue as the overhanging heaven, that spread
And wind among the accumulated steeps...

However, with Shelley, Coleridge, Byron, Senancour, and other Romantics we have passed to the nineteenth century and its full expression of the theme of 'mountain glory'.

Eighteenth-century painting offers analogies with the developing awareness seen in literature, as a few examples may illustrate. Vernet was a major and surprisingly early painter of wild nature as illustrated by storms at sea, as will shortly be noted, and he excelled from the 1740s on in painting craggy rocks and waterfalls and the like. He rarely painted mountains, however, though he did execute one celebrated painting, *La Bergère des Alpes* (1763). In this work the bare mountain tops are vividly presented – and yet they are firmly in the background. What dominates in the picture are the green, fertile slopes, the well-bred flock of sheep, and the clean and leisured figures of the pretty shepherdess and her attentive admirer. Much the same is true in *Le Matin sur terre: la pêche en rivière* (1766) also. The high mountains, misty in the pink early-morning light are clearly depicted but form only a tranquil setting, like the two waterfalls, for the valley-dwellers at work at their fishing. In both cases there is clearly aesthetic appreciation and also detailed realism as regards the mountains, but they remain scenery, a setting for the pastoral idyll in the foreground, just as the High Alps were for Saint-Preux. It was in England that certain painters would shortly go further: most notably Cozens around 1770 and Loutherbourg, after his move from France, in the following two decades and more; wild Wales and the Lake District became favourite subjects during this later-eighteenth-century period. But if Vernet is comparable with Rousseau, the analogue with Saussure and Ramond is (apart from Swiss landscape-painters such as Linck, Hackert, Bourrit, and a few others) another young Englishman who followed Wordsworth to Chamonix near the turn of the century – namely, Turner. In his many Alpine scenes one finally finds in painting the wild sublimity of mountains – just as of wild waters in his many seascapes. Here, as with the English Romantic poets, one has finally arrived at a sense of deep affinity between the human spirit and nature in even its most savage forms.

The French seem for the most part to have remained more ambivalent than the English. Numerous private visitors toured the Alps in the later century, and Mme Roland notes that by 1777 a trip to Switzerland has become all the fashion. Once again, many individuals may have been ahead of the mainly urbanised writers and painters. Publication of a work like Bourrit's *Description des Glacières* (1773), followed by his later, similarly illustrated travel-works, attests to a demand – and not only from Goethe, Walpole and Reynolds, all of whom subscribed to it, or from Louis XVI who gave Bourrit a pension on the strength of it.[13] Yet it is impossible to verify how many of the visitors were from France or from elsewhere. One estimate of visitors to Chamonix in the 1783 season – the first inn there had opened in 1765 – put the total at 1,500 but adds that of those three-quarters were British. But certainly there is a contrast of attitude between French writers on the one hand and their contemporaries in both England and Germany. Goethe, for example, had been exhilarated by the mountain scene from his youth – as *Werther* already shows:

Monstrous mountains invested me, abysses lay before me, and mountain torrents plunged downward, the rivers flowed before me, and woods and wilds resounded; and I saw all the unfathomable forces in the depths of the earth working and creating within each other.[14]

That is one of Werther's letters and was written even before Goethe visited the Alps for the first time.

By comparison, in France even early Romantics like Mme de Staël and Chateaubriand years later remained luke-warm. Mme de Staël could describe the valley at Chamonix as 'one of the most imposing spectacles that Nature has given to man'; but she rarely visited it even though she lived nearby at Coppet on Lake Geneva, and one notes that it remains for her a 'spectacle'. Chateaubriand is celebrated for his depictions of what he called 'fearful and sublime nature' in the form of storms, but is more guarded about the high peaks. He went to Mont Blanc in 1805, stayed at Chamonix and climbed up to the Mer de Glace. But his account, in *Voyage au Mont-Blanc*, is surprisingly ambivalent and even critical. He praises mountain scenery in the distance, even declaring that 'there are no beautiful landscapes without mountains on the horizon', and he especially admires the view of the setting sun upon the summits of the Savoy Alps as seen from Lausanne. But those who live close to the mountains are deprived of such vistas, he continues; they also lack air space, and from the depth of their valley they rarely see the sun except at midday: theirs is 'a sad place to live'. He acknowledges that others attribute 'sublimity' to mountain views; he himself is doubtful and even says: 'These heavy masses are in no way in harmony with man's faculties and the weakness of his sense-organs.' Nor does he accept Rousseau's happy view of the peasants living in these mountains: 'I could only see in those "famous" Alpine chalets dreamed up by the imagination of J. J. Rousseau unpleasant huts filled with the manure of the herds and the smell of cheeses and fermented milk', inhabited (he adds) by 'wretched mountain-dwellers'.[15]

In short, it appears that the mountain themes found in English and German writers of the period are largely absent amongst French authors even in the first decade of the nineteenth century (Senancour excepted, and he was Swiss, significantly) – though David's painting of *Napoleon Crossing the Alps* suggests that the writers may have lagged behind. In French literature one has to await *later* Romantics. Meanwhile we must leave the 'misérables montagnards' to their fate and descend to the sea – a second vivid illustration of wild nature.

For countless centuries men had sailed the seas out of necessity: to fish, wage war, explore. Yet as far as one can tell they had largely felt it to be alien, something to be feared rather than enjoyed. Likewise, those who did not go to sea do not seem to have shared at all our enthusiasm for sea-views, for looking at the sea from a holiday hotel or a cliff-top. Indeed, houses in coastal towns were normally built with their backs to the sea, away from the wind. (Even in a maritime country like England the first complete terrace of houses facing the sea was apparently

not built until 1808 – the Royal Crescent at Brighton.) The
common attitude in the eighteenth century and before was that
expressed by Dr Johnson when he deplored 'the sterile
uniformity of the ocean' and by a foreign princess who thought
it 'boring, disagreeable and unbearable': 'it is intolerable to see
only air and water'.[16] As noted earlier in this chapter, for Bishop
Burnet the very existence of seas and irregular coastlines was
one more sign that the world is fallen.

It is true that in England seaside resorts were being
developed from before the mid-eighteenth century, but the
motives for that were medical – in order for the visitors to be
'dipped', by burly female 'dippers', into the otherwise dull
salt-water or, alternatively, to drink it.[17] (That too is perhaps
relevant to our subject as a whole, as one instance of the idea
that what is natural is or may be good for us.) Scarborough was
the first English resort – from around 1740 – largely because it
had well-tried spa water for drinking as well as the North Sea,
and soon afterwards Dr Richard Russell at Brightelmstone
would be urging the health-value of dipping before breakfast –
the start of a spartan tradition with the further merit of leaving
the day free for more enjoyable, social pursuits. Dr Russell's
Dissertation on the Use of Seawater on Diseases of the Glands, first
published in Latin in 1750, is rarely read today, one imagines,
but Brighton is much indebted to it and as much as a century
later the French historian Michelet would praise Russell as 'the
inventor of the sea'.[18] What it illustrated was the view that the
sea is good for us but in no other way interesting. Other resorts
developed for the same health reasons: Eastbourne, Deal,
Portsmouth, Exmouth, and in the North a tiny hamlet called
Blackpool. Weymouth was likewise established, although not
until 1789, when George III's doctors recommended it after his
first attack of madness, a fact still commemorated by his statue
on Weymouth promenade. Many people went to these resorts
– something which by 1782 William Cowper was mocking in
his poem *Retirement* – yet still for their health rather than for
pleasure in seeing the sea.

That was in England. In France the natives were to be even
more laggardly in their appreciation of the sea than in regard

to mountains. The numerous 'maisons de campagne' were largely built inland even on the Côte d'Azur, we noted. Cannes, for instance, remained a minute fishing village until after 1830, and even then it developed only thanks to Lord Brougham, who was forced to stop there by an outbreak of plague in Italy. (One finds *his* statue close to the pier at Cannes.) Nice did expand earlier, but mainly because a colony of English – some consumptive and some eccentric – began to winter there. (The 'quartier' across the river from the old town of Nice was built originally for the English and the first Nice hotel was apparently called the Hôtel de l'Angleterre, though the name of the Promenade des Anglais came later.) The only real resorts in France were at Calais, Boulogne and Dieppe, and they were, precisely, for the English coming across the Channel. The French themselves would only go to the seaside – day trips excepted – towards the mid-*nineteenth* century. When, in 1763, nearly a century before that, the English novelist Smollett insisted on bathing in the sea at Nice, some French doctors, we are told, 'prognosticated immediate death'.[19] In fact, French resorts established for the French rather than for the English seem not to have grown up until the 1840s and 1850s – Dinard, for example, followed by Trouville in the 1850s, made particularly fashionable a little later by the Empress Eugénie, who was painted by Boudin standing in the wind there in 1863.

To revert to eighteenth-century England, it is difficult to say when people began to enjoy looking at the sea and at storms, whether over sea or on land. Thomson's *The Seasons* (1726–30) and Collins's *Odes* (1747) seem to have been in advance in their reactions.

> Vapours, and Clouds, and Storms: Be these my Theme,
> These, that exalt the Soul to solemn Thought,
> And heavenly musing. Welcome kindred Glooms!
> Wish'd, wint'ry, Horrors, hail!

These lines of Thomson express an exultation which most people would not have understood; the same may even have been true twenty-five years later, as the readers of Burke's *Enquiry* found him illustrating his notion of 'the sublime' by reference to wild waters, as when he writes of a flood in Dublin:

'It gives me pleasure to see nature in these great though terrible scenes. It fills the mind with grand ideas, and turns the soul in upon itself.' It would take Blackpool a little time to catch up with Burke – but catch up it would; a Regency guide to the resort offers as a prime attraction the chance to view a stormy sea – 'a singular, but yet awful combination of the pleasing and the sublime'.[20] That translation of Burke into advertising copy implies that by the early-nineteenth century there was a fairly widespread taste for looking at the sea in real life, but that taste was probably still relatively novel. (The early history of seaside resorts is still too neglected for one to be at all sure.)

Literature and painting were probably earlier in conveying an enjoyment of wild seas and of storms over land as well, and if so for the obvious reason that representations on paper or canvas are less dangerous and chilling than the reality. Almost suddenly, in English and also German literature, Thomson and Collins and, in Germany, Brockes, were no longer isolated figures but were joined by Falconer in *The Shipwreck* (1762), Klopstock in *Die Frühlingsfeier* (1759), Goethe in his *Wandrers Sturmleid* (1771), and above all Macpherson's Ossian, with his evocations of rocky coasts and raging seas. Falconer offers a representative example:

> Loud, and more loud the rolling peals enlarge,
> And blue on deck their blazing sides discharge;
> There, all aghast, the shivering Wretches stood;
> While chill suspense and fear congeal'd their blood…
> Sick earth convulsive groans from shore to shore,
> And nature shuddering feels the horrid roar.

Van Tieghem concludes a chapter on eighteenth-century depictions of the sea in European literature as a whole by claiming that they do not go very far and that only the nineteenth-century Romantics gave to the sea 'a place in poetry which it had not achieved before them'.[21] But whilst these earlier writers may not respond, may not exult, as much as Byron, Lamartine, Hugo or Heine, they do seem to be at least moving towards the perception that there is psychological affinity between man and even untamed and dangerous nature. The notion of 'the sublime' does, of course, postulate such an affinity since danger, terror, a sense of infinity, are by definition part of the 'sublime' reaction. Yet what the theorists may lead us to think, these eighteenth-century English and German poets lead us to feel.

French writers, here again, remained silent for longer. Rousseau says nothing of it, and though Delille's *Les Jardins* (1782) does describe a wild sea, just off Nice, the scene seems artificial. Even Bernardin de Saint-Pierre was unattracted by the sea in his earlier years; 'I detest the sea', he wrote in 1767, and in the following year: 'There is hardly any sadder sight than that of the high tide.'[22] Yet his *Voyage à l'Ile de France* (1773) contained vivid seascapes and a storm scene, and in 1788 he gave the first real shipwreck scene in French literature. This was in his novel *Paul et Virginie*, at the moment when the good ship Saint-Géran is wrecked in sight of land. All swim safely to shore except the heroine Virginie who, refusing to take off her clothes, is drowned as a martyr to female modesty. In part Saint-Pierre is advancing his story and seeking to rouse our sensibilities at the tragedy; but what is significant for us is that he makes of the wild seas a major element in this scene of elevated emotion:

The sea, swelling from the wind, rose ever higher with each moment, and the whole channel between this island and the île d'Ambre was but one vast sheet of white foam, with yawning abysses of deep black waves. The foam piled up at the heads of the bays to a height of six feet and more, and the wind...carried it over the steep coastline for more than half a league into the land.[23]

Yet even at that date Saint-Pierre remained an isolated exception.

As to the evidence of French art, in earlier French paintings the sea had usually been depicted as calm and with humans and their buildings safely dominating the foreground. This was true not only of seventeenth-century French painters; it remained true in (say) Watteau's *Embarquement pour Cythère*, and the sea in Boucher's *Triumph of Venus* is likewise calm and sunny. But then there comes a puzzle. It is posed by the numerous storm-scene paintings of Vernet (albeit he also often showed the sea in tranquil mood). These were not the work of his later years alone; the dates of some of them are 1746, 1750, 1754, 1756, and so on, as well as later – that is, thirty or forty years before Saint-Pierre's literary descriptions, though, incidentally, Vernet lived on to depict the drowned Virginie lying chastely on the tropic shore. In part such paintings obviously resulted from the artist's own feelings. It is said he once had himself tied to a ship's mast in order to study and enjoy the reality of an ocean storm (an event actually painted by his grandson), and when commissioned to paint the port of Sète in a realistic manner, he depicted it as seen through a storm at sea. And yet painters tend to depict what their clients will purchase, and as regards Vernet we know he was often asked to present wild scenes, albeit over land more than sea. A quotation given by Mornet lists these requests to him:

Two landscapes with waterfalls, rocks, tree-trunks, etc.; a rural scene, with rocks, high mountains, torrents, waterfalls, tree-trunks...; a truly horrifying wind-storm...; waterfalls with muddied waters, rocks, tree-trunks, and a frightful and wild scene.[24]

Such preferences, as well as the storm paintings themselves, surely suggest that the new taste for wild nature belonged to the patrons as much as the artist. Diderot's *Salon* reviews show that at least he shared the same taste. 'Everything that astonishes the soul, everything that imprints a feeling of terror leads to the sublime. A vast plain does not astonish one as does the ocean, nor a tranquil ocean as does a storm-tossed ocean.'[25]

Loutherbourg, a little later, would illustrate the same fondness for storms at sea. Born in Strasbourg in 1740, he lived in Paris until 1771, when he left for London. He painted numerous landscapes similar to Vernet's: storms and mountain torrents in particular. Diderot greatly liked his work also; of a *Shipwreck* of 1771 he writes in his *Salon*: 'This subject is moving and filled with naturalness; it speaks to the soul.' One can just add that Loutherbourg continued in the same genre after moving to England – in, for example, his *Smugglers landing in a storm* of 1791, with Conway Castle in the background – wild Wales again – or, two years later, his *Shipwreck with banditti*. We shall also meet him again as theatrical designer for a Covent Garden portrayal – with highly dramatic storm effects which he arranged – of the death of Captain Cook. But Loutherbourg, being later, presents less of a puzzle than Vernet. Are Vernet's storm paintings substantially ahead of French sensibility at his time? Or is it that most French writers are substantially behind in registering a new feeling that was already shared by patrons, Diderot, and others, as well as Vernet himself?

The latter is probably truer, though without the former being wholly untrue. Saint-Lambert, for example, in his theoretical 'Discours' of 1769 which prefaced *Les Saisons*, defines what he understands as nature in its 'sublime' expressions at no greater length than in describing the other moods of nature – as if there was no need to instruct his reader in especial detail. Such a case may be significant, but uncertainly so, for it is striking, none the less, that his definition should be so comprehensive:

[Nature] is sublime in the immensity of the skies and seas, in the vast deserts, in the infinity of space, in the darkness, in its unlimited strength and fecundity and in the innumerable multitude of its creatures. It is sublime in the great natural phenomena such as earthquakes, volcanoes, floods and hurricanes.[26]

Saint-Lambert, perhaps too neglected a writer, here crisply surveys a range of 'sublime' phenomena, including storms at sea and over land alike, which it is hard to believe only he and a few others appreciated. Others of them – such as night and earthquakes – could well have been taken here to illustrate a distinction that by the later-eighteenth century had become commonplace between, primarily, the 'beautiful' and the 'sublime'. Saint-Lambert goes further and juxtaposes four distinct aspects of nature, as we saw, but the more frequent comparison may have been the simpler one – as when the lower slopes of mountains were said to be 'beautiful' whereas their peaks were 'sublime'.

It need hardly surprise us if the 'agreeable and cheerful' and the 'great and beautiful' attracted more observers than the 'sublime' – and than the 'sad and melancholy', defined by Saint-Lambert in an unenthusiastic manner as offering 'few sensations' and 'few ideas'. It is obviously easier to feel in harmony with the tranquil and unthreatening. Man can believe he is on equal terms with pastoral nature, even collaborating with it as he tills his fields and constructs his landscaped gardens. By contrast, wild nature overwhelms or may overwhelm us. What the minority of eighteenth-century people we are concerned with in this chapter managed to achieve was so to enlarge their appreciation of nature that they could inwardly accept nature's ultimate power over us. Nor were they depressed by this; on the contrary they felt almost strengthened by their sense of that power: hence the near-exultation, the mood of almost transported affinity which they sometimes expressed. Why was this so?

They sensed, firstly, that man might tap, as it were, the force and energy of wild nature and also the elemental truths it could teach. At the more comic level it was even argued that one would gain strength for love-making by being in a mountain area. Sébastien Mercier declared: 'Love, in this wild area, has more strength and dominance', and the same view may underlie the Comtesse de Polignac's claim that 'Switzerland is the land of the lover', as well as of the poet and the painter.[27] But there were far more weighty assertions than those. If the pastoral landscape is inhabited by happy peasants and contented animals, the desolate moors and mountains also have their characteristic residents. There is the hermit who withdraws to contemplate, away from society's distractions. In Scotland there was developed also a notion of the Highland clansman, praised for his virtues by such as Adam Ferguson in his *Essay on the History of Civil Society* (1767) and endowed in due course with an ancient tradition – the equivalent amongst the high mountains of Rousseau's peasants in the Alpine valleys.[28] Furthermore, it was at this period precisely that 'high culture' took up the long tradition in 'popular culture' of the *good* bandit or outcast. Hobsbawm has shown just how widespread, for centuries and in diverse countries, this notion had been amongst the oppressed peasantry, but in the later-eighteenth century – 'the golden age of bandit-heroes', in his words[29] – it moved into the literature and painting of the cultivated: Schiller's Karl Moor in *Die Räuber*, Goethe's Götz, the banditti painted by Loutherbourg and others, and Rob Roy – all prior to such Romantic instances as Byron's Corsair and Hugo's Hernani. The revival of the William Tell legend offers another and somewhat special

instance.[30] As regards France, a popular tradition since the
late-sixteenth century was transferred to the Théâtre Français
by Lemierre's successful play in 1766; his Tell became a symbol
of liberty – for Bernardin de Saint-Pierre as early as 1773,
writing to Mme Necker to ask material for a study; for Florian
in his last work; above all for the French revolutionaries – well
before Schiller's *Wilhelm Tell* in 1804 gave the definitively
influential version that would inspire Rossini. And the relevant
point here is that wild nature not only offers greater safety but
also seems to transmit something of its strength and purpose
to those who live amongst it.

Yet perhaps the principal human inhabitant of the mountains
was first depicted, once again, by Gray, in *The Bard* (written
1755–7):

> On a rock, whose haughty brow
> Frowns o'er old Conway's foaming flood,
> Robed in the sable garb of woe,
> With haggard eyes the Poet stood;...
> And with a Master's hand, and Prophet's fire,
> Struck the deep sorrows of his lyre.

And the final lines describe a suicide that consummates his
union with wild nature:

> He spoke, and headlong from the mountain's height
> Deep in the roaring tide he plung'd to endless night.

This wild-haired figure quickly became admired, not least by
writers and artists. Loutherbourg, Richard Bentley, Blake,
Fuseli, John Martin: all these illustrated Gray's bard. Other
writers too would be conscripted to the bardic profession:
Homer; Shakespeare as viewed by Young and, in French
translation, Letourneur; Ossian above all; even Dante. Diderot
too, at the same time as Gray, was linking poetic genius with
wilder nature in his *De la poésie dramatique* (1758):

What does the poet require? Shall he prefer the beauty of a pure and serene
day to the horror of a dark night...? Shall he prefer the sight of a tranquil
sea to that of rough waves?...Poetry demands something enormous, barbaric
and wild.[31]

And Goethe, a little later, would make the link between artistic
creation and wild nature even more intimate – as when Werther,
writing of 'the stream of genius', refers to 'its sublime floods'.[32]

It is perhaps surprising how comparatively quickly the earlier and long-standing notion of the writer or artist as an urbanised, court-centred entertainer was replaced in the later-eighteenth century by this concept of the writer or artist as a solitary, unsociable genius, and what underlies it is a claim that is no less arresting. Man can be inspired by a power beyond himself, the power of untamed nature, utilising and speaking through him, and indeed, alongside these bardic prototypes of the primitive wise man, earlier and simpler peoples were likewise praised for the insights expressed in their primitive mythologies and in folk ways and cultures. This is seen in Britain in a cult of the ballad and especially in Thomas Percy's *Reliques of Ancient English Poetry* (1765), albeit with some softening of the wild scene, and one finds it also in the cult of the 'minstrel' – not only in Beattie and Walter Scott but even in the explorer Hawkesworth as he admires, in the early 1770s, 'the bards and minstrels of Otaheite'. It is evident too, in Germany in particular, in the rising interest in Nordic sagas and, to some degree, in interpretations of the medieval, or again by the inspiration given to a composer such as Haydn by folk music and dances. The bard is thus a special instance of a wider trust in the natural, speaking through uncivilised and elemental man.[33]

He would be taken up by the Romantics in due course, who would preserve the old man to some extent – notably in representations of King Lear upon the storm-blown heath. But they would also devise a younger version, move him to a more urban and comfortable setting and present him as the Romantic poet–prophet, like themselves. Yet the link with wild nature remained, as in Vigny's *Moïse* or Hugo's *Ce qu'on entend sur la montagne*, to give French examples amongst many others. (One can add that this notion of the genius inspired by uncontrolled natural forces is still with us, but – in his older guise – he now has Einstein's white, flowing locks or – in his younger form – is presented as a brilliant if unkempt mathematician deserving academic promotion at the age of 27.)

Man can tap nature's energy in these and other ways: here is a first reason for the mood of exultancy. He can do so – and here is a second reason – because man's higher self is in tune with nature in its wilder forms: they speak to his imagination and his soul. For Burke the Dublin flood 'fills the mind with grand ideas, and turns the soul in upon itself'. For Diderot Vernet's *Shipwreck* 'speaks to the soul', and his *Entretiens sur le fils naturel* stress the same link. The man of genius leaves the town for the world of nature, which is 'the sacred abode' of enraptured 'enthusiasm', and even more moving than the meadows and fertile countryside are the forests and 'their secret horror', the mountain torrent, 'a cave which inspires him', or, as in the third *Entretien*, the storm in which Dorval stands in exhilaration, his own inner turmoil matched by that around him.[34] Here, as often in the Romantics later, what is sometimes mocked as 'the sentimental fallacy' is in reality a reflection of a wider trust in the harmony between man and nature and in man's privileged ability to combine with its superior power.

Thirdly, most of the eighteenth-century observers who exulted in nature's wildness were able to do so because they remained confident that this is God's world, that His providential care for man is still at work even when man feels most endangered. Indeed, for most of them their Christian faith was not weakened but strengthened by their awareness of savage nature: it revealed the full majesty of God, just as the beauties of pastoral nature exemplified His goodness. Their view remained that of the Anglican Church's *Prayer to be used in Storms at Sea*: 'But now we see how terrible thou art in all thy works of wonder; the great God to be feared above all.' Even though in a few cases perceptions of nature became 'secularised' in the eighteenth century the great majority were led towards religion by the awe-inspiring power of nature rather than away from it. Gray found the Grande Chartreuse 'pregnant with religion and poetry'. Klopstock, in *Die Frühlingsfeier*, is not finally fearful of the storm because he sees it as a manifestation of the Almighty. For Cowper, in *Retirement*,

> Ocean exhibits, fathomless and broad,
> Much of the power and majesty of God.

Ramond gazing at the Swiss Alps around 1780 could write:

'The imagination believes that it is glimpsing an image of eternity and welcomes it with religious fear' – much as Rousseau's Saint-Preux had declaimed of a mountain view: 'This spectacle has about it something magical and supernatural.'[35]

In short, it is only in a few eighteenth-century instances that one senses that the links with Christian belief are loosening – that nature's power and majesty are beginning to be viewed as independent of the power and majesty of God, that nature may become a rival deity to God. Pantheism of this kind developed in the nineteenth century; Spinoza, for instance, was seen as an atheist in the eighteenth century but was re-interpreted as a religious thinker in the nineteenth.[36] And pantheism was certainly fostered by the admiration of wild nature we have been noting in its early development. Soon Shelley would observe of Mont Blanc:

> The secret Strength of things
> Which governs thought, and to the infinite dome
> Of Heaven is as a law, inhabits thee!

Senancour's Obermann would find in an Alpine waterfall, likewise, 'a mysterious expression of the world's energy'. Byron too would marvel at the Alps rather than at their Creator:

> Above me are the Alps,
> The palaces of Nature, whose vast walls
> Have pinnacled in clouds their snowy scalps,
> And throned Eternity in icy halls
> Of cold sublimity...

It is notoriously difficult to determine where a particular writer is pantheistic rather than Christian: Wordsworth and Lamartine provide two well-known examples of the problem. In the late-eighteenth century Diderot was pantheistic, if anything, and was not Christian, but others are in a more ambivalent position. What of young Goethe, for example? His Werther, marvelling at 'the swarming life' around him, feels 'the presence of the Almighty'. But he also writes of 'the glowing inner holy life of nature', of 'the consuming power which lies hidden in the whole of nature', and he resolves 'to keep henceforth exclusively to nature'. 'Nature alone is infinitely rich, and she alone forms the great artist.'[37]

What above all of Ossian, Macpherson's Celtic bard? Ossian's works, from 1760 onwards, became the object of an astonishing admiration throughout Europe, and almost more so after 1800 than before. His popularity extended from Turgot, Hume, Diderot, Goethe, Blake, Haller, Schiller, Lessing, Klopstock, Herder (fewer British than French or Germans) to Napoleon, Lamartine, Byron, and many others, including such painters as Ingres and Gros.

A primary source of the cult of Ossian lay in his landscapes – landscapes, precisely, evoking nature's wild sublimity. These were 'a revelation' for the whole of Europe, according to Van Tieghem in his study of *Ossian en France*. Rocky Scottish coasts battered by foaming seas, barren moorlands rising into the mists, desolate lakes over-shadowed by leaden, threatening skies, turbulent waterfalls beneath a cold (not a Romantic) moon: such was the natural scene, almost totally devoid of humanity, which appealed so deeply to Macpherson's admirers. Young Werther preferred Ossian even to Homer – the archetypal bard himself – and read from his works on his final visit to Lotte before going off to shoot himself. An earlier letter reflects his and Goethe's own response:

To stroll across the heath, with the gale roaring around me, which leads in streaming mists the spirits of our fathers through the vague light of the moon. To hear from yonder mountains, amid the roar of the forest stream, the half-obliterated groaning of the spirits from the caves, and the lamentations of the girl who is grieving herself to death...

And within this scene there is, needless to add, 'the gray-haired, roving bard', who 'looks wailing toward the good evening star which conceals itself in the rolling waves of the ocean' – for the blind Ossian, led by the young Malvina, is second only to Gray's bard as example of the primitive seer.[38]

But the question which arose amongst Ossian's admirers in the late-eighteenth century concerned his apparent absence of religious belief. His hunters and warriors have many moral virtues, it was felt, but not rooted in any notion of divinity. As Van Tieghem puts it: 'Truth to tell, this absence of religion astonished, and often scandalised',[39] though some defenders like Harold and Cesarotti denied he was an atheist. His depiction of natural landscapes – and this is the relevant point here – seems similarly unrelated to any religious feeling, Christian or pantheist. Humanity is absent from the scene – apart from the odd unkempt bard or savage warrior – and God is absent also. Nature itself and alone, at its most empty, provokes the sense of wild sublimity.

4

SCIENCES OF NATURE

In this chapter our concern is with a European phenomenon in a special sense. The science of Newton and Buffon, Stahl and Haller, Needham and Maupertuis, Priestley and Lavoisier, was heedless of national boundaries; to take mainly French examples here is not to ignore the reality of constant international intercourse. Furthermore, science in the eighteenth century was a subject of deep interest to the educated public as a whole, not an esoteric mystery as it has increasingly become. We now can hardly hope to follow the specialised complexities of our modern sciences and sub-sciences and their technical languages; then, by contrast, science comprised a vastly smaller body of knowledge, was far less sub-divided, more general and unified, to the point where it was often described as the single subject of 'natural philosophy' – a name still preserved for a few British university professorships of physics, still reflecting the former dream of a united science and the belief that this would be best based upon physics. Furthermore, its researches then were not only a matter for professionals; numerous 'amateurs' themselves contributed, by carefully-noted observations, by forming collections, and the like, to the flowering of the sciences and fully shared the scientists' own sense of excitement. And this in turn ensured that information was readily available. To take the case of France alone, works of scientific popularisation multiplied – some of them, like Buffon's, as important for the scientists as for the general reader. Fontenelle's *Entretiens sur la pluralité des mondes* (1686), the Abbé Pluche's *Le Spectacle de la nature*, in eight volumes from 1732 to 1744, Réaumur's seven-volume *Mémoires* about insects (1734–42), Voltaire's *Eléments de la philosophie de Newton* (1736), supremely, Buffon's *Histoire naturelle* from 1749 to 1789, in numerous volumes,

often with splendid coloured plates to convey the basic
messages even if one did not read all the text: these are just a
few examples out of many. And though we cannot know
altogether reliably, some of these works seem to have been the
best-sellers of the century. Mornet, in a classic study of the
holdings in 500 private libraries in France, counted 220 copies
of Buffon and 206 of Pluche – clearly more numerous than even
very successful works of literature like *La Nouvelle Héloïse* (165)
and Voltaire's *La Henriade* (181), and far more so than (say) the
Encyclopédie (82) or Rousseau's *Discours sur l'inégalité* (77) or –
with just 7 copies found – Diderot's *Lettre sur les aveugles*.[1] As
well as books, scientific articles were commonly provided in
the journals of the day and the amateur enthusiast could readily
consult also the *Mémoires de l'Académie des sciences* and the
equivalents from other groups of scientists, such as the Royal
Society in Britain.

Science was thus accessible, and very readily so, to a broad
general audience of educated people, and hence it becomes very
relevant to our subject to ask how the new knowledge and ideas,
diffused so widely and fascinating to so many, affected their
'general view' of nature, their 'image' of the world around them.

A single chapter is bound to simplify and can pick out only
a few salient developments. And even so the most major of all
the innovations linked with science will have to be taken for
granted, since it dated from an earlier age: that determination
to study nature as *objectively* as possible that was the very essence
of 'the scientific revolution' which by the mid-eighteenth
century was already well under way. It was within that common
framework that the changes gradually emerged.

One has to start, as always, by asking what went before, what
overall 'impression' of nature had previously prevailed – and
in many minds, even by the later-eighteenth century, still did
prevail. The Renaissance view has usually been linked with
'animism', with a stress (to use the old Latin distinction) upon
Natura naturans, nature as creative and animate, rather than
Natura naturata, created and fixed as what it is, and that view
has often been related to an Aristotelian concept of science as
opposed to the concept that would shortly replace it. For the

seventeenth century saw a major movement that led to a new synthesis of explanations. This is most often connected with Descartes and his many followers but was also distinctive of other major scientists before and after him: for example, Copernicus, Galileo, Kepler, Huyghens – and in many ways also Isaac Newton, notwithstanding the later quarrels, in France around 1730, between Cartesians and Newtonians.

The scientific work of the seventeenth and early-eighteenth centuries had been shaped above all by mathematics and, reliant on it, physics. The use of Arab numerals had replaced the use of Latin numerals only at the start of the seventeenth century, and even that in itself allowed a distinct advance. For Descartes in his *Discours de la méthode* mathematics offers the model for all 'clear and distinct' knowledge, and for Galileo likewise the hidden harmony of the world, soon to be uncovered by science as he believed, lies in the mathematical laws which underlie it. And the view of nature that emerged from the achievements of all these mathematicians and physicists – and of other scientists whose work was developed under their influence – was the view of 'mechanism'. Nature is a perfectly-ordered machine, operating in a fixed, unaltering way in accordance with the laws of mathematics. It is a perfect 'clock', created by the Divine Clock-maker (to whom, most famously, Voltaire would appeal). It is a completed and immutable system, determined in all its operations, generating no novelties, and in that way it is passive, not active in the manner of 'animism' earlier. This was the model assumed for several decades (and well into the eighteenth century) for the whole range of natural phenomena: fixed stars; fixed plant and animal species; animals as machine-like automata, as Descartes argued to the later annoyance of La Fontaine; the preformationist view of human and animal reproduction, which we must return to shortly; the circulation of the blood described by Harvey as a mechanical system – the examples are endless. If we ask what emotion such a world may inspire above all, the answer is surely not so much pleasure in its beauties or its creative powers, not so much the Renaissance affection for 'la Mère Nature', as respect for a perfect order, eternally the same, established by the Perfect Creator. It is also a somewhat grey, geometric world, composed in essence of such monochrome abstractions as 'extension' and 'motion'. Pascal – an outstanding mathematician and physicist as a young man – wrote in a famous 'pensée': 'Le silence éternel de ces espaces infinis m'effraie' ('The eternal silence of these infinite spaces fills me with dread'). In some ways this reflected a strikingly novel view: the music of the spheres is hushed; the notion of the world as transitory and soon to end has gone; the spaces are now infinite, not limited to God-established circles. The mechanical world is in this way something to admire or to fear, as with Pascal, rather than to love. It is also, since no more than a machine, something for man to utilise and seek to control; Descartes invites us in his *Discours* to make ourselves 'masters and possessors of nature' – less to collaborate with it harmoniously than to dominate and exploit it.

The massive figure of Newton too looms up inevitably in the fortunes of this tradition; his most important work was significantly entitled *The Mathematical Principles of Natural Philosophy*. Yet he initiated – outstandingly so, we all know – as well as inherited, and the move away from the Cartesian outlook began with Newton and his disciples. Whatever one's judgement as to how far he broke with mechanism, Newton undoubtedly loosened its hold on scientific thinking and to that extent prepared the way for what would follow. Two major points demand mention even here. Above all he stressed empiricism and the experimental method as central in scientific methodology, extending and emphasising the approach found earlier in Bacon, Gassendi and Pascal by contrast with the Cartesians' more *a priori* 'esprit de géométrie'. He thereby encouraged his admirers – and they were countless during the eighteenth century – to look at nature before they reasoned about it – and the more they looked, the more they discovered. Secondly, Newton did not see the world as a *completely* perfect, self-maintaining machine. Occasional corrections are needed for its operations; the system has to be attended to from outside itself. Whereas in Descartes' physical world God's work was limited to the original act of Creation – to providing that 'flick of the finger' Pascal found so inadequate – for Newton, an ardent Christian, God is still actively involved with His world: God, he declared, is a 'powerful, ever-living Agent'.

Against this background, what was most novel in eighteenth-century science? First and most dramatically it brought a veritable explosion of scientific observation. This was the first age – the so-called age of empiricism – when scientists really looked at nature closely, in all its complex and many-sided realities and established the crucial role within science of experimentation. In the mid-seventeenth century Pascal had seemed eccentric when he carried his tube of mercury up the Puy de Dôme and thus demonstrated the variations of air-pressure. A hundred years later experiment had become one – though not the dominant one – of science's established methods. And it was this empirical leap-forward that above all accounts for the rise during the eighteenth century of a wide range of new sciences: marked advances in chemistry, and the establishment of geology, botany, biology, and zoology, even if in some cases the name of the new science would not be coined until the following century. Within each of these sciences the primary emphasis was upon observing and classifying the sheer multiplicity of phenomena. Linnaeus, the great Swedish naturalist, born in 1707 – like both Buffon and the Swiss botanist and physiologist Haller – offers a good example. His much-consulted *Systema Naturae* was based upon observing thousands of different species of plants, and it established the classification system within botany still in use today. Nor is it a coincidence that the Natural Gardens at Kew were created in the period from 1730 to 1750 – so that by 1789 well over 5,000 species were growing – or that the Paris Jardin des Plantes was immensely extended in the mid-eighteenth century, above all by Buffon, its 'Superintendant' from 1739 to 1788. Geologists went to the mountains to chip away at the rocks; amateur botanists like Rousseau loved to gather new flowers; when Linnaeus died, Sir Joseph Banks adroitly bought his vast collection and later bequeathed it to the British Museum, to add to the biological exhibits gathered earlier by Sloane; shells, insects, fossils – these and much more were enthusiastically collected and grouped by professionals and amateurs alike. The impact of explorations overseas during the century was hardly less important. Most Pacific expeditions took a naturalist as a matter of course; Hodges and Banks went with Captain Cook, Commerson with Bougainville, for example. They brought back descriptions, drawings, even specimens, of new plants (like the bougainvillea or the versatile bread-fruit) and of unknown, strange animals like the kangaroo.

One may almost feel that the motto of eighteenth-century science was 'observation for observation's sake', but what matters here is that the outcome was a tremendous extension in people's awareness of the range, the marvels and the beauties of the phenomena of the natural world. And amongst all the resultant developments there was one general feature of especial relevance: the rise of the 'life sciences', though the term itself, 'les sciences de la vie', was not used in French until a later date. Even the earlier-eighteenth century had little notion of the differences between living and non-living matter; the great distinction was between matter of all kinds on the one hand and soul or spirit on the other. In the seventeenth century people had still discussed 'the generation of rocks', as if rocks were like animals and produced baby rocks; now people became aware that if nature is in part 'dead' matter, in part it is also alive – and that it is so in a distinctive way.

The distinctive way in which 'life' operates was a crucial issue of contention throughout the century. Some remained largely under the influence of mathematical physics in discussing it, whilst others were more affected by the life sciences. Thus the 'philosophes', for example, seem to have been divided. D'Alembert and Voltaire, Helvétius and d'Holbach remained in the former camp, whereas Diderot moved into the latter – perhaps the underlying reason for his quarrel with d'Alembert in 1758 – or at least he was struggling towards that different allegiance, with many of the ambivalences so characteristic of his most honest 'esprit de dialogue'. Almost at the start of his *Pensées sur l'interprétation de la nature* (1753), Diderot declared: 'We have reached the moment of a great transformation in the sciences.' And he then defines this great change as the substitution of 'experimental philosophy' (as he calls it) for

mathematics: that subject is admirable within its self-enclosed
sphere but has little to do with the real world, and he even
predicts that within a hundred years only three great geo-
metricians will be left![2]

The outcome – seen in Diderot uncertainly, more clearly in
others like Goethe a little later – was the gradual replacement
of the mechanistic concept of nature by a new concept, by a
re-interpretation that saw nature as creative, dynamic, organic,
and self-developing. The debate between mechanism and
'organicism' has even been described as 'the key to French
thought in the eighteenth century'.[3] Whether that is an
exaggeration or not, the rise of organicism was certainly the
second distinctive way in which men's views of the natural were
gradually changed, alongside the empiricist explosion of factual
awareness. The leading figures were scientists – like Buffon and
Maupertuis in France – but even they and most other scientists
within the century remained, like Diderot, ambivalent. Only
with Lamarck and Darwin did the anticipations of 'transformism', for example, that are found in Maupertuis, Buffon
and Diderot become triumphant, and even then with well-
known difficulty and opposition.

A major illustration is found in views on the phenomena of
reproduction of both men and animals, and a particularly
striking instance may serve as an example of the new perceptions.
In 1744 a Swiss naturalist, Abraham Trembley, published a
book entitled, somewhat wordily perhaps, but significantly so
in its wish to stress facts, *Mémoires pour servir à l'histoire d'un genre
de polype d'eau douce, à bras en forme de cornes*. It was all about that
engaging creature, the hydra. The hydra is still much studied,
not least by school science pupils, and university biology
departments still find it of exceptional interest. Trembley first
studied it in 1740 and observed a number of astonishing things
about this humble dweller in ponds and ditches – so much so
that the scientist Réaumur declared: 'I could hardly believe my
eyes', and added that it was 'the strangest and most embarrassing
novelty ever offered to the eyes of those who study nature'.[4]
Others were equally intrigued: Charles Bonnet, Maupertuis, La
Mettrie (who used the discovery to re-inforce his materialism,

as he believed), Diderot (whose *Rêve de D'Alembert* later imagines 'human polyps' living on Jupiter and Saturn), and many others – including Rousseau (who lists 'extraordinary' reproduction in his *Discours sur les sciences et les arts* in 1750 as one of the principal problems for science and philosophy).

The hydra was originally thought to be a plant (as some, like Voltaire, went on insisting) but is in fact an animal, of the family of coelenterata, belonging to the same broad group as anemones and jelly-fish. What astonished Trembley and his contemporaries was its method of generating new hydra and also of regenerating lost parts. It can reproduce by budding new hydra on itself which then float free of the parent. Second, it can reproduce sexually; it is an hermaphrodite with both ovary and testis, though their respective ripening times are such that no hydra can fertilise itself. Thirdly, and most amazingly, if one cuts a hydra in two or more parts, each part will grow into a complete hydra. Trembley also turned a hydra inside out and found it could then re-organise itself back to its normal form. It can also re-grow amputated tentacles, and is thus in this way as well as in its means of reproduction a creature which seems to have a striking ability to create new life. Its operations appeared, in short, radically to challenge the doctrine about animal and human generation that prevailed, despite some disputes, by the earlier-eighteenth century.

This was the theory of 'preformationism': all creatures develop from a pre-formed embryo contained (some, the ovists, maintained) in its mother's egg or (others, the animalculists, contended) in its father's semen. And some scientists (Bonnet, for example) added to this the notion of 'emboîtement' – the claim that the 'germs' of all future generations are already contained within the egg or the sperm; this means, indeed, that Eve (or Adam) contained all the embryos of all future humans within herself (or himself). The conclusion is that the future creature will basically be what is already contained in the embryo. Nature merely develops what is already there and, in fact, has always been there since God's act of creation. There is thus no perception that a new individual may be an unpredictable product of its mother and father and therefore be a genetic novelty. For the ovists, the father's semen provides lubrication for the growth of the embryo within the mother; for the animalculists, the mother's womb is a favourable site for the growth of the embryo contained in the father's semen. But essentially the offspring is pre-formed, firmly fixed as what it will be, before any sexual act occurs. It follows from this belief that the preformationists were opposed to the idea of spontaneous generation and in favour of fixity of species.

This is a mechanistic theory, clearly enough, and the hydra certainly seemed to create difficulties for it. Even Trembley was not altogether happy about his observations, though on different grounds: he believed animals have souls; if by chopping up one hydra you get several, do several souls come into existence, and how? This was one reason, indeed, why La Mettrie as an anti-Christian welcomed the discovery: it could be used to query the reality of a soul in humans also as well as to suggest that nature contains within itself – with no need for help from God – a creative, organising capacity.[5] Others struggled to reconcile the old theory with the hydra – most notably, Bonnet, a relative of Trembley – and this was not the first difficulty the theory had dealt with, one may add. The problem posed by an offspring resembling both of its parents had been countered by the argument that the parent not carrying the embryo could still affect its characteristics through (for the ovists) the father's fluid or (for the animalculists) the mother's food to the embryo – or even by the power of her imagination (as argued earlier by Claude Perrault, brother of the fairy-story writer and a respected scientist). Another difficulty had arisen over hybrids, where the dominant characteristics of one parent are passed to the offspring. Some thought hybrids rarely occurred: God only allowed them occasionally for His special reasons and hybrid sterility is far more common. Others, like Réaumur, thought hybrid phenomena would allow us to decide between ovism and animalculism – but even so they did not abandon the assumption that either the mother or the father pre-dominated and held the pre-formed offspring. Yet again, as regards re-generation, the ability of the green lizard to re-grow its tail had been noted in 1686, and of the crayfish to re-grow its limbs in 1712, well before the hydra was observed in 1740. The answer of Réaumur and others was that the particular creature contains a preformed tail or limb within its skin-cells. Modern biology's 'DNA coding' amounts to much the same thing: hence the present interest of biologists in the hydra.

But if some managed to preserve their preformationist convictions, others were more open-minded. For educated but non-professional observers the evidence of the hydra was probably far from conclusive. All the same, it was, first, the object of interested surprise and, secondly, a puzzle that served to weaken the broad assumption that nature is largely passive – to weaken but not (in so far as one can tell) to destroy it. For them the particularly challenging evidence would be posed by a German family called Ruhe some twenty years later, a case that was studied by Maupertuis, who was in Berlin as the director of Frederick the Great's Academy of Sciences. He had earlier, in 1744, examined albinism in Negroes, but the Ruhes were even more decisively interesting. Some of them had *six* fingers on each hand – an extremely rare occurrence: the father in the first generation, his *daughter* in the second, and *her son* in the third generation. The conclusion Maupertuis drew is obvious: *both* sexes contribute in a major way to forming the offspring. A similar phenomenon was found too in tobacco-plants and also, by Trembley, in maize. If this is so, then pre-formationism cannot be correct; both ovists and animalculists are wrong, and the process of generation allows for variations not fixed in advance. In that case, moreover, the doctrine of the fixity of species is called into question, and that is in turn to open up the whole possibility of theories of transformism and of evolution as they would be developed by Lamarck, then Darwin, and others.

It is not necessary here to ask how far Buffon, Diderot and others went along the evolutionary road: Roger and other scholars have evaluated in detail their anticipations of the nineteenth-century theories.[6] Of them all Maupertuis would seem to have gone furthest: he came close to prefiguring Lamarck's theory of variations through the transmission of acquired characteristics and also Darwin's belief in chance 'mutations' – 'productions fortuites', as he said of the Ruhe family's extra fingers. His first major work, *La Vénus physique*, created widespread interest, moreover: published in 1745, it was already in its sixth edition six years later. Thereafter, unfortunately, Voltaire attacked and damaged his scientific reputation, and Buffon had much greater impact at the time. We may best take him, therefore, briefly to illustrate the new insights and, as well, their limitations.

Buffon's stress on the observation and description of facts was already clear in his preliminary discourse on method in the very first volume of his *Histoire naturelle* (1749). He was sceptical, by contrast, of abstractions, and it was this which led him to query the notion of fixity of species, in the form given to it by Linnaeus's system of classification for plants and animals. For Buffon Linnaeus was imposing his own abstract categories upon the facts; the Linnaean species are mere fictions, and nature consists in reality only of individuals. Buffon likewise rejected preformationism: 'There are no pre-existing germs, no germs contained to infinity the ones within the others but there is an organic matter that is always active.'[7] There exist 'living organic molecules', he would suggest later in his *Histoire des animaux*, which help to explain reproduction of all kinds – by budding in plants and in the hydra as much as by sexual means.

Yet his notion of these 'organic molecules' was in fact still mechanistic, as Roger and others have noted.[8] Each molecule, he contended, contains, as it were, a miniature version of the creature or plant itself. One may think this was to reintroduce preformation at the microscopic level after abandoning it at the macroscopic level. In short, the tension between mechanism and organicism and the contradictions born of that tension remained in Buffon's system: hence conflicting interpretations of his position by scholars – either that he at bottom believed in fixity of species or that he was a precursor of transformism. The fair conclusion is probably Lovejoy's: he was divided between 'two opposing forces'; 'his work both fostered and hindered the propagation of evolutionary ideas in biology'. Strikingly enough, Buffon and Linnaeus seem to have moved to similar middle positions. Linnaeus modified his earlier defence of fixity and abandoned the view that there are never new species; species, he would finally declare, 'are the work of time'. They are modified through variations, in particular variations brought about through hybridisation, even though they remain still, he suggested, within very broad species fixed by God.

In brief, in Buffon and, to a lesser extent, Linnaeus alike, the movement from mechanism towards organicism is under way, but the movement is hesitant and only partial. Much the same appears to have been true of others at this time. Diderot, for example, contended in his *Rêve de D'Alembert* (1769) and his *Principes philosophiques sur la matière et le mouvement* (1770) that matter has an innate power or force that is capable of producing all the changes in the world, and it has been claimed that the *Rêve* is a 'most important step forward' in conceptualising the notion of 'the organism'. And yet the same scholar concludes that Diderot's 'universe is holistic, but not organicist'.[9] A similar, entirely understandable tentativeness is seen even in the so-called 'vitalists' in the second half of the century, scientists like Bordeu, Bichat and Barthez centred at Montpellier. In England earlier Joseph Needham had postulated the presence of a 'spontaneity' within nature, an 'organic principle' which he termed 'vitality' – a notion discussed in Diderot's *Rêve* in opposition to Voltaire's mockery. The 'vitalists' revived this idea of a 'vital principle', even trying to conscript Newton's 'law of attraction' to help, but they seem to have got little further. Neither they nor Linnaeus nor even Buffon achieved the further step to the notion of an evolutionary 'family tree' – one species descended from another from another. For that one has to await Lamarck's *Philosophie zoologique* of 1809. Yet what they did achieve, to a greater or lesser extent in each individual instance, was an essential preparation for nineteenth-century theories of evolution. They criticised the old machine model of the natural world; they moved towards the new organicist model. The utterly predictable *order* of nature was being replaced by the unpredictable, dynamic *power* of nature, capable of throwing up novelties and variations not fixed in advance. Creative energy from *within*, not static design from *without*, was increasingly being perceived as a fundamental characteristic of the natural world.

This general move from a mechanist to an organicist notion is paralleled in the other sciences in various ways. In cosmology, for example, the concept of fixed stars was attacked. Kant in 1755 contended that there is an unlimited number of galaxies and that 'the Creation is never finished or complete'. In chemistry the quarrel – which has been called 'a landmark in the history of chemistry'[10] – between Joseph Priestley, defending the notion of phlogiston in the air, and Lavoisier, attacking it, has been interpreted as a conflict between a mechanist and an organicist explanation, and one can note that for the latter, in his *Réflexions sur le phlogistique* (1785), oxygen is 'vital air'. Medicine too reflected the controversies – in regard, for example, to the cause of the plague.[11] In fact, the new notions of 'organism', 'organic form', of self-development, generated from within, not produced by externals – these were to have profound, wide-ranging repercussions.[12] In a later chapter we shall see their impact on people's ideas about *women*, but as well organicism affected theories about the origins and development of languages, ideas about society and the law and perhaps about economics. Above all it transformed concepts of human history and of the nation – as is beginning, for example, in Herder, from whom (Isaiah Berlin and others have suggested)[13] Hegel would take them over: for Herder the unfolding development in nature moves all the way from the first galaxies to the latest changes in European history. Indeed, to generalise, one may well think that 'organism' was becoming the decisive 'analogy', 'image', 'metaphor', in European thinking. Even geology reflected the development: even the apparently unchanging realm of rock came to be seen as being in a process of *becoming* and not of inactive *being* – as we must note shortly in relation to a third major development brought by eighteenth-century science: what has been termed 'the discovery of time'.

Prior to that, however, one or two important generalisations should be mentioned. We have seen, first, that men were observing nature in far more detail than previously and over

a much wider range both of sciences and also of areas of the
globe, and consequently were being led to marvel all the more
at its rich diversity. What is noteworthy is that the scientists'
observations paralleled and confirmed that more vivid awareness
and depiction of nature by landscape-painters, literary writers
and others seen in earlier chapters. Science and the arts
converged on similar conclusions (as we shall observe again in
regard to Pacific exploration). Moreover, as we noted, men were
beginning to conceive of nature less as a static 'order' than as
an active 'power', changing, transforming, even (some already
believed) progressing, and here too there were resemblances
between the sciences and the arts. Both increasingly stressed the
energy and *creativity* of nature, whether it be shown in Trembley's
hydra or Stubbs's savage lions or William Blake's tiger or
Goethe's sense of teeming life between the grass-blades, or in
the human realm, as with the emerging notion of the 'inspired'
poet and artist. Nature, wrote Buffon concurrently, is an active
power 'that embraces everything and animates everything'; it
is 'a ceaselessly active worker, able to make use of everything'.[14]
We today may suffer from having 'two cultures', of the sciences
and of the humanities in isolation from each other, or at least
from a partially-fractured culture. In the eighteenth century,
by comparison, there was a single culture in which the sciences
and the arts alike moved towards a fuller appreciation of nature.
Each was conscious of the other and was influenced by it.

The question obviously arises as to whether this organicist
or at least partially organicist image of the natural world
represented a movement away from Christianity towards a
purely 'naturalistic' outlook. Contrary to the claims of some
scholars, one may think – and here is a second generality – that
Christianity was strengthened as well as weakened. It is not only
that most of the scientists were Christians or at least deists and
that even a thinker like La Mettrie does not entirely rule out the
possibility of God's existence. Far more important, Christians
drew positive re-inforcement from these new perceptions,
scientific and artistic alike, for their belief in God's providential
goodness. The argument for God that had most appealed to
more mechanist minds was the argument from Design; indeed,

mechanist science greatly strengthened the evidence for a
Divine Clock-maker. If, now, a less pre-designed, pre-formed
view of the world is adopted, that tends to weaken the
argument. But if so it is replaced by two considerations that
are, arguably, even more appealing to the Christian. The first
and more important of them relates to the beauty and beneficence
of nature revealed by closer observation. Earlier scientists like
Réaumur and Newton who were Christians had appreciated the
'marvels' of God's creation, but for them they were mainly
marvels of machinery. Réaumur, for example, finds in nature
'many surprising mechanisms', and claims that there is no
demonstration of God's existence more within the compre-
hension of mankind. The Abbé Pluche, as mechanist as the
scientists, tells us that nature is a splendid 'watch', whose
springs 'only operate to teach us something quite different from
what we see'.[15] By contrast, Christians and deists after them
increasingly appealed to nature's lavish creativity as evidence
less of God the perfect mechanic than of God the loving,
providing Father. Rousseau, Bernardin de Saint-Pierre, and
Chateaubriand are three French examples – and so also, in
Britain, are hymn-writers of the time. In *The English Hymnal* one
finds Addison's version of the argument from design: 'The
spacious firmament on high'; by contrast, the following hymn,
by Thomas Moore some decades later, stresses instead the
beauties of nature: 'Thou art, O God, the life and light/Of all
this wondrous world we see.' And the next hymn after that,
from Bishop Heber in the early-nineteenth century, goes even
further in harnessing observation and love of nature to the
Christian cause:

> When spring unlocks the flowers to paint the laughing soil;
> When summer's balmy showers refresh the mower's toil;
> When winter binds in frosty chains the fallow and the flood;
> In God the earth rejoiceth still, and owns his Maker good.

(It is easy to read too much into such examples, and yet one
may wonder if it is wholly co-incidental that when the Physiocrats
were preaching that true economic value lies in the 'good
earth', Claudius (1740–1815) was writing another hymn:

We plough the fields and scatter
The good seed on the land.)

For many Christians another factor was also relevant, given their belief in God's active intervention in His world. Although some of the new scientists – including Haller and Bonnet – certainly had worries, all the same the emerging organicist notion allowed far more scope, as it were, for divine Providence than had mechanism; Christians could and did contend that nature's novelties show God's *continuing* work and care for man. The more conservative of the theologians were undoubtedly antagonistic – as was manifest in (say) the Sorbonne's attacks on Buffon. It is true also that the notion of fixed species had fitted well with the Bible story of Noah's Ark. And yet it was scientists like Bonnet or Linnaeus who had most strongly affirmed it; the quarrels had been scientific far more than religious. Indeed, the idea of fixed species had originally been in the nature of a revolutionary theory propounded by scientific mechanists. (At the popular level even in the eighteenth century some continued to believe that any species could produce almost any other – that a woman could give birth to a rabbit, say.)

One must not assume as a corollary, however, that what refreshed some Christians' faith in God, with whatever hesitations, must have damaged the secularist, naturalistic opposition. On the contrary, the anti-Christians were no less encouraged, as is well illustrated by La Mettrie, finding support for his materialism from observations of the hydra, and by Diderot's thinking too. For both of them the new insights served to encourage their attempts to replace 'God' by an alternative, 'Nature'. Its wonders – which they saw as clearly as the Christians – and its powers of organic development inspired confidence in them. They rarely anticipated Lamarck's bleak descriptions of evolution's methods a little later, or Darwin's presentation of the struggle for survival in nature, any more than did the Christians. One should not project the nineteenth-century conflicts between scientists and the churches back on to the eighteenth century; for the present the mood on both sides was largely hopeful.

Much the same was true even in regard to the third major development in eighteenth-century science that demands attention: what has been termed 'the discovery of time', to which we must now turn. It is striking to recall that almost all scientists up to and including Newton took for granted that the world was no older than some 6,000 years, as calculated from the Bible. One story recounts that when Newton made calculations that required it to be some 50,000 years old, he concluded that his calculations must be erroneous – not for fear of church reprisals but because, like most others, he took it for granted that the Bible was literally true. A few other scientists and thinkers were more puzzled and postulated longer periods of past time: Montesquieu, Hume, Diderot, for example. Moreover, they did so, by and large, without conflicting on this issue with the church. It was easy enough to argue, as Buffon in his *Epoques de la nature* and Cuvier later both did, that the 'days' of the Creation were longer than our earthly days or that unrecorded time had existed for God's work *before* the start of those final days of the creative act. Consequently the eighteenth-century arguments about 'time' were mainly scientific, in contrast to the nineteenth-century controversies with biblical fundamentalists.

What was involved in the arguments, none the less, was a marked re-adjustment of imagination and of men's notions of the world. With some 6,000 years at one's disposal one could begin to conceive of development in *human* history but not, to any significant extent, in the vaster area of *natural* history. The 'idea of Progress' in human history had developed from the later-seventeenth century onwards, from almost a century before Buffon would significantly choose *Histoire naturelle* as the title of his life's work, and this chronological gap need not surprise us, nor need the relative timidity of even Buffon's eventual lengthening of time to some 50,000 to 80,000 years. Moreover, without more time the machine 'model' of the world was distinctly more persuasive than the new organicism. We all know that many changes in nature are slow; with only 6,000 years available it is reasonable to assume things have always been much the same – a largely static order and not a developing process.

Here, as in regard to the debates around reproduction, we can take no more than a few illustrations of the discoveries that gradually led to so immense a change and that would finally, in a later age, lead most people to believe that Nature had had and continued to have all the time she needed in order to exercise her dynamic power. The 'expansion' of time was derived from three major areas in particular, of which the development of the idea of progress in human history was the first. In practice the assertion that human civilisations reveal a continuing improvement provided an almost inseparable context for speculations about the history of the world as a whole, and above all, perhaps, it helped to counter the long-held belief that both man and nature had *degenerated* since the Fall. Second, the actual scientific debates often centred on the biological issue of fixed species: if species merge into one another, how much time is required for the changes to take place? 'Lack of time' was often invoked by the defenders of fixity. Third, geological discoveries and discussions were to prove especially decisive. Our illustrations here may thus be best chosen from this rapidly expanding science.

Geology takes us back, as when considering 'wild sublimity' in nature, to the mountains. Indeed, we noted then that some of the scientists who lingered to praise their savage beauty, from Haller in *Die Alpen* to Saussure in 1787, originally went there for scientific reasons. In the outcome, their geological hammers, tapping carefully away, were to be major implements in transforming our whole concept of time and thereby of nature.

It had been known for many centuries that sea-shells and fossils are found in mountain areas, but the development of geology and of the earth sciences generally from the early-eighteenth century on – and even with Hooke and Steno in the seventeenth – drew renewed attention to them. Their presence did not in itself pose problems for either scientists or Christians. Most saw them as solid evidence that the Flood had indeed occurred; it appears that the pious geologist Scheuchzer went to the Alps in 1718 explicitly to look for fossils that would confirm the Bible story, and the Abbé Pluche, for example, embraces the same view in his *Spectacle de la nature*. But problems gradually became more evident. If, at the time of the Flood, the mountains were roughly as high as now, where has all the water gone that would be needed for so deep a flood? If they were not then raised above the general surface, how in a mere 6,000 years have they become so high? Again, given that the Flood only lasted for a few months, how could so many shell and fossil deposits have been laid down? Moreover, deposits are found in quite obviously separate layers of rock, which could thus surely not all have been formed during that limited duration of the Flood. For example, even by 1720, in regard to Réaumur's description of a bed of shells in Touraine, Fontenelle had surmised that though the Flood must have left many traces on earth, the shells of Touraine were certainly not among them but must have been deposited there 'very slowly and gently' over a much longer period than a year. Some reacted by saying that God had created the fossils for unknown reasons of His own. Others, most notably Voltaire, were more ingenious: some of the shells on mountains are not really shells; some were dropped by pilgrims and crusaders; some were left by mountain lakes drying up. In his controversy with Buffon in 1749 and again in his *Dictionnaire philosophique* entry 'Des Coquilles', the sage of Ferney tried everything to preserve his belief in a static creation of limited duration.

In other ways the problem lay less in the fossils themselves than in the rocks which contained them. In 1751 the French geologist Guettard while returning from the Naples region and travelling up the Rhone valley noticed at Moulins, near Montélimar, that both the milestones and the pavement-stones were of a black rock remarkably similar to that of the Vesuvius area he had just left. The stones, it transpired, came from the Massif Central. Were they volcanic – as later became quite clear? If so, why were there no records, verbal or written, within a mere 6,000 years of the eruptions required? Even Guettard himself, in a paper to the Académie des Sciences in 1752, may not have grasped the full significance of those milestones, and it was Nicholas Desmarest a little later who made the first detailed study of a volcanic activity that demanded a far longer period of time.

However, as in regard to fixity of species, so in geology it was Buffon who took the steps that would ultimately prove decisive. Fossil evidence led him to suggest, as early as his *Théorie de la terre* (1749), a longer time-scale than the apparent Biblical one, and in the 1770s he went much further and on different grounds. First, how long must it have taken for the Earth, the other planets and their satellites to cool down from a white heat to their present temperatures? (Incidentally, it had been a similar calculation about the cooling rate of molten iron that had given Newton the result he assumed must be mistaken.) Buffon, in 1774, concluded that the planets were 74,832 years old and also that life could exist on Mercury, Venus and Saturn and most of their satellites but not on the Moon or Mars (which were already too cold) or on Jupiter (which was still too hot). His time-estimate may have been much too short, but its psychological impact was considerable, and especially when re-stated in his *Epoques de la nature* of 1779. Another calculation brought him to a similar result. If the mountains have been formed by sedimentation, how much time must have been needed to build them up to their present heights? On his figures a 6,000 ft mountain, for example, would have required at least 14,000 years. In short, whether one took the 'Neptunist' hypothesis of Werner (namely, that sedimentation built the continents) or the 'Vulcanist' theory Buffon finally favoured and which Hutton would shortly propound (that heat and volcanic activity were responsible), one reached the conclusion that the earth is far older than 6,000 years and also that its configurations are constantly changing. 'The surface of the earth has taken different forms in succession', Buffon wrote; 'even the heavens have changed, and all the objects in the physical world are...caught up in a continual process of successive variations.'[16]

His system was in many ways speculative, and geologists in the early-nineteenth century, such as Hutton, William Smith and Lyell, would replace it. Yet what he and others like

Maupertuis achieved was to break through what one may call 'the imagination barrier'. Thereby they directed men's ideas and attitudes along a road which later generations would follow further, ever extending the time available for nature's creative, transforming processes, and radically altered men's perspectives upon the world and its history.

5

DEATH AND DESTRUCTION

Yet time brings death and destruction. Of all the problems faced
by those who allege the beneficence of external nature this fact
surely poses the most severe and apparently insoluble.
Furthermore, its challenge was becoming all the more disturbing
during the eighteenth century, at least for the greater minority
than previously who wished to believe in that beneficence. The
historians of the age were very significantly extending
knowledge of past and lost civilisations. In 1681 Bossuet in his
Discours sur l'histoire universelle had largely confined world
history to the story of the Greeks, Romans, Jews and Christians,
but now it was ever clearer from study, exploration and
excavation that numerous other cultures too had risen, pros-
pered and then decayed. Gibbon, as he sat at the Roman
Capitol, was only the most celebrated of those who were
depressed by a sense of the seemingly recurrent and inevitable
'decline and fall' of great empires over the centuries. It has
been argued, indeed, that there runs in Enlightenment thought,
for all its confidence in the idea of progress and the possibilities
of reform, a deep 'historical pessimism'.[1] Nor could the ruins
of the past be explained solely as the outcome of human actions.
Natural disasters such as, most dramatically, earthquakes and
volcanic eruptions had clearly been prime agents also. In an
hour or two the lava from Mount Vesuvius had eradicated the
cultures of Herculaneum and Pompeii – towns that were even
now, in the mid-eighteenth century, being excavated, revealing just how much nature, not man, had destroyed. Most
traumatically and vividly of all, the Lisbon earthquake in 1755,
having been preceded by minor tremors elsewhere, including
London, resulted in the deaths of thirty to forty thousand
people during a few Sunday morning hours. For Voltaire, most

famously, the 'optimism' of Leibniz and his followers – and, indeed, his own earlier confidence – no longer seemed tenable.

Sudden mass death on this scale is dramatic and all the more arresting for being infrequent and unpredictable. Nevertheless, in the last analysis it exemplifies, obviously enough, a phenomenon that is universal and utterly inevitable: individual death, nature's always successful destruction of man. Personal death has brought its sufferings, distress and dilemmas in every period, but over the ages men's responses to it have changed in distinctive ways, as Philippe Ariès has most recently described in his *Essais sur l'histoire de la mort du moyen âge à nos jours* and *L'Homme devant la mort*. Earlier, he claims, death had been 'tamed death', met with a calm ceremonial, often arranged by the dying person himself, surrounded by his family and friends – including children, moreover, who featured in most paintings of death-bed scenes right into the eighteenth century, in contrast to our own practice of shielding children from death. By then, however, it appears that death was becoming even more personalised than previously, even more deeply felt. Life itself was still held more cheaply than by most of us now; execution for trivial offences, torture to the point of death, and acceptance of cruelty in normal life remained commonplace. Dying in general still impinged far more upon the living and thus was far more familiar than for us today who rarely see the discreet cortège moving to the out-of-town cemetery or crematorium. Life-expectancy was so much shorter than for us, even though rising somewhat in the eighteenth century, that in a community of (say) 1,000 there would almost every week in every year be a funeral procession – bearing a well-known inhabitant, moreover – along the main street, with church bell tolling. Frequently – until the late-seventeenth century at least – there were in France more deaths than births; only after 1750 did an excess of births become normal, and even then with occasional reversals as in Anjou in the later part of the century.[2] Yet despite this continuing 'familiarity' with death – and even with the dead themselves as one walked into church close to their burial-place – grieving seems to have become even more

intense than earlier. Later chapters will note family expressions
of what Stone has called 'the rise of affective individualism':[3]
one good example lies in the heightened reactions to what Ariès
terms 'thy death' as opposed to 'tamed death', leading, for
instance, to the wish to have a personal grave for the deceased
by contrast with a family burial-place or the even more frequent
communal grave.

The problems provoked by death and destruction were thus
all the more preoccupying than before, and certainly the
detailed studies by Robert Favre on *La Mort dans la littérature
et la pensée françaises au siècle des lumières* and by John McManners
on *Death and the Enlightenment*, as well as the works by Ariès
and by Michel Vovelle, Pierre Chaunu, and François Lebrun,
have made abundantly plain the near-obsession with death of
Enlightenment thinkers like Voltaire and Diderot in particular
and of numerous others in the later-eighteenth century.

For many, if not all traditional Christians death was hardly
a 'problem' at all, however reluctant they were to die or to lose
their loved ones – nor was Lisbon or Pompeii. Compelling
answers had long been accepted and were still accepted by the
majority. First, human sin and the Fall bore prime responsibility.
'The wages of sin is death'; 'in Adam all die': such was the
basic conviction. Man's Fall brought nature's Fall, moreover,
as was noted earlier: volcanoes and earthquakes had not existed
in the world God created – a view reiterated by John Wesley,
for example, in relation to the Lisbon disaster. Furthermore, in
the belief of Wesley and others God commonly intervenes in
this world, sending eruptions, plagues, and the like to punish
men for their particular sinfulness. Lisbon for Wesley in his
Serious Thoughts (1755) was God's visitation on Catholic
wickedness and especially the Inquisition, and in a letter later
he approvingly wrote: 'There is no divine visitation which is
likely to have so general an influence upon sinners as an
earthquake.'[4] Others thought the Portuguese were being
punished for their pride in being a great commercial power, and
many Spaniards saw the seemingly miraculous preservation of
the Giralda tower on Seville Cathedral, despite the tremors
spreading from Lisbon, as evidence of God's favour towards

them as compared with their neighbours. And in France a Jansenist argued that the disaster marked the anniversary of the destruction of Port-Royal des Champs in 1709; Portugal had harboured the Jesuits who lay behind it and was rightly getting its just, if delayed deserts. Lisbon provoked wide-spread apprehension, indeed, lest God would extend His wrath to others: the students at Cambridge, the Vice-Chancellor reported, were unusually quietly behaved after the earthquake; a general Fast-Day was held in England in February 1756; in France Mme de Pompadour offered to give up using rouge. Orthodox Christians had a second conviction also that gave them consolation in the face of death: it is a merciful release 'out of the miseries of this sinful world'. Although terror of eternal torment in Hell appears to have been provoked, even as death approached, by many a French Catholic priest,[5] death remained, at least potentially, the gateway to eternal bliss, just as in England the Anglican too died 'in sure and certain hope of the Resurrection to eternal life'. And, thirdly, the Christian could claim that some misfortunes may in reality be for our good: they may serve to warn us against our sin, and they may strengthen our moral character. God's goodness can be trusted even when we do not perceive His intentions, and whilst some Christians were worried or puzzled, the majority were largely satisfied – or at least reconciled and comforted.

If orthodox Christians thus had their answers to death and natural disaster along these lines, so also – at the opposite extreme – did some of the unbelievers, those who rejected any notion of the benevolence of nature. Hume put their view well in his *Dialogues concerning Natural Religion*: 'The whole presents nothing but the idea of a blind nature,...pouring forth from her lap, without discernment or parental care, her maimed and abortive children.' Helvétius seems to reach the same conclusion: nature is a wholly material and determined system ruled only by chance; and so also does Diderot in his early work, *Lettre sur les aveugles*. For his Sanderson the world manifested 'an unceasing tendency to destruction', 'a transitory symmetry', 'a momentary order'. And Buffon too, though not holding their extremer anti-religious views, appears to have achieved a serene acceptance: 'Everything changes in nature, everything deteriorates, everything perishes.'[6]

Yet for others the problems were unavoidable and pressing, and amongst them one can distinguish two main groups: first, Christians and deists whose belief in God was above all based on belief in the goodness of the natural world; secondly, unbelievers who wished to replace faith in God by faith in nature. Voltaire is one illustration of the first group, as his *Poème sur le désastre de Lisbonne* especially shows – a work of which, significantly, there were no fewer than twenty editions in 1756 alone. God is the perfect clock-maker whose perfect design operates without further divine intervention; how, then, is Voltaire to explain the occurrence of Lisbon-type phenomena, since the traditional Christian answers are not available to him? His consequent uncertainties have been fully examined by others, and Favre in particular has shown his deep, persistent preoccupation with the fact of death.[7] He may have found palliative and partial answers – and the last line of his poem stressed 'hope' – but finally, it seems, he remained in unhappy scepticism.

Rousseau belonged to the same broad group but was even more deeply anxious to preserve his trust in nature's goodness, for that was the bedrock of his faith in God. It is thus in no way surprising that he should have responded to Voltaire's questionings with alarm and antagonism – as, indeed, did others, including Herder later, who would maintain against Voltaire that nature's destructiveness is perhaps only 'apparent'. Rousseau's 'Lettre sur la Providence' of 18 August 1756 is a classic illustration of his struggles to reconcile belief in nature with the fact of death. Many died at Lisbon, he suggests, because they delayed to pick up their clothes, paper or money; a quick death, as at Lisbon, is best in any case; moral evil is the work of man, and 'the greater part' of our physical evils are also our own fault; death 'is almost only an evil' because of the preparations we make for it; moreover, given the immortality of the soul, this life is unimportant and finally irrelevant. And from such arguments he concludes: 'I see everywhere that the evils to which nature subjects us are far less cruel than those which we ourselves add'; we can trust in 'a beneficent Providence'.[8]

If deists like Rousseau were disturbed, so also were materialists such as Diderot. It is striking to realise that on this issue believers and unbelievers shared a common cause. Diderot, having rejected belief in God and Christian morality, was seeking to base a replacement ethic on exactly the same conviction that the natural is good. 'O Nature, everything that is good is contained within your bosom! You are the fruitful source of all truths!': thus declaims his Dorval, and to preserve that faith Diderot was led, despite his empiricism and his exceptional honesty of mind, into assertions that almost equal in comicality Saint-Pierre's notorious claim that God designed the melon for convenient eating *en famille*:

Water, air, earth, fire, everything in nature is good: the hurricane rising towards autumn's end shakes the forests and, striking the trees against each other, breaks away and separates out the dead branches; the storm too beats the waters of the sea and purifies them; and the volcano, pouring out from its gaping side floods of glowing matter, carries into the air the vapour which cleanses it.[9]

Such evidence seemed persuasive to him, but by contrast the fact of our dying remained for Diderot a more intractable and anguishing dilemma; he illustrates more movingly than almost any of his contemporaries the attempt, crucial to his system, to reconcile death and nature.

The studies mentioned earlier have very fully described the wide variety of responses and 'counter-measures' in regard to death that were advocated by the 'philosophes' and others. The briefest summary may suffice here, however, in order to justify a basic conclusion. They strongly attacked the church's exploitation of death to terrorise the dying into conversion. Diderot's *La Religieuse*, for example, presents the stark contrast between the Mother Superior's despairing, terrified death and Suzanne's tranquil, patient, still loving end,[10] and a similar comparison is seen in Saint-Pierre's *Paul et Virginie* between the deaths of Virginie and her aunt. They campaigned for measures to improve health and thus extend life. They urged a better attitude towards death, moreover. The unbelievers contrasted

the stoic calm of 'le philosophe mourant' with the Christian's
dread of divine judgement – instancing as the best approach the
Ancient models of Socrates, Lucretius, Cicero, Cato and Seneca
and the more recent examples of serenity offered by Bayle,
Chaulieu, the Abbé de Saint-Pierre, and Mme de Pompadour.
The believers too urged an alternative to terror: the truly
composed Christian death, concluding a life of Christian virtue
and faced with trust in God, the 'belle mort' of Julie described
at the end of *La Nouvelle Héloïse* and the serene *Death of the
Paralytic* painted by Greuze. They all deplored, furthermore, the
mood of black-robed distress or of horror with which death was
commonly surrounded – the assertion we noted in Rousseau
and that would shortly be well illustrated by one of Diderot's
German admirers, Lessing, in his attack in 1769 on Christian
representations of death as a skeleton and his controversy to
show that the Greeks portrayed it as sleep, 'the ancient cheerful
image of death'.[11]

Yet one conclusion is surely clear: all these measures or
attitudes only help to soften the blow; they do not resolve the
apparent enmity between nature and man that is indicated by
the universality of human death. It is true that Christians
retained their hope in an after-life and that the increasing
number of illuminists, occultists and the like at this date also
trusted in their continuance into another life through
metempsychosis or reincarnation – but in both cases the appeal
was to the supernatural, precisely, in order to remedy the
destructiveness of the natural. Nature itself remains guilty, even
if one argues with Rousseau that the crime is not as heinous
as it might appear.

The astonishing fact, however, is that despite intensified
personal grieving and a heightened awareness of decline and
fall in human history, despite a weakened conviction in some
minds in the reality of an after-life, and despite Lisbon and other
evidences of natural disaster, nature and death were brought
together and were reconciled, as it were, in the outlook of at
least a minority. The manifestations of this feature of later-
eighteenth-century intellectual and cultural history have been

fully illustrated by the historians of death, but one may wonder whether even they have fully stressed its significance or considered the sources of the arresting contrast between old and new. For the traditional Christian death is the final separation *from* nature, except a few transitory bones, a little dust and ashes; for a few in the eighteenth century, including some Christians, and for many more since then, death was to be re-interpreted as an absorption *into* nature, or, to put it in a different way, nature was to be recruited as God's best undertaker.

A single but vivid juxtaposition taken from literature may serve to illustrate the extent of the contrast. Celebrated scenes in Prévost's *Manon Lescaut* of 1734 and in *Atala* of 1801 by the Catholic Chateaubriand present the same melancholy event: both describe a lover at the burial of his beloved; in both instances the setting is the untamed, wild landscape of North America; in both episodes sensibility is all-pervasive. One can add, moreover, that the earlier novelist was in advance of his time in his appreciation of external nature, as his novel *Cleveland* especially shows and also his collection of travel accounts across the world, the *Histoire générale des voyages*. None the less, the two descriptions, though separated by less than seventy years, are in marked opposition in the role and emphasis they give to nature as the background for the burial they are describing.

For Manon's Des Grieux, as he digs her grave, the dominant fear is that her body will be devoured by nature in the form of wild animals – 'become food for wild beasts'. Fortunately the earth is sandy and he is able to make a grave within it, but even then he wraps her in his own clothes 'to prevent the sand from touching her'. Those are small details in the passage; what is still more significant is that it is almost wholly concerned with what he felt and did, with his mental reactions, and that it contains no evocation of the world of nature whatever, except the references to wild animals and the sand.[12] In sharp contrast, in the scene where Atala is buried – a scene far more dominated by Christian references, moreover, than Prévost's – the natural world is omnipresent. She lies on a bed of mountain plants, a magnolia in her hair, and her lips are compared to a rose-bud. Far more important, nature attends her burial and its mood is in total harmony with the human event. The moon rises 'like a vestal virgin in white', coming to weep over the coffin of a companion and friend and to tell to the woods 'that great melancholy secret it likes to recount to the old oaks and to the age-old shores of the seas'. The priest dips a flowering branch into the holy water itself and uses it to scent the evening air, 'perfuming the night with the balms of heaven' – the very image of a union of natural and supernatural. Nature and man are in unity, even to the extent that (Chateaubriand can write) 'the name of God and of the tomb sounded from every echo, every torrent, and every forest'.[13]

Chateaubriand's preferences – expressed again later by his wish to be buried himself on a rocky headland above beetling cliffs and a wild sea near to St Malo – were neither original nor peculiar to him. Literature and life alike in the later decades of the eighteenth century illustrated an increasing conviction that nature is the most fitting place for interment, not the church itself or the town churchyard, and for memorials to the dead as well as for their graves. Once more England is ahead of France in its literary evidence of the novel view – and most notably so in Gray's *Elegy written in a Country Churchyard* (to stress its full title). Only a few years before, in 1743, Blair's *The Grave* had evoked the traditional and didactic picture of tormented spirits rising from the darkness deep below the ground:

> Rous'd from their Slumbers
> In Grim Array the grizly Spectres rise,
> Grin horrible, and obstinately Sullen
> Pass and repass...

For Gray, by contrast, in their country churchyard, 'beneath those rugged elms, that yew-tree's shade', 'the rude Forefathers of the hamlet *sleep*', at peace and undisturbed, and the poem's *Epitaph* makes the union between the dead and nature even closer and explicit.

> Here rests his head upon the lap of Earth

– the lap, that is, of Mother Nature, identical, it almost seems, with (in the poem's final line)

The bosom of his Father and his God.

Gray's gentler view of death as sleep (anticipatory of Lessing's essay later) and his evocation of a simple burial-place amidst nature would be immensely appreciated in France once, after a short time-lag, it was translated – first by Madame Necker in 1765 and frequently thereafter, by Chateaubriand, Cabanis, Lamartine, and many others – and its themes would be much borrowed by the authors of the new 'poetry of tombs and ruins' that proliferated in the later part of the century both in France and elsewhere. Goethe's Werther expresses the wish to be buried under two linden trees within the churchyard. Saint-Pierre's Virginie is buried 'near the church' and at the foot of a clump of bamboos, her body 'covered with flowers', on a mountain-slope and within sound of the sea. Delille in *Les Jardins* evokes a grave for himself set beneath trees and by a stream and bearing, after sprinkling with holy water, a cross. Rétif de la Bretonne goes even further and wishes the dead to be interred at random in the fields. Behind all such wishes lies a new appreciation that is well caught by Delille, addressing the mourner:

> Venez associer les bois, les eaux, les fleurs,
> Tout devient un ami pour les âmes sensibles.

From being the last enemy, nature is now 'a friend'.[14]

The same perception was fully expressed in life as much as in literature and not only in the growing preference for simpler burials and tombs. This very period in France saw a move away from the age-long practice within Christendom – in contrast to the Ancients – of burying the dead in or close to the church, as near to the altar as one's wealth and status made possible, and towards creating cemeteries out of the town. Though Turgot had worried about the loss of agricultural land involved, at least one revolutionary edict later would even prescribe the type and number of trees to be planted. The explicit reasons for the campaign and, in due course, for the legislation in favour of burial-places in the countryside or at the town's outskirts lay in the increasing health hazards created by over-filled urban cemeteries, but the sharp break with tradition on so emotive a matter seems to have been less resisted, after an initial period from 1763, than one might have anticipated. An obvious advantage was to avoid the multiple and crowded graves of the town churchyard, given greater space; that accorded with the growth of a more personalised grieving, as noted earlier, and made possible the provision of a special and individual resting-place for the deceased. Yet the quite rapid acceptance of the new locations surely suggests also that even amongst the public at large there was perhaps a growing sense that 'returning to nature' was an apt conclusion to one's life. It is significant, moreover, that the plans adopted for the new cemeteries very commonly postulated banked trees and a natural irregularity as opposed to landscape formality. To give one example, the cemetery of Père-Lachaise, developed in the first decade of the nineteenth century and situated outside Paris at that date, was designed on the hill-top on the pattern of an English garden, with winding pathways and with the tombs shadowed by irregularly-banked trees, to form a version of the Elysian fields, which today's visitor can still re-capture and contrast with the straight avenues and the rectangles of the rest.[15]

Many of the upper classes expressed the new attitudes similarly, siting tombs and monuments in their informal gardens – as at Bagatelle in the Bois de Boulogne, Méréville (with a memorial to Captain Cook included), and numerous other places. And of them all the most celebrated and frequently visited was at Ermenonville, where Rousseau's tomb stood on the lake's small island beneath the poplar trees, a simple natural setting for nature's best friend, as was widely felt. The tomb's inscription was provided by the Marquis de Girardin himself: 'Ici repose [and again the notion of sleep and rest is invoked] l'homme de la nature et de la vérité.' ('Here rests the man of nature and of truth.')

Nor was the mood created here and elsewhere, or that was expressed in the literary and artistic works of the age, usually one of despair or alternatively, as with such earlier 'graveyard poetry' as Blair's, a mood of salutary didacticism, reminding us sternly of our mortality. Some scholars of the period's poetry of tombs and ruins have perhaps exaggerated the frequency of such attitudes: Favre thinks this literature was anguished and expressive of an 'aspiration towards death'; Mortier, though offering much evidence to the contrary in his study, can suggest all the same that the cult of ruins is the focus of a 'cultural *malaise*'; others have linked the new feelings with the rise of the Romantic 'mal du siècle'.[16] Melancholy is certainly present but, often enough, it is a gentle melancholy, 'une douce mélancolie' as Diderot, Saint-Pierre and others all put it, linked with a degree of acceptance and softened by trust in God or nature or both. Diderot especially responds to the aesthetic appeal of ruins: he is the inventor, as Mortier judges, of a new 'poetics of ruins'. Thus, for example, Hubert Robert's depiction of the Louvre in ruins, with nature's vegetation growing over them, absorbing man's works back into itself – an increasingly favourite theme – inspires him with a 'noble sadness'. 'The ideas which ruins awaken in me are great ideas.'[17] Saint-Pierre's *Etudes de la nature*, similarly, included sections arrestingly entitled 'Plaisir de la ruine' and 'Plaisir des tombeaux', and in his first *Etude* he claims that even 'suffering and death are evidence of nature's goodness'.[18]

The distinction between such a response and what Saint-Pierre termed by comparison 'a black melancholy' is especially explicit, contrary to Favre's suggestion, in writings about ruins, and here again one finds evidence of the new attitudes to nature that concern us here. This is seen in a contrast that was frequently drawn between distinct kinds of ruins: those created by man as the result of wars and other human folly and vice and those created by time and nature. Saint-Pierre's two sections, and that on the 'Ruines de la nature' give an especially striking instance. The moral lesson is certainly stressed: ruins and tombs of all kinds illustrate our 'misery' and the 'vanity' of human achievements. They serve also to remind us of God and immortality, and the 'melancholy' they inspire is or should be 'religious'. But he then draws the comparison between the human and the natural as the cause of ruins. Man-made ruins provoke only 'horror', he claims, whereas the ruins of time and nature give us 'pleasure' – 'by casting us into infinity' – and he adds that the older the ruins, the greater our pleasure, whether they are of man's works or within nature itself. 'The ruins in which nature fights against the art of men inspire a gentle melancholy. It shows to us here the vanity of our world and the perpetuity of its own.' As to such ruins as crumbling rocks, these accord with 'the infinitely wise designs of nature': 'nothing is destroyed in it which is not made good'. This principle that nature always builds even as it destroys is illustrated, he submits, even by the way plants and flowers grow over human ruins, thus forming 'charming contrasts'. And, predictably, he ends by preferring simple tombs amidst nature to cathedral catafalques. It is particularly in the countryside that 'suffering takes on a sublime quality'; 'it rises up with the graveyards' ancient yew-trees; it extends with the plains and hills around; it unites with all the impressions of nature'.[19] Chateaubriand, a little later, adopted this same distinction between ruins that are the 'work of time' and those that are the 'work of men'. The latter, as when he goes to visit the temple of Poseidon at Cape Sounion, pain him, but the former, he declares, 'have nothing unpleasing, for nature works along with the years' – and flowers spreading over the ruins are again valued.[20] Similarly, his contemporary, Mme de Staël, finds 'a singular charm' in viewing the ruins at Tivoli; 'they are mingled with the trees, with nature; they seem to be in harmony with the solitary torrent, the image of time itself, which has made of them what they are'.[21] In these and other cases death undoubtedly provokes regret, but the melancholy is not bitter nor – most relevantly here – is it in revolt against nature.[22]

The question that arises, however, is *why* that melancholy is not in revolt against nature. Many in the nineteenth century – and a few even in the eighteenth – would be troubled by their perceptions (as de Sade enjoyed and exploited his) of 'Nature, red in tooth and claw', as, for instance, were Vigny, Leconte de Lisle and Tennyson amongst other poets of 'the struggle for survival'. One thus wonders how the later-eighteenth-century minority was able to take so much more kindly a view, how it could apparently feel that a reconciliation was possible between belief in nature's goodness and the fact of death. The sources of that reconciliation have perhaps been left largely unconsidered by even the most distinguished of recent historians of death in France.[23]

The answer may lie – one should put it no higher – in some of the notions that were being concurrently advanced by eighteenth-century science, as outlined in the previous chapter. If so, one also has a further example of the inter-relationship of science and humane culture at this period which was referred to there.

Of those notions the 'discovery of time' was the most pertinent, and a first but minor and perhaps finally cosmetic illustration is provided by the cult of remembrance in the future and, for the happy few, down the long ages. The expressions of this cult have been frequently described and with ample justification. Monuments, as well as tombs, dedicated to out-standing individuals were erected – as, say, the Marquis de Girardin's 'Temple de la Philosophie' at Ermenonville, with its columns celebrating Descartes, Voltaire, Newton, Montes-quieu, Penn, and Rousseau, or in Madame d'Houdetot's park at Sannois. Louis XV accepted in 1768 a plan for a 'Panthéon' as part of a re-design for the Louvre, 'a gallery in which would be placed busts and monuments erected to the Geniuses of the Nation' – though the project was only realised later, of course, and in a different site and form. The promise of remembrance in marble could be matched by literature too: hence, reviving the earlier elegiac tradition, a spate of 'éloges' and 'épîtres' amongst late-eighteenth-century poetry; hence Diderot's own emphasis as editor of the *Encyclopédie* upon 'portraits' of the illustrious like that devoted to Montesquieu; hence the success of Palissot's periodical *Nécrologie*, founded in 1764 to give obituaries of the famous; hence above all the notion that one can live on through one's own creations, along, also, with those they depict. Posterity will remember; posterity will keep us in that way alive. Such was the view, and it was greatly encouraged, obviously enough, once one envisaged time as continuing long into the future, if not for ever.

Yet this is an ancient notion, as we all know – found in the

Death and destruction

Old Testament, in the classics and elsewhere, long before eighteenth-century ideas about time. Furthermore the hope of 'remembrance' is far from meeting the particular problem at issue: it is *humans* who confer this form of immortality, not nature itself. The same is also true, one can notice in passing, of a different defence against death's finality that was requested by a small number of people at this time. The parents of Mme de Staël were preserved, visible, in great bottles of alcohol, and Jeremy Bentham can still be viewed in his glass-sided box at University College, London. Yet here again it is human initiative at work, not nature (as still today in those cases where corpses are being deep-frozen or preserved in stout containers).

Diderot does wonder if nature can help in another way, and this hopeful question warrants mention since there is little that is more deeply moving in the age's writing than the letter to Sophie Volland in which he envisages that if they are buried in the same grave their remains may perhaps still be in contact with each other:

> Those who have loved each other during their life-time and who ask to be buried side by side are perhaps not so foolish as one may think. Perhaps their ashes press together, are mingled and united with each other! I do not know. Perhaps they have not lost all feeling, all recollection of their earlier state... Oh, my Sophie, there would thus remain for me the hope of touching you, feeling you, loving you, seeking for you, being united and merged with you, when we shall no longer exist.[24]

That is indeed a slender hope, however. More substantial were other consolations, it would seem, that were offered by nature as re-interpreted by the new sciences. They may not be totally satisfying – we and our loved ones still die – but at least they may allow us to cling to an affection for the natural world even whilst we grieve.

In the first place, it was increasingly argued, death is biologically useful. It is a process within organic nature whereby one species lives upon another, upon another. What dies is not lost but is essential for the sustaining of future life, and so a writer like Robinet can note in *De la nature* (1761) that nature takes 'as much care to destroy what it makes as to construct it'.[25] The dying leaf falls and feeds next spring's growth, and likewise with man. Rousseau's Julie dies in autumn, the perfectly appropriate time to die, as others like Delille, Saint-Lambert and Mercier also felt.[26] And Rousseau had already invoked the same belief when he struggled to justify God's ways at Lisbon; in his letter to Voltaire he contends that it may be 'necessary to the conservation of the human race that there is a circulation of matter between men, animals and plants' and that thereby 'what hurts the individual contributes to the general good'.[27]

It is surely clear how fundamentally these beliefs rested upon thinking of nature not as mechanically passive and static, with everything in it already 'pre-formed', but as organic and dynamic, utilising what has existed to create novel forms for the future. Furthermore, another scientific doctrine was often postulated in this context – an ancient idea but now being re-asserted by such scientists as Lavoisier. Matter is indestructible and is thus never lost. D'Holbach, for example, in his *Système de la nature*, attacked those who fail to see that the decomposition of a body does not necessitate the destruction of its elements: 'The whole of nature continues and is conserved only by means of circulation, of transmigration.'[28] In short, not only is nature organically conceived *able* to utilise what is past for what is future; since nothing is ever destroyed, it *invariably* does so. The two doctrines of organicism and of matter's indestructibility, if taken together, give certainty that, in one sense, we survive eternally. As Boulanger put it in his *Anecdotes de la nature*:

> Crois moi! Rien ne périt dans ce vaste univers,
> Rien ne s'anéantit, tout se survit, tout change.[29]

It is noteworthy too that Saint-Pierre's wise old man, seeking to console Paul after Virginie's death, invokes the same idea. As well as reminding him of the Christian promise of eternity in the world-to-come, he uses it to promise eternity in this world also: 'But Virginie still exists. My son, observe how everything on earth changes and nothing is lost. No human art could destroy the smallest particle of matter.'[30]

There is also, thirdly, the possibility of quite specific survival: we can live on, almost identifiably, in our descendants. One good example, relying upon a particular set of scientific observations that were mentioned earlier, is provided by Diderot's appeal to the hydra. The hydra when cut up is in that way dead, and yet it lives on in the new hydra that result. Thus he writes to Sophie: 'When the polyp is divided into a hundred thousand parts, the original generative creature no longer exists, but all its principles are living.'[31] Even more significantly, the new understanding of reproduction given by cases like that of the Ruhe family had shown that human individuals themselves survive – genetically, as we would now say – in their offspring and, in turn, in their descendants. Here is a quite direct and personal continuation of oneself in one's progeny. Of the father, the Abbé Rémi writes: 'Your name will be passed on...to others, by means of whom you will journey triumphantly across the centuries, under the auspices of nature.' Sylvain Maréchal summed it up when he declared: 'The father of a family is eternal.'[32]

'Eternal'? Yes, since time has ceased to be finite, limited in its past and soon to be terminated by the end of the world and the Day of Judgement. Buffon might calculate that the earth would be too cold for humans after 93,291 years, but others were more hopeful, as we noted with Kant and Hutton. An arresting transformation follows. Previously time had been both restricted and ultimately irrelevant compared with the timelessness of our supernatural future in the after-life. Now – and especially, of course, for those who doubted the very reality of the supernatural and the after-life – it was time itself which became endless, timeless. 'Everything is destroyed, everything perishes, everything passes', begins Diderot in the *Salon* of 1767, but he continues: 'There is only the world that remains, there is only time that endures' – a lesson taught by ruins. And in a letter to Sophie in 1760 he writes: 'Nature which has condemned us to undergo all sorts of affliction has willed that time should assuage them despite ourselves;...almost nothing withstands the consolation of time.'[33] Here and for others of Diderot's age the new scientific perceptions of time have affected directly the new responses to death. Man lives on after his death not *outside* finite time but *inside* timeless time. This chapter began by noting that time, Buffon's 'great workman of nature', brings death and destruction, but now time has been transformed into a foundation of our hope for eternity.

This reconciliation of nature and death, if such it be, was achieved by only a limited number in the later-eighteenth century. For the great majority death remained as fearful as in previous ages; the reality (to quote Lebrun's moving conclusion) lay in 'the poignant sight of men, women and children struggling or resigned, disarmed in the face of death'.[34] Yet one may well ask finally – and notwithstanding the claims of Ariès and others that death in our own time has become 'forbidden death' – whether the minority view has not now become 'democratised', implicit in the reactions of many people in at least the Anglo-Saxon countries, and found its symbol in the modern crematorium. Set often in the suburban countryside, with winding ways, lawns and irregular groups of trees as in the informal gardens of those earlier days, it serves Protestant Christians and non-Christians alike, and the ashes of the deceased are scattered upon the rose-beds to renew their growth, within, precisely, the 'garden of remembrance'. Inside the chapel itself and then in that garden outside it two concepts of immortality are suggested; since the eighteenth century the mourner has been able to seek consolation in either or both of them. It is fashionable amongst intellectuals to mock with Evelyn Waugh in *The Loved One* at that Californian burial-place, Forest Lawn Memorial Park, but perhaps the novelist – secure, moreover, in his Catholic faith – stayed on the surface and failed to wonder why so many of the bereaved feel it so appropriate. Even the name – fusing the appeal of both pastoral and untamed nature, and of the hope of remembrance too – perhaps reflects a yearning by many modern people, and not least among those who drive past it, under the Los Angeles smog, on the crowded freeway to San Bernardino: a yearning to be reconciled, at peace at last, with the world of nature – if not in urban life, then at least in rural death.

6

TRANSOCEANIC PERSPECTIVES

Westward to Tahiti

The great age of exploration overseas was the eighteenth century even more than the sixteenth: one could almost claim that the 'Enlightenment' was as much geographical as intellectual in its dimensions. In this chapter we must consider the greatly widened transoceanic perspectives upon nature and the natural that resulted.

The voyages ranged more extensively than ever before: from Greenland to Patagonia in the Americas, and much deeper into their interiors than previously; in Africa from Guinea and the Congo to Abyssinia, the Cape of Good Hope, and the island of Madagascar; in Asia from Persia to Ceylon and the East Indies. There was also the rather special case of China, admired in Europe as a major and more ancient civilisation. The fragmentary tales, myths and hearsay brought back by previous explorers from Columbus, Diaz, Vasco da Gama and Magellan onwards, and by such circumnavigators of the world as Francis Drake and Tasman, were increasingly replaced now by facts about wider areas of the globe. These journeys, vastly more numerous than in earlier centuries, were undertaken above all for reasons of commerce and colonisation, but they also led to a rich proliferation of knowledge and awareness. Just as the biological sciences at the same time were being created on the basis of closer and more extensive observation, so also with geography and anthropology. It is thus no surprise, for example, to find Linnaeus, the great classifier of plants, also classifying the different types of men and developing the notion of 'races' of human beings. In 1740, in the second edition of his *Systema Naturae*, he had distinguished four varieties of man:

white European, red American, dark Asiatic, and black African. By the 1758 edition he would be noting two further varieties: wild man – mute, four-footed, and with shaggy hair – and human 'monsters', like giants and pygmies and other dwarfs. Those additions, a mere eighteen years later, clearly derived from yet more information brought back after yet more journeys – of which, in fact, one motive, however secondary, was often quite explicitly scientific. Intellectuals like Buffon pressed for more exploration for scientific reasons, and expeditions not uncommonly took an officially appointed naturalist along with them; Commerson went with Bougainville, for example, and William Hodges and Joseph Banks with Cook. Nor was it only scientists who keenly followed the discoveries. There was a markedly increasing interest amongst the educated public in general. Curiosity about foreign countries had been fed earlier by the 'exotic' and often erotic details of works like Chardin's *Voyage en Perse* (1686) or Dufresny's *Amusements sérieux et comiques* (1699), portraying a Siamese in Paris, or, a little later, by such epistolary novels as Montesquieu's *Lettres persanes* (1721), in which such details were used partly to attract the reader and partly to provide a contrast with Europe and the pretext for a criticism of its institutions. More and more what began as a titillated and casual interest deepened into a wish for better authenticated and detailed information – or so it would seem from the many publications in the eighteenth century of actual travellers' accounts, such as those included in Prévost's collection, *Histoire générale des voyages*, in twenty volumes from 1746 on, since publishers in all ages publish for a market they believe to exist. To look at one particularly useful bibliography of such accounts over the whole period from 1500 to 1800 is to recognise at once the astonishing increase in their number in the eighteenth century compared with the two previous centuries and, furthermore, the striking geographical range which these works collectively covered.[1]

All the new knowledge thereby publicised was fascinating above all because of the many novelties it contained. But it was also to prove to be highly relevant to major ideological debates in the later-eighteenth century and beyond, to provoke strong disagreements even between otherwise mutually sympathetic thinkers, and to play a very significant, even if ambivalent, role in modifying men's views of the natural in human form as well as of external nature.

Today, two centuries later, now that so little of the world and its population remains unknown to outsiders and when journeys across it have become routine air flights, it is hard to recapture the moods of curiosity and astonishment amongst educated Europeans of the time. A detailed illustration may thus help to set the scene for this chapter, and it is especially pertinent to choose, out of countless others, the case of one particular French expedition to the Pacific Ocean, partly since its discoveries were to have a special impact and above all because the major novelty of all novelties during these years lay in the exploration of that particular area of roughly one-third of the entire earth's surface. The Pacific was hardly known before the eighteenth century. Dutch and other traders had visited the East Indies and discovered something of the north-western coast of 'New Holland' long before Cook landed on its eastern coast. Others, since Magellan more than 200 years previously, had ventured up the western coast of South America. It has been calculated that between 1698 and 1725 alone, and from France alone, some 168 ships sailed into the 'South Sea', many of them more profitably than for investors in the Englishman John Law's 'South Sea Bubble'. Frézier in particular thoroughly explored in 1717 the shores of present-day Chile – and he lived on to be consulted by Bougainville himself half a century later. Yet if the Pacific's coastal fringes were becoming familiar, the myriad islands scattered over the ocean were unknown or at most conjectured, as contemporary maps illustrate. For the golden age of Pacific exploration did not come until the late-1760s, thanks above all to the voyages of Bougainville and Cook, culminating in 1770 in the latter's landing during the first of his three expeditions on the eastern seaboard of Australia. Here we may consider as an example the experiences of the French explorer – though Cook's discoveries were to have almost as great an impact even in France – and Bougainville's arrival in due course at an island, a mere thirty-five miles in length, lost in the vast ocean and totally unknown to any Europeans (indeed to anyone other than its natives and their neighbours) prior to 1767 – the island of Tahiti.

In 1759 Quebec City, defended by the French commander Montcalm, had fallen to the English troops of General Wolfe, both leaders being killed. The negotiation of the French surrender and evacuation fell to a young colonel, aide-de-camp to Montcalm – Louis Antoine de Bougainville. When he returned home in 1760, it seemed natural to him and others that France should try to compensate for her loss of the North American territories. French defeat in the Seven Years War had not helped morale either; colonisation elsewhere seemed the obvious alternative, the more so as the perfidious British were similarly engaged. After a brief but abortive expedition to the Falkland Islands, Bougainville, now in the navy, was allowed by Louis XV, almost as a consolation prize, to undertake a sea journey round the world, with two ships provided for it, the frigate *La Boudeuse* and a storeship *L'Etoile*.

He sailed from France in December 1766, complete with the 'Royal Botanist and Naturalist' Commerson (whose valet later turned out to be a girl – the first girl, probably, to go round the world). His expedition lasted over two years, and his account of it was given in his *Voyage autour du monde*, published in 1771, two years after his return. He called first at the Falkland Islands for the official ceremony ending French colonisation there and handing the territory to the Spanish. After considerable delay at Rio de Janeiro, in November 1767 he entered the Magellan Straits – and met, like so many others before and since, with appalling weather. But at last in late-January 1768 his two ships finally entered the Pacific, with the crew singing the *Te Deum* to celebrate their deliverance. The relevant part of what followed concerns his landing at Tahiti – discovered by an English expedition under Samuel Wallis, in the *Dolphin*, the year before, and to be visited by Captain Cook the year after. The date was 4 April 1768; the island seemed attractive, despite poor anchorage, and the natives very friendly, especially the young females. Bougainville comments:

I ask you: how could one keep at their work 400 Frenchmen, young sailors, who had seen no women for six months?...Sailors and soldiers alike hurried to get to the hatchway, and never was a capstan heaved so briskly.[2]

One scholar aptly remarks: 'On that day the legend of Tahiti was born.'[3] Even Bougainville himself felt that the island's inhabitants provided strong evidence for the view that man in his natural state is good and is only corrupted by civilisation.

His account of 'la nouvelle Cythère', as he called it with a classical reference, in contrast to Cook who would patriotically term it 'King George's Island', is given in chapters 8, 9 and 10 in his *Voyage*. Parts of it deal with anchorage troubles and geographical items, but the most important features concern firstly external nature, and secondly human nature. In chapter 9 he describes his visit to the interior of the island and his delight at its beauty and beneficence:

I thought I had been transported into the Garden of Eden; we crossed a plain of grass covered with beautiful fruit-trees and intersected with rivulets that maintained a delightful coolness in the air, without any of the disadvantages brought by humidity.

The climate is equally attractive, the temperature being warm but not over-hot, and there are none of the insects which often plague tropical lands. 'The climate is so healthy that, despite the hard labour we had to undertake,...no-one fell ill.'[4] The strength and good health of the natives, even living in houses always open to the weather, is further evidence of the healthy air – and, as well, he claims, of the good way of life led by the inhabitants.

The 'natural' on Tahiti also included the natural humans he saw. Bougainville was much impressed by the spontaneous kindliness of the natives, though he does admit that they have defects. They wage war against other islands with great cruelty, killing all males and capturing the females. They are also very superstitious and dominated by their priests. Their form of government is autocratic and the kings and nobles have power of life and death over their inferiors; typically, they alone can eat meat and fish, whereas the rest live on vegetables and fruit. He adds that, comparably, wives are totally subject to their husbands; infidelity results in death unless the husband has agreed to it, as, however, he commonly does.

Indeed 'jealousy' hardly exists, whether about wives or about property. 'It would seem that as regards the absolute necessities of life, there is no personal property and everything belongs to everybody.' 'Day and night the houses are open. Everyone gathers fruits from the first tree he encounters, or takes them in any house he enters.' The natives neither guard their belongings nor lock their dwellings. True, they did steal from the sailors, to their chiefs' disapproval – but Bougainville himself excuses this as caused by mere curiosity about totally new objects. At bottom they are naturally warm: 'everybody greeted us with friendliness'; 'everywhere we found hospitality, ease, an innocent joy and every appearance of happiness'.[5]

This is true especially of their sexual attitudes – the aspect Diderot would take up in his polemical *Supplément au voyage de Bougainville*. There is no guilt or embarrassment but only a natural delight in physical love; there exists total sexual freedom, except for married women, and there is an actual encouragement of the unmarried girl, especially since one or two children will be a welcome dowry to her future husband. The sailors are invited into the natives' houses, given a meal, and offered a daughter of the family – with the neighbours gathered round, flowers strewn on the floor, and musicians. 'Here Venus is the goddess of hospitality and her cult admits of no mystery' – a situation that embarrassed some sailors, says Bougainville, though he drily adds with discreet negatives: 'All the same, I cannot guarantee that anyone failed to overcome his reluctance or to conform to the local customs.'[6]

One may interject here that the English sailors on *The Dolphin* in the previous year had found the maidens more mercenary. Then they had charged for their services, asking for nails, according to the account – first a 20-penny nail, then a 30-penny, then a 40-penny – 'and some were so extravagant as to demand a 7 or 9 inch Spick'. It later became all too evident, as the ship set sail, that the nails had been removed by the sailors from the fabric of *The Dolphin*. Bougainville reports no such commercialism – and perhaps the girls had found nails of limited

use on Tahiti – and nor does Captain Cook after he landed the
year after Bougainville. Cook was in fact more distressed than
Bougainville by the Tahitians' attitude, but he confirmed the
general picture:

More than one half of the better sort of the inhabitants have entered into a
resolution of enjoying free liberty in love, without being Troubled or
disturbed by its consequences…The Men will very readily offer the Young
Women to Strangers, even their own Daughters, and think it very strange
if you refuse them.[7]

In reality the French expedition stayed for less than a
fortnight. A few of the sailors angered even these placid natives,
who asked them all to leave. Bougainville took with him a
Tahitian male, who offered to visit France. They sailed via New
Guinea, came very close to discovering Australia – which might
even be French-speaking now if they had – and arrived back
at St Malo in March 1769. The Tahitian, Aotourou, interested
the Parisians and charmed them by his pleasant, quiet-spoken
good manners. Sad to report, however, they tired of him, and
on his way home a year later he died of smallpox off Madagascar.
In this particular, ironically, he was much less fortunate than
his equivalent in England, Omai, brought back by Cook, of
whom we are told that whilst 'the honoured and beloved guest
of King George III and Society', he was 'inoculated by Baron
Dimsdale, who later treated Catherine the Great, with the
newfangled smallpox vaccination of Dr Jenner'.[8] Yet enthusiasm remained, in theory at least, and some of Bougainville's
colleagues were even warmer than he. Thus Commerson, who
wished to name the island 'Utopie', claimed to have found there
'the state of natural man, born essentially good',[9] and Fesche's
praise for Tahitian life was even more all-inclusive:

If happiness consists in an abundance of everything needed for living, in
inhabiting a splendid land set in the most beautiful of climates, a land that
produces all these things, so to say, without any need for cultivation, in
enjoying the best of health, in breathing always the purest and most salubrious
air, in leading a free, gentle, tranquil way of life,…then I say there is not
a happier people in the world.[10]

Information about Cook's first journey soon strengthened such
enthusiasms, moreover. Hawkesworth's account, which also

included versions of the views of Cook and Joseph Banks, was published in 1773 and reached the conclusion, like Commerson, that 'these people have a knowledge of right and wrong from the mere dictates of natural conscience'.

Awareness of this idyllic island was further reinforced by paintings and drawings by the expedition artists[11] – and in France even decorative wallpaper showing Polynesian life was produced. The aim was in part to portray both the scenery and the natives' life as exactly as scientists would expect, but their own enthusiasms also are easily discerned along with their transposition of the artistic tradition of the 'ideal landscape' – not forgetting in addition their responsiveness to the newer tastes for mountain and ocean wildness, especially in renderings of Antarctic scenes. Hodges's *A View taken in the Bay of Oaitepeha (Tautira), Otaheite* offers a characteristic example. The composition is modelled on the classical landscapes of Claude which he admired, but within this framework the gentle Italian hills are replaced by the steep inland mountain peaks of Tahiti and olive and cypress trees give way to accurately depicted plantations of bread-fruit and coconut trees, whilst in the foreground, in place of well-bred shepherdesses roaming in Arcadia, naked Tahitian maidens are disporting themselves. Hodges is thus stressing the same two elements of the Tahitian idyll as Bougainville and his fellows: a beautiful and bountiful external nature; a liberated and thus happy human nature.

Many others who have never been to the Pacific quickly took up the topical themes: novelists, poets, theatrical producers. Thus, to give first a single example from England, if one had gone to the 1785 Christmas production at Covent Garden one would have seen *Omai, or a Trip Round the World*, a favourite production with King George himself. The play's plot was preposterous, ending with Omai enthroned as King of Tahiti accompanied by his queen from London and thus called Londina, and there was a finale with a choral tribute to Cook, whose portrait was lowered to the stage. The settings and costumes were planned by none other than Loutherbourg (whom we last met being praised by Diderot for his paintings of wild nature and who had moved to London by then). Joshua

Reynolds was at the production's first night and expressed 'the utmost satisfaction at all the landscape scenes'. This is not surprising since Loutherbourg indulged his love of wild nature to the full and included a red moon, in eclipse, hail-storms, moonlight, sunrise, snowy rocks, a 'dreary ice island', and, predictably, a storm at sea, not forgetting a final parade of Pacific island representatives.[12]

As regards France, it is clear just how rapidly the 'myth of Tahiti' was developed and exploited.[13] Already in 1770, even before Bougainville's account had appeared, Bricaire de La Dixmerie published *Le Sauvage de Taïti aux François*: Aotourou is imagined expressing his criticisms of French politics, manners and society, and Tahiti is held up as a model of Rousseauist natural society. Sébastien Mercier in 1771 included in *L'An 2440* a chapter that envisaged one of Bougainville's sailors deserting to stay on the island. (Reality was to imitate fiction with the mutiny on *The Bounty* later.) A novel, *Lettres taïtiennes*, by Mme de Monbart; the Marquis de Sade's *Aline et Valcour*, a novel whose hero Sainville sails to Tahiti to find his beloved Léonore and in which the idyllic island of 'Tamoé' is contrasted with the 'anti-Tahiti' illustrated by the island of 'Batua'; a play by Delisle de Sales, *La Vierge d'Otaït*; Rétif de la Bretonne's utopian novel, *La Découverte australe*: these and a variety of other works between 1770 and 1789 all illustrate the literary utilisation of the explorers' information. And in them Tahiti was in general presented in the ways already noted: as, first, an exotic, beautiful, all-providing land; and, secondly, a land whose people live happily by following only their feelings and impulses, especially sexual, and by their freedom from European notions of property, power and religion, who are – in brief – 'noble savages', challenging by their very existence the values and systems of European society.

Tahiti's discovery provides one particularly colourful and widely-popularised example of a diffusion of knowledge that could be illustrated from numerous other instances. Some, and perhaps many, eighteenth-century readers would go no further than the exotic interest of all the travel details and of Aotourou and Omai. For others, however, the consequences were more far-reaching, and it is these that must now be considered.

As regards men's changing appreciation of external nature they were relatively straightforward and uncontentious. First, the developing 'sciences of nature' of the age were immensely stimulated by the discoveries of the explorers and their naturalists. Drawings and paintings of exotic scenery and life and of a host of previously unknown plants, flowers and animals were made and reproduced for European readers. Many actual specimens were brought back also and large collections of Pacific ethnography established, and these were to be as fascinating to contemporary scientists as moon rocks and dust in our own time, as Bernard Smith's study of *European Vision and the South Pacific* reveals with particular clarity (he also stresses the contribution which all the new observations made to the rise of theories of organic evolution). For the time being, moreover, it seemed that the new scientific knowledge could be enjoyed without intellectual anxieties, with few of the religious difficulties that would arise from Darwin's comparable voyage in *The Beagle* some seventy years later. By the mid-nineteenth century the existence of the kangaroo, for example, would threaten belief in the literal infallibility of the Bible story of Noah's Ark; in the late-eighteenth century the kangaroo was still an innocuous and intriguing new species. And indeed a second consequence for many Europeans of these revelations of an unknown world was yet further to extend their faith in God and His perfect goodness as creator of a world containing so many wonders and beauties. The new knowledge – or so it seemed in general – did not so much conflict with the old theology as reinforce it, and any storm clouds of impending conflict were geological, as in Buffon's work, and not biological. A third, if lesser consequence was artistic. Smith in particular has shown that observation of the marked differences between Europe and the Pacific in regard to types of plants and animals alike did much to encourage in art the notion of 'typical landscape' – of landscapes differing distinctively from one another by virtue of their flora and fauna. Finally, and more generally, the discoveries extended awareness of just what marvels nature could achieve, and to that extent they weakened further the old notion that the natural world is merely an uninteresting and unlovely vale of tears prior to the spiritual life-to-come. Bougainville's and Cook's descriptions of the Tahitian 'garden of Eden' and 'the treasures poured out by nature' upon it do not, strictly speaking, clash with the Christian postulation of a 'fallen world', as the very reference to Eden implies. Yet they are none the less suggestive of a quite different response, conscious of nature's qualities rather than its defects. Their reactions had been anticipated prior to the landings on Tahiti – notably by Rousseau in *La Nouvelle Héloïse* (iv, 3 and 10) where Saint-Preux gives accounts of his protracted journey across the oceans with Anson's expedition. He has to withstand harsh rigours, from wild seas and storms, but feels amply rewarded by the natural splendours of the Pacific islands on which he lands:

I stayed for three months on a deserted and delightful island, that offered a gentle and moving image of the age-long beauty of nature and that seemed to have been confined to the end of the world in order to provide a refuge for persecuted innocence and love.[14]

Now, some ten years later, the explorers' true-life accounts persuasively confirmed Rousseau's evocation. (*O tempora! O mores!*: it was from Saint-Preux's 'delightful island of Tinian', two centuries later, that the plane took off to drop its atomic bomb on Hiroshima.)

Nature's children

Saint-Preux does not only respond to an idyllic external nature, however. He also declares his horror as he observes the once happy natives in the lands he visits reduced to misery by European greed and cruelty. Overseas exploration did not only affect men's appreciation of the outside world of nature in the scientific, religious, artistic and more general ways just noted. It also entered – and perhaps more significantly so – into the ideological disputes of the time in regard to the natural in human form. Previous chapters have observed changing attitudes to the world around us, but the eighteenth century was distinguished above all by a wide-ranging 'rehabilitation', as it has been called, of human nature itself, by the claim – whether confidently or tentatively expressed – that man is not 'fallen' through the sin of Adam any more than is the creation as a whole.

This claim, made against the assertions of many Christian centuries, had numerous precursors, notably during the Renaissance period, but it was the age of the Enlightenment that made the decisive moves away from the dominance of orthodox Christian teaching. Whatever moments of historical pessimism one may find, revaluation of human potential is nevertheless clearly in the direction of optimism, towards the assertion that man is naturally more good than sinful, to put the matter at its lowest, and especially if he can be protected against the corrupting effects of certain forms of society, government, religion and education. Its hopefulness about man is illustrated most strikingly in the century's development of the idea of progress – of progress not as an historical inevitability, as for Hegel, Marx and others in the following century, but as an improvement in society and human life that can be ensured by men's good will and reasoned determination. Here the 'philosophes' are appealing to the values of civilisation at its best. Some of them also show their optimism in another way: by urging us to follow above all our personal emotions and conscience if we wish to achieve the happiness of ourselves and others. This trust in the goodness, potential or actual, of the 'natural' individual – before education and civilisation have 'corrupted' him – rests in fact upon an even greater confidence about man than the reasoning and empirical arguments of a Voltaire, and in the thought of some of the 'philosophes' consequently there is sometimes a tension, even a contradiction, between two somewhat differing assessments of human nature, between two separate injunctions – the one being to follow civilisation, reason and science, and the other to 'follow nature'. The tension was sometimes evident in their theoretical arguments, and it was also manifested in their complex attitudes to certain 'images of the natural' in human form, images which incarnated this second, more extreme suggestion that man is

'naturally good' and is not the morally neutral 'blank sheet'
postulated by Locke and his French 'sensationalist' followers
any more than he is the depraved sinner of Christian orthodoxy.

Later chapters will be concerned with others of these images
of the natural human being as they emerged and were
popularised in later eighteenth-century France – with 'the
natural child', 'the natural family', 'the natural woman', and
'the good peasant'. But of all these images probably the first,
chronologically, to achieve significance in European thinking
was that of 'the noble savage'.

The notion of the noble savage had had a long history well
before Dryden in 1670 wrote the now familiar lines in *The
Conquest of Grenada*:

> I am as free as Nature first made man,
> Ere the base laws of servitude began,
> When wild in woods the noble savage ran.

The Ancients had dreamed of a 'Golden Age' – a dream
revived to some extent during the Renaissance by those who
admired classical civilisation. The Hebrew and Christian
religions had posited an idyllic 'Garden of Eden' before Adam
and Eve fell from happy innocence into sin. And the accounts
of some at least of the earlier explorers seemed to confirm the
same notion of man's original happiness when in the state of
nature. Christopher Columbus was only one of those who
praised the good will and generous nature of the American
Indians: 'These people are without any religion, not idolaters,
but very gentle, not knowing what is evil, nor the sins of murder
and theft.'[15] A companion of Magellan in 1522 likewise admired
the natives of Brazil for their goodness: they live by natural
instinct, naked, and survive to the age of 140. It was such
reports which would lead Ronsard to idealise the American
savages in his 'Complainte contre fortune' and Montaigne by
the late-sixteenth century to write his essay *Des cannibales*,
though admittedly he was utilising them to highlight his
criticisms of European man. 'We may well call them barbarians
in relation to the rules of reason, but not in relation to ourselves,
for we surpass them in all sorts of barbarism.'

Yet theirs was far from being a universally-held view, and there was indeed a fervent debate concerning the savage around the end of the sixteenth century.[16] The early explorer of North America, Cartier, for example, called the Canadian Indians 'the most miserable people there can be in the world'. Leo the African in the sixteenth century – who, unlike the Portuguese a little earlier, had moved from the West African coast into the interior – could praise the inhabitants: 'The Blacks are of good life and are faithful... They devote their time to pleasure and leading a cheerful existence.' But he also called them 'brute beasts without reason, without intelligence'. Churchmen throughout the Middle Ages had likewise argued that 'wild men' might not even possess 'human' souls at all but might be like animals; a thirteenth-century encyclopedia edited by Thomas of Cantimpré, for instance, conjectured that pygmies did exist, yet were not human but midway between man and ape. Even in 1520 Paracelsus could write of such wild men: 'In speech they are like parrots, and have no souls, unless God be pleased to join them in the bonds of matrimony with those who have souls.'[17] As late as 1537 Pope Paul II needed to issue a Bull declaring the natives of North and South America to be human – at least if they were converted to Christianity. This failed to inhibit the Spanish conquerors from exterminating numerous of the disgusting heathens for their own profit.

Comparable mixed reactions persisted in the seventeenth century. Some seventeenth-century missionaries, especially Jesuits in Canada like Père Le Jeune, the Jesuit Superior at Quebec, continually praised the Red Indians in their reports, and a few of them even wondered whether they might not be free of original sin itself, so innately virtuous did the Hurons in particular seem to be. And an explorer like Lescarbot, even more boldly, described the natives as 'more human and good than many who bear the name of Christian'.[18] By the end of the century this favourite view was being quite widely expressed – in Aphra Behn's novel *Oroonoko* (1688), of which a French translation in 1745 would prove very popular; by Shaftesbury as he contrasted European corruption with the 'simplicity of manners and innocence of behaviour which has often been known among mere savages'; and by that gentle Quietist bishop Fénelon. In his novel *Télémaque* (1699) (later translated by Hawkesworth) he describes (in Book VI) the mythical land of La Bétique, where wise and happy primitives live in harmony with nature – an evocation which Rousseau would recommend in *Emile* as appropriate reading for Sophie.

But others were distinctly less enthusiastic. For example, Hobbes used the North American savages to illustrate his very concept of man's life as 'solitary, poor, nasty, brutish and short', and early in the eighteenth century Père Gabriel Marest described the Illinois Indians as 'cowardly, treacherous, frivolous and inconstant, thieving by nature, ... brutal without honour'. Less sanguine missionaries than the Canadian Jesuits seem to have agreed with him – and especially those who were working amongst the Negroes. Père Loyer in West Africa declared that 'of all the nations on earth the most wicked, knavish and ungrateful is that of the Negroes'. Père Lavit says of the Guyana natives that they live 'like animals, with no form of worship and with hardly any knowledge of natural law'. Père Labat, in his five-volume *Nouvelle Relation de l'Afrique occidentale* (1728), whilst approving of some Negro practices, could even refer to 'the vices attached to the colour black'. The reference here is to the belief held by many Christians that the blacks were not only miserable but deserved their misery. They are the descendants of Ham, cursed by Noah, and that curse in the Book of Genesis was even invoked to justify Negro slavery. The theologian Bellon de St-Quentin, for example, asserted in 1764 that slavery is not contrary 'to natural law, nor to the written law of God, nor even to the law of the Gospel'; it is willed by God Himself – as well, he adds, as being socially useful.[19] There is in fact a fairly clear distinction to be drawn between views on Negroes on the one hand and views on Red Indians, Polynesians and other natives on the other. The Negro had an unusually bad press, as Roger Mercier's study of *L'Afrique noire dans la littérature française* makes clear.

We have moved into the eighteenth century – often claimed to be the age of a marked resurgence of the notion of the noble savage – and must now enquire how far this is true and how far the 'resurgence' actually went. How far is the praise of the inhabitants of Tahiti characteristic of wider opinions about the savage?

There was undoubtedly a deepening of interest created by the many fresh explorations during the century. At its start a thinker like Bayle, sceptical of human goodness, had appealed to the customs of other societies mainly in order to question French practices and support his pleas for greater toleration. A generation later the notion was emerging that primitive societies have a whole distinctive culture of their own, preferable in some ways to that of Europe. Works like Prévost's *Cleveland* (1732–9), whose hero becomes king of a tribe of South American Indians and marries the heroine by their rites, and Rameau's ballet, *Les Indes galantes* (1735), illustrate a fresh awareness which numerous others would also show as they invoked their own versions of the noble savage. For some he would be a more 'refined and rational' figure; for others, like Rousseau in his *Discours sur les origines de l'inégalité*, a rather wilder, more passionate creature.[20] But however he was presented, by the middle of the eighteenth century, one might have said, the apotheosis of the noble savage was at hand.

With some observers and within limits it was so, as we shall see, but this was also the age of what has been authoritatively described as 'the dispute of the New World'. Gerbi's detailed study under that title concentrates on the Americas and shows that side by side with praise for their inhabitants there was scepticism and trenchant criticism; even greater doubts abounded about the Africans and, after an initial honeymoon inspired by Bougainville and others, uncertainties grew about the Polynesians as well – not least, by around 1780, about the Maoris of New Zealand and the Hawaiians, who gained especial notoriety.

The mood of criticism and doubt must not be neglected, since one would otherwise infer from Rousseau and other enthusiasts a quite unbalanced picture. How, before one turns to more intellectual critics, may it have seemed to many an educated but more casual observer in Europe towards the century's end? Two examples must suffice.

For Englishmen the killing, on 14 February 1779, of Captain Cook on Hawaii during his third voyage was especially horrifying, but it seems to have been hardly less so for the French. In 1788, for instance, one could have viewed in Paris a 'pantomime', without words, entitled *La Mort du Capitaine Cook*.[21] (In 1789 one could have seen it in England too, at Covent Garden – just four years after *Omai*.) Even the *Avertissement* of the play poses the contrast between civilised man and savage – and in somewhat tendentious terms, referring to 'the tragic death of Captain Cook, assassinated by islanders on whom he was heaping kindness'. (In historical reality Cook seems to have led an expedition to capture hostages after an alleged theft from his ship and thereby to have alarmed the natives.) Exotic interest is also acknowledged: the 'pantomime' shows 'the dress, manners and dances of the savages of the South Sea' on the island of 'O-Why-e'. But the death of Cook itself is the central subject and is depicted as the direct result of his moral superiority over the natives: he defends a wife against attacks by her husband (III, 10); he protests against the cruelty shown to a prisoner (III, 26).

Such was the message at the Théâtre de l'Ambigu-Comique in Paris in October 1788, and earlier cases had provoked similar reactions. In 1772 a French captain, Marion de Fresne, and others were killed by the Maoris – who had already shocked Cook by their cannibalism. The news horrified many Europeans, and the French writer Crozet was even prompted to contend that 'among all created animals there is nothing more savage and dangerous than the natural and savage peoples themselves'. Rousseau was still alive and Crozet told him of the massacre. It is said that Rousseau asked if it was possible that the good children of nature could really be so wicked. One feels he doubted it, but many others thought the wickedness was clearly established.

What, however, of the 'dispute' in more intellectual terms? Is the savage noble or ignoble? The leading proponents of the 'ignoble' view were Buffon and de Pauw. The American savages are degenerate in various ways, they argued. This is in no way their fault but results from the climate and country in which they live; this degeneracy is likewise observed in the plants and animals of the New World. 'Living nature is much less active there', claimed Buffon, 'much less varied and, we may even say, less strong.' The 'philosophe' Raynal could even mention 'the excessive height of the mountains of Peru' as parallel evidence.[22] De Pauw – the most influential proponent of these views through his *Recherches philosophiques sur les Américains* of 1768 – alleged indeed that many animals lose their tails, dogs their bark, and birds their song. Many agreed with this degeneracy view, one may note, and were repelled rather than attracted by the travellers' tales. Just one example amongst others is found in Oliver Goldsmith's *The Deserted Village* of 1769, where he evokes Nature in Georgia:

> Through torrid tracts with fainting step they go,
> Where wild Altana [Alatamala] murmurs to their woe.
> Far different there from all that charm'd before,
> The various terrors of that horrid shore;...
> Those matted woods where birds forget to sing,
> But silent bats in drowsy clusters cling;
> Those poisonous fields with rank luxuriance crown'd,
> Where the dark scorpion gathers death around;
> Where at each step the stranger fears to wake
> The rattling terrors of the vengeful snake;
> Where crouching tigers wait their hapless prey,
> And savage men more murderous still than they...

It is worth quoting Goldsmith at that length since he gives the broad impression of someone sympathetic to the natural and with neither a theological nor a scientific axe to grind. Many Europeans shared this general view, it seems, including an intellectual as eminent as Kant. He originally had a high view of savages, but by 1775 – influenced by de Pauw, it appears – he had come to judge them much less favourably: 'the American people are incapable of civilisation'. And in his *Religion within the boundaries of pure reason* (1793) he would cite the Maoris and the Red Indians to support his conviction that all men are evil.[23] The settlers as well as the natives, some also thought, were affected by the climate. Raynal, to give an example from a progressive, claimed they had 'visibly degenerated' and 'their minds have been enervated like their bodies'.

This posed a distinct puzzle for Raynal, since, like other 'philosophes', he also admired North America as the land of liberty and of frugal farmers leading lives of rural virtue and prosperity.[24]

There were naturally attacks on the thesis of de Pauw, and even Buffon rejected part of it, later saying that the Americans, though immature, are strong and handsome. More direct attacks came from Pernety (powerful enough to provoke a reply from de Pauw in 1770), from Bonneville and Delisle de Sales, and others, but 'the dispute' certainly did not cease. On the contrary, it was reinforced in particular by William Robertson's *History of America* in 1777 and, two years later, by the murder of Cook – something more immediate and clear-cut than any book. Gerbi concludes, indeed, that Cook's travels and death reinforced a realistic attitude and, far from strengthening, actually undermined the notion of the noble savage.[25] Certainly, the argument remained alive into the nineteenth century, so that, for instance, one finds Joseph de Maistre – understandably, given his Catholic orthodoxy – agreeing with de Pauw that savages are depraved.

It was thus in the face of counter-attacks and considerable scepticism that certain later-eighteenth-century writers and others re-expressed the noble savage idea. The interest which they thereby aroused is clearly to be explained first and foremost by the novelty of their illustrations. To account for the curiosity of most of those who read the travel books, novels and plays one need not look much further than the mere differences between the familiarities of Europe and the oddities of the transoceanic natives.

Yet there is also no doubt that the 'noble savage' appealed to both the writers and some of their readers for other reasons. The good native provided useful evidence in favour of a variety of current notions and causes. This is true even of some Christians: they wished to contrast the unhappy sinfulness of European society with the happy virtue of simple natives, and to that end, as has often been noted, Christian missionaries were major agents in reviving the notion of the noble savage. Yet it was even more helpful in the eighteenth century in support cf more radical positions. For those like (say) Morelly or Rousseau who were attacking social inequality and the evils of property or money, primitive society provided a ready instance of a better and happier community. For those like (say) Diderot who were attacking political tyranny and lack of individual freedom it could be presented as run by mutual consent, as prospering by its very lack of government and social organisation. For those who were urging their readers to follow their own feelings or the inner light of conscience, or to make happiness their moral end, the savages could be invoked as already successful examples. For those – and Diderot is again a good instance – who wished to question dogmatic Christian morality, and notably Christian sexual inhibitions, the natives once more provided an appealing illustration in favour of following the natural. For those who were convinced of cultural relativism – Herder, for example – the sheer diversity of practice and outlook described by the explorers came as obvious grist to the mill. Yet again, those opposed to colonial exploitation – such as Marmontel in *Les Incas* (1777) – or who were campaigning against slavery naturally invoked the evidence that allowed them to contrast the unhappiness imposed by European intervention with the basic goodness or innocence of the exploited natives and with the happiness enjoyed by those natives – the Tahitians being a favourite case – who were not yet subject to colonialists or slave-traders.

These appeals to the example of the noble savage were very often well-intentioned and for ends one can easily approve of. Yet it is clear that they were largely for ulterior purposes. Except in the last instance of opposition to slavery they were in order to achieve improvements within *European* society of one sort or another. Granted the attacks on the slave-trade and the warnings by a few observers that the Europeans were destroying the values of primitive societies, the majority of writers were nevertheless not centrally concerned with the natives themselves. Just as many of the natives were being cruelly exploited for economic ends, so too they were exploited (less cruelly, undoubtedly) for intellectual ends – to justify one ideological position or another – and likewise they were exploited too for financial gain by writers, publishers and theatrical producers.

All of this underlines the need to make a basic distinction between two quite different questions. Firstly, why did the noble savage interest so many late-eighteenth-century thinkers and readers? The considerations just listed seem an adequate answer to that question. Secondly, however, how was the savage actually 'perceived' and evaluated by those who invoked him and claimed to admire him? For there is an obvious potential conflict: between the values of 'civilisation' and those of 'nature'. Diderot in particular, as a leading exponent of Enlightenment ideas, believed that reason, science and social re-organisation would immensely improve the quality of human life: yet these were precisely what the noble savage was apparently managing very happily to do without. Hence, at bottom, the ambivalence found in Diderot and even in Rousseau – uncertainties which reflect the tension in Enlightenment thought mentioned earlier between following reason and following emotion and natural impulse.

It is many years since Lovejoy, in a classic essay, demolished Voltaire's gibe that Rousseau wished mankind to go back onto all fours. The truth about 'the supposed primitivism' of Rousseau's *Discours sur l'inégalité* and his alleged advocacy of a return to nature is rather different. As Lovejoy showed, the *Discours* 'represents a movement away from rather than towards primitivism', albeit with a wavering 'between conflicting tendencies'.[26] One need not repeat his arguments, but three other points about Rousseau's essay are especially pertinent.

First, its long opening section is directed towards establishing that inequality in the state of nature as he conjectures it was far from having 'as much reality and influence as our writers claim'. It cannot therefore be attributed to the will of God or to inborn human traits; it has been acquired by the formation of societies and the wish to safeguard private property. In short, Rousseau seeks to prove the savage guiltless primarily in order to prove that society and property are guilty. Secondly, he clearly regards the savage as morally innocent and not as good, as being in a pre-moral condition. Even his pity for others is instinctive. 'One could say that the savages are not wicked precisely because they do not know what it is to be good.' The savage has not yet appreciated his freedom of will – 'the specific, distinguishing characteristic of man'. 'Left by nature to instinct alone', the savage is limited to desiring food, sleep and sex and to fearing pain and hunger. Moreover, Rousseau explicitly denies to primitive man the possibility of perfectibility and the social virtues unless there occurs the 'fortuitous coincidence of several outside causes' – and those are causes which take man, precisely, out of his primitive condition. Potentially perfectible, man can become actually so only on the condition of ceasing to be primitive. Thirdly, if we ask which stage of society's evolution is favoured by Rousseau, it is clear the answer is that moment shortly after the first forming of societies which he calls 'the true youth of the world'. Men are already developing the vices of jealousy and acquisitiveness, but this condition remains 'a happy mean between the indolence of the primitive condition and the irrepressible operation of our pride'. And it is this condition that is illustrated, Rousseau believes, by many of the explorers' accounts, by 'the example of the savages who have almost all been found at this point'. That example makes him wish mankind could have stayed at that stage for ever, and he even conjectures that man was in fact made to remain in it always. Alas, humanity moved on to metal-working and agriculture and the social consequences which they imposed – and was thereby lost.[27]

It seems undeniable that Rousseau was attracted to the 'noble savage' (as contrasted with primitive man); in a note he remarks how rarely such people, even when brought to Europe, choose to abandon their own ways. He vividly and influentially held out to his readers the picture of a tantalising, near-utopian way of life, but at the same time he saw that it had within it the seeds of its own corruption, and, moreover, he fully realised that there was no possible going-back. As regards the later development of societies, he refers to 'the inevitability of this development', and for him the only possibility lay in a going-forward to some new freer, more equal, more natural society than that of eighteenth-century France. In short, in

Rousseau's view the noble savage is to be sharply distinguished from the primitive, but what even *he* inspires is a nostalgic wish for what might have been but can no longer be. Only in a few respects can the noble savage still teach us – notably, in the treatment of children. That apart, it is time for us, in Rousseau's opinion, to hasten to the Swiss market-place and agree our social contract.

What of Diderot? His ideas are conveyed in a variety of essays, 'contes', and fragments and, understandably, they also developed over the years, as Benot, Duchet and others have shown.[28] Here, however, we may take the particularly good test-case provided by his *Supplément au Voyage de Bougainville*, written between 1771 and 1773, though not published until after his death: it largely concerns the Tahitians, of all savages the most often praised, and it has been claimed to be 'one of the most comprehensive and enthusiastic panegyrics of primitivism in the century'.[29] Clearly Diderot had been interested and charmed by Bougainville's account and was alarmed that Tahitian life might be degraded, as in other colonial conquests, by European interference. Yet one may doubt whether this work was seriously committed to the notion of 'the noble savage' or even to a serious evaluation of it.

It is noteworthy, first, that Diderot is distinctly selective in his use of his source-material. The explorer himself had indicated the defects of the Tahitians: almost always at war; killing all male captives and using the females for sex; 'very superstitious' in religion; in no way liberal in government. By contrast, although Diderot notes the cannibalism and cruelties practised on the 'île des Lanciers', his portrayal of Tahiti is decidedly idyllic and one-sided. Whilst the interlocutor A may enter mild reservations, B and the Tahitian Orou together clearly represent the work's primary contentions, and their picture hardly amounts to a factually comprehensive and balanced presentation of what Bougainville had discovered. There is a suppression of contrary evidence to a greater extent than could be explained by unconscious selectivity.

Secondly and more crucially, Diderot is not in reality contending that the natural ways of the Tahitians are morally good, that they are 'noble', but only that they are innocent and happy and can teach something to Europeans. As Orou declares: 'We are innocent, we are happy, and you can only harm our happiness. We follow the pure instinct of nature.' Even the work's sub-title indicates the moral neutrality of the Tahitians' sexual attitudes in particular: 'Dialogue sur l'inconvénient d'attacher des idées morales à certaines actions physiques qui n'en comportent pas.' Later, the discussion in Part IV of the work is centred on identifying what in human reactions and behaviour is 'natural'. 'Is marriage natural?', asks A – to which are added 'gallantry', 'coquetry', 'constancy', 'fidelity' and 'jealousy'. On most of these B replies in the negative or remains uncertain, and he concludes with the striking statement: 'Vices and virtues, all are equally natural.'[30] This has been interpreted as showing in Diderot's thought 'a disintegration of the concept of nature'; if so, however, it did not take him unawares but was contained in the sub-title itself. It has even been argued to the contrary that the *Supplément* reveals its author's increasing doubts about the 'nobility' of the savage and shows in him 'a new tension between his primitivism and his belief in enlightened civil society', a 'combination of admiration and mistrust for the Tahitian'.[31]

However that may be, the *Supplément* leaves the clear impression that his principal preoccupation was with European issues and with questions of moral and social principle related to them. This is true of almost all the subjects at the focus of the work: the rigidity and 'unnaturalness' of prevailing church morality; the concept of 'property' and of 'ownership' of persons, whether of wives by their husbands, of subjects by their rulers, or of natives by colonialists; the conflict between our natures and prevailing religious and civil codes; his major argument that any ethic which frustrates the natural will be ineffective and may also, on that same ground, be considered false; support for the utilitarian moral position. On most of them the Tahitians provided him with appealing illustrations currently in the news, which he could utilise as a foil to European attitudes – much as (say) the Persians had served for Montesquieu earlier in his *Lettres persanes*. But it is doubtful if they were ever at the centre of his concern, other than as regards their exploitation by colonialists. His so-called 'primitivism' is perhaps not significantly more than a pretext or device for discussing situations 10,000 miles distant from Tahiti.

Rousseau and Diderot were certainly not untypical, as Duchet in particular has argued from a rather different standpoint. They were in fact far warmer about the savage than most other contemporaries, yet she discerns in them and other 'philosophes' an 'ambiguous' outlook, and she also concludes, as we have done, that the true debate within their writings is not about the savage but about European problems. Indeed, she goes further and seeks to 'denounce the myth that the *philosophes* were anti-colonialists'. Their only campaign against the exploitation of the Negroes and Red Indians, she contends, was for the remedy of mere abuses and in order to 'civilise' them by Enlightenment standards. Thereby the 'philosophes' contributed to and implicitly connived in maintaining the *status quo*. 'Liberation of the Negroes, protection of the Red Indians, and the civilising of the savage are only elements in the same structure, despite appearances, that of the colonial ideology.'[32]

Her thorough study demands a fuller discussion than is possible in this chapter, yet she does seem to come close at times to saying that to favour slavery is to be colonialist and that to attack slavery is also – 'despite appearances' – to be colonialist. Her argument, though subtly presented, is perhaps at bottom a version of the position which some Marxists have held in claiming that the whole notion of the noble savage was a 'cover', as it were, for continuing exploitation, that it represented the ideology of the slave-trade. This view, one may think, has to contend with distinct difficulties. First, we have seen an extensive campaign by Buffon, de Pauw, Robertson and others to deny nobility to the savages of America. Hugh Honour concludes that by the late-eighteenth century the dominant image of the Red Indian in European minds was not of a noble savage but of a weak, backward, even degenerate creature.[33] After the killings of de Fresne and Cook the Polynesians hardly preserved a higher reputation. If 'cover-up' there was, it was ill-coordinated, to say no more. Secondly, at least some of those who sought to justify slavery invoked precisely the savage's *ignobility* to support its continuance, as we noted earlier in regard to the curse of Noah. Thirdly, the Negroes – of all the savages those who were most often taken into slavery – were precisely those who were least often depicted as noble, as Mercier's study amply shows; it was almost as if their slave-status itself prevented their being regarded as noble. Fourthly, those who came closest to embracing the noble savage idea were precisely those who expressed the strongest opposition to slavery. Enlightenment intellectuals like Voltaire, d'Holbach and Raynal were more doubtful about the savage's nobility – and were significantly less outspoken against slavery, albeit sincerely committed to the values of justice and equality. Raynal, for example, calls for an improvement of the slave's lot, mainly for reasons of the Europeans' self-interest, rather than for abolition, though he thinks that this will gradually come; he remains as 'ambivalent' (in Mercier's word) as he was about the nobility of the savage. Michèle Duchet may well be correct to discern in some of the 'philosophes' she studies a less than total commitment to anti-colonialism; what she may perhaps neglect is the relationship between that and their very ambivalence about the savage himself. By contrast, one may reiterate against any claim to the contrary that those who came nearest to believing in the natural goodness of the savage were also major campaigners against the slave-trade. This is true to some degree earlier in the century, with Prévost and the Abbé Pluche, for instance; later it was most obviously true of Saint-Lambert and Bernardin de Saint-Pierre.

Both writers were to be leading members of the Société des Amis des Noirs founded in 1788 (just a year later than the British Society for the Abolition of the Slave Trade) and whose pressure helped towards the abolition of slavery in all French colonies by the Convention on 4 February 1794. (The trade would, alas, be restored by Napoleon in 1802.) But, as well, they had earlier had considerable impact on public opinion by their writings. Saint-Lambert, in *Les Saisons* (1769), that version of Thomson we met earlier in relation to new views of external nature, inserted into his section on 'L'Hiver' a note attacking

slavery, a polemical passage which Mercier can even declare to
be 'the origin of the whole anti-slavery campaign' in France,
and in the same year he also wrote an influential short story,
Ziméo. He accepts that some recent discoveries have brought
the benefits of commerce and industry and new foods like rice,
but most earlier explorations have been characterised by the
'cruelties' and 'perfidies' of the Europeans. The discovery of
the Americas created much unhappiness for the natives of Peru,
Mexico and elsewhere, but Africa above all still continues to
suffer from colonial exploitation:

I learn that the Negroes used to live in peace, but that the English, the French
and the Portuguese, with a devilish art, have sown and maintained divisions
between these peoples, who sell to them their prisoners of war.[34]

Saint-Pierre first expressed his views in his *Voyage à l'île de
France* (1773), and the book had a frontispiece depicting a Negro
with 'the instruments of slavery' and illustrations by Moreau
to bring out the slavers' cruelty. Plate IV, for instance, shows
a chained Negress with two frightened children and a Negro
being whipped by a European. Especially influential, however,
was the slave episode in his *Paul et Virginie* (1788). In Mercier's
view this novel was 'the decisive work' and the episode itself
'had a decisive impact on opinion': 'the emotion aroused by
a moving story [he judges] had achieved more than the best
reasoned deductions'.[35] The mothers have gone to church;
Virginie is behind at their house when a runaway Negress slave
appears outside:

She was as emaciated as a skeleton, and her only clothing was a scrap of
sack-cloth across her loins. She threw herself at Virginie's feet, who was
preparing the family meal, and cried to her: 'My dear young lady, have pity
on a poor fugitive slave; for the past month I have wandered in these
mountains, half-dead with hunger, often pursued by hunters and their dogs.
I am fleeing from my master, who is a wealthy planter from the Rivière-Noire;
he treated me in the way you see.' And she showed her body marked by deep
scars from the lashes she had received.[36]

Virginie feeds her and begs the slave-owner (naïvely, no doubt)
to pardon the escapee and take her back. He swears to do so,
but soon after the Negress is seen to have been shackled by him,

her feet chained to a block of wood and with an iron collar around her neck.

Other writers campaigned as well: Raynal, despite his 'ambivalence', in Book xi of his *Histoire des deux Indes* (1770) to which Diderot also contributed; physiocrats like Turgot; certain poets such as Roucher; Necker; Condorcet in a pseudonymous work of 1781; Sébastien Mercier; and others. It would be wrong to claim that the only opponents of slavery were those who believed in the innate goodness or innocence of natural man. Nevertheless, there is a tendency in that direction, and some historians, unlike the Marxists, have seen the noble savage idea as a major factor behind the anti-slavery movement.

Yet it has to be noted that even a Bernardin de Saint-Pierre is not a totally convinced believer in the *goodness* of the noble savage. First, he makes plain that he does not trust nature alone as a moral guide. The *Avant-Propos* to his novel very significantly declares, as a 'great truth', that 'our happiness lies in living according to nature and virtue'. The prudent addition of 'et la vertu' reflects his belief as a Christian (however close he strayed to heresy at times) that, finally, moral teaching must complement natural inclination – as, indeed, one also sees in the novel's stress on the instruction given to Paul and Virginie by their mothers and Le Vieillard. Secondly, a deal of paternalism remains in Saint-Pierre's attitude to the natives – both to the servants Domingue and Marie and to the slaves. They are in reality presented as above all innocent children of nature who need protection and guidance from the *good* Europeans to escape the evils created by the *bad* Europeans and in order to remain in their natural state of carefree yet, ultimately, subservient contentment.

All this points to a perhaps disappointing conclusion. The 'image' of the 'noble savage' proved in the outcome to be less effective and enduring than other 'images' of the time in representing the idea of man's natural virtues. It is, as it were, the image which failed to establish itself.

It may well be significant that the Romantics in the following decades would embrace, for example, the notions of the good child and the good peasant, not to mention the inspired bard, but would not significantly accept or develop that of the noble savage. In England there is Southey (another who attacked slavery) in his *Songs of the American Indians* (1799), but even in his case two later poems, *Madoc* (1805) and *A Tale of Paraguay* (1814–25), seem to place Christian values above Red Indian values. Wordsworth has occasional poems only about the savage, and in *The Excursion* seems, like Keats also, to be unfavourable. Byron, notably in *The Island*, stresses less any nobility than the savage's passionate violence. German Romantics say, understandably, little, excepting only *Die Spanier in Peru*, Kotzebue's play of 1796. In France, likewise, Chateaubriand stands virtually alone amongst the Romantics, with *Atala* and *Les Natchez*, a work that he originally planned prior to his Catholic re-conversion as an 'epic of natural man' and that was inspired by his visit to North America. He vividly evoked external nature in America, leaving us with memorable evocations of Niagara Falls, of 'Une nuit chez les sauvages de l'Amérique', with the world around depicted as in harmonious sympathy with Chactas and Atala, amongst other descriptions. Yet even in him, as in Saint-Pierre, one finds a sympathetic cautiousness regarding the natives. His noble savages – Chactas is the major example – are Christian or near-Christian as well as being savages, and it has also been well said of *Atala* that it is overshadowed by the author's sense – like Rousseau's before him – that primitive ways are inevitably doomed to extinction. Chateaubriand re-affirms the idyllic view of the Tahitians in particular, in *Le Génie du christianisme* – here 'nature had placed a people as lovely as the sky which saw their birth'. And yet the dominant mood is sadness, for his major impression is of the ruins of the past; man here 'resembles the blind Ossian seated on the tombs of the Kings of Morven'. 'Oh, the vanity of men's pleasures! The first flag that one observes on these enchanted shores is that of death.'[37] Much the same is true, one can add, of representations of Atala and the other Red Indians by such Romantic painters as Girodet and Delacroix a little later, and it had already been anticipated at the very end of *Paul et Virginie*, as Saint-Pierre describes all that remains after the death of his characters: 'No-one since you has ventured to cultivate this desolate land or to re-build these humble huts. Your goats have become wild; your orchards are destroyed; your birds have flown away.'[38]

The conclusion must be that even those who rejected de Pauw's thesis about the degeneracy of the savage perceived him as being at best innocent or, perhaps, 'noble', provided that Christian teaching strengthened his natural inclinations, and, secondly, that they also feared – from Rousseau to Chateaubriand and on to Delacroix – that time and civilisation had triumphed over him. In the nineteenth century and especially in American literature the noble savage would remain a symbolic figure, but as the representative of different values in a different debate. For French utopian thinkers of the new period North America, in particular, continued to be a principal location for the ideal community – but now peopled not by Red Indians but by white enthusiasts for the simple life who would emigrate from Europe. Prior to the cult of negritude and of a wider primitivism in our own century the noble savage became no more than secondary as an image of natural virtue. He was not, after all, 'natural *man*' but only one of 'nature's *children*'.

7

HAPPY FAMILIES:
(1) The age of innocence

'The greatest contribution of the eighteenth century to the advance of civilisation': thus concludes John McManners about the emergence of our modern European image of the family.[1] Its central elements comprise a husband and a wife who marry for love and who thereafter rear, with caring attention and within the privacy of a home of their own, a small number of children whom they regard as both interesting and basically lovable. And whilst this 'nuclear family' ideal may not always be achieved, as we know from the incidence of divorce and wife- and child-battering and other symptoms of unhappy domestic life, it remains the concept which most of us in Europe, North America and related cultures still cherish and aspire to follow.

Yet this concept certainly seems to be more a cultural artefact than the outcome of a biological imperative, as we may sometimes believe. Even today most of the world's inhabitants probably do not share it, as we can confirm by observing the customs of arranged marriages and of family life and control that prevail in (say) the Muslim Near East and the Indian sub-continent and that often persist amongst immigrants from such areas to Europe. Furthermore, it has become ever clearer from the pioneering scholarship of Philippe Ariès and others since him that even within Europe our present notion of the family is relatively novel, that it rests upon attitudes and assumptions which most of our own ancestors did not hold and at least some of which they would have dismissed as foolish or even denounced as sinful. As Ariès concluded in his study of *L'Enfant et la vie familiale sous l'Ancien Régime*, 'the whole evolution of contemporary customs is incomprehensible if one disregards this prodigious growth of family feeling'.[2]

Since Ariès's book of 1960, studies of family history in

Europe and America have proliferated, as the bibliography to this and the following chapter may serve to illustrate, albeit, even so, it is highly selective. Controversy too has proliferated and still continues. Thus, for example, several scholars of medieval Europe have trenchantly criticised his assertions that the child was largely ignored, even by its parents, during the Middle Ages, that the very notion of childhood was largely absent. They grant that generalisations – whether from Ariès or themselves – must be hazardous, given the range of countries, centuries and social classes involved and since the source-material is inevitably more fragmentary than for more recent periods since the invention of printing; as one of them comments, 'The history of medieval children is as complex as the history of any social group, and even more elusive.'[3] Nevertheless, the evidence they cite against Ariès's claims – from literary and artistic works, from medical and paediatric writings, and from views on education, for example – certainly seems to require the contrasts he drew to be at the least qualified and softened as regards medieval perceptions of the child.

Yet to believe this does not invalidate the comparisons pertinent to this and the succeeding chapter. First, the medievalists' arguments do not challenge (or seek to) the general claim that cultural attitudes to the family and marriage and to women and children within them have substantially changed over the centuries. Beyond doubt there were anticipations of later views in earlier times, whether one judges these to be isolated exceptions or not. This is notably true, for example, of the Renaissance humanists. Parental duties were stressed by, amongst others, Erasmus in *Puerpera* (1516) and Montaigne later, and comparable sympathies were expressed by other late-sixteenth-century French moralists like Scévole de Sainte-Marthe in *Paedotrophia* (1584) and Charron in *De la sagesse* (1601). All the same, the earliest swallows do not make the summer or abolish the differences of the seasons. Secondly, the medievalist critics themselves do not seem to deny that the child was at an earlier stage disregarded for the most part, that it was rarely considered to be of any distinctive interest but was seen merely as a small adult-in-the-making, a status symbolised even by its miniature adult clothing, or that even when its parents were indulgent, they were so in a mainly casual and emotionally uninvolved manner. Whereas Ariès attributes such disinterest to the Middle Ages, however, they assign it to the 'barbarian' centuries, when 'the barbarian child grew up within an atmosphere of affectionate neglect', when the views of St Augustine and others prevailed that 'the innocence of children is in the helplessness of their bodies, rather than any quality of soul'.[4] The issue, in short, is as to dating, but on either view the contrast survives – between medieval and post-medieval for Ariès, between pre-medieval and medieval for his critics. And a third point is most directly relevant here. Whatever be true of the Middle Ages, and accepting that attitudes developed even within those centuries, historians of the following, early modern period in Europe have amply shown the reality of later changes. The family's social role and organisation and the intellectual and cultural assumptions affecting prevailing views on the family and its members were all alike evolving as between the sixteenth and earlier centuries and the seventeenth and eighteenth centuries. Moreover, the evidence clearly suggests that the newer attitudes became more influential in family practice only during the course of the seventeenth century – and even then less in France than amongst the English and Dutch middle classes and the Puritan settlers of North America. The scene may thus be usefully set for a study of the French example in the eighteenth century by summarising the developments as sketched by Stone's work on *The Family, Sex and Marriage in England, 1500–1800*. Whilst the datings he proposes for England are decidedly earlier than they would be for France (as the author himself stresses), the basic evolution is similar in both countries.

Until the sixteenth century and beyond, he concludes, the model was of the 'open lineage family'. This relatively large, 'extended' family was based upon kinship, not upon the married couple, and given the high mortality-rate it was marked by a frequently changing membership. Family relationships were rarely close and intimate, and each member's life was largely carried on in public, with little chance or even thought of personal privacy. The individual was always subordinated to the interests of kin or village or, in due course, of the state, and as regards marriage his or her partner was arranged by parental decision. The period from the sixteenth to the seventeenth centuries was 'a transitional stage' in Stone's view; it witnessed the growth of the 'restricted patriarchal nuclear family'. Deference was now paid less to one's kin than to state, king and church, and this favoured a strengthening of the nuclear unit within the wider family and also of the father's power within it – partly by analogy with the rights of kingship within society as a whole. As regards France, one may interpolate, a perfect example of this phase is seen in Rétif de la Bretonne's idealising evocation of his own village family and father in *La Vie de mon père*, published in 1779 though referring back in time. From the seventeenth century in England and elsewhere, however, Stone continues, there emerged our present-day model of the 'closed domesticated nuclear family'. Patriarchal control within the family grew weaker, and the young gained more freedom to choose their own pattern of life and, most notably, their own spouse. Affection became more frequent and important in marriage, and for this and other reasons there developed a stronger emotional 'bonding' within the family group than previously. More attention was paid to each child's upbringing, and there was more grief if it died; one even finds a deliberate limitation of family size deriving (it seems) from greater concern for the wife's well-being and the existing children. Concurrently, and in part as a consequence, greater privacy was sought in terms of domestic architecture as well. Life in earlier ages had been led almost wholly in the company of the other members of the extended family, with the servants, and even, at night or in winter, the animals also all inhabiting the same few rooms. Several people would sleep not merely in the same room but in the same bed – and the fact that inn-keepers too habitually crammed four or five into their beds suggests a wide acceptance of communal sleeping as well as communal living. Nor was this necessarily the product of economic hardship; to visit the upper floors of the Palace of Versailles, to take the supreme case in which money would have been of no relevance, is to observe that the bedrooms, even of the King and Queen themselves, were open to each other. In sharp contrast, as nuclear family feeling increased and a higher valuation was placed upon personal privacy, parents and children withdrew ever more firmly from the society around them into their own exclusive dwelling, and, in particular, the bedroom door became the norm, an invention so original that even now social and cultural historians dispute as to its significance as a cultural indicator.[5] Stone also claims the dumb-waiter is a parallel innovation in the cause of greater privacy: to be able to eat *en famille* without the servants present.

Between the English and Dutch and the American Puritans and, on the other hand, the French there was (in Stone's words) 'an astonishing time-lag'.[6] Though perhaps it is not quite as long as the hundred years that he suggests, we shall shortly note all the same that amongst the upper classes in the earlier-eighteenth century in France it even became more and not less fashionable to neglect one's children and to send them away to wet-nurses. Yet gradually the tide was turning, even at that date. The first campaigners, like the sentimental moralising dramatist, Nivelle de La Chaussée, in *L'Ecole des mères* (1744), were at work, and painters too were already depicting more family groups. Watteau in his *Famille*, Lancret in *Enfance*, and Boucher in *Famille de l'artiste* and *Le Déjeuner* offer early examples prior to Chardin and Greuze, and probably their portrayals often reflected the wishes of their patrons as well as their own sympathies – very much as was suggested in relation to paintings of wild external nature.

However that may be, it was none the less the later-eighteenth century in France which saw the full depiction and elaboration of the new family images. We today may be tempted to accuse many of the relevant books, paintings and arguments of displaying sentimental banality, but in reality they amounted to a propagandist campaign for radical change that can be understood only in the context of their time. When, say, Chardin depicts the caring mother with her contented children in such paintings as *La Mère laborieuse* and *Bénédicité* or when Diderot praises Greuze's rendering of *La Mère bien-aimée* because it 'depicts most movingly the inestimable happiness and value of domestic peace',[7] they are pleading for a new ideal against the realities of their day – notably, against widespread neglect of their families amongst the better-off and also against certain traditional Christian teachings, especially about children and women.

The composite image, we noted, has three central characters, albeit with a few affectionate animals like dogs and birds in attendance at the margin of the family circle. The mother and father, their relationship with each other and their treatment of their children will be the subject of chapter 8; here, first, we must consider the children themselves.

The concept of the child in West European Christendom seems to have moved in broad outline from stage to stage, albeit with undeniable overlappings at any one time as between different countries (or even areas within them), different classes and even different individuals within the same country or class. In the first – whether one attributes its attitudes to the 'barbarian' or medieval periods or finds ample evidence of them in the eighteenth century or, indeed, in the neglectful treatment of some children to this day – the child is far less at the centre of parental attention than (say) in the average present-day European family. Even if some regard is paid to his physical needs, special mental qualities are rarely attributed to him, and such specific provisions as children's toys and games (or even the modern concept of Christmas as above all a children's festivity) are almost wholly absent. The child may be valued for his future contribution as an adult but is only infrequently found interesting *as a child*, it would seem – a view also reflected in cultural forms. Whereas in Ancient Greek art, for instance, he was presented as an obvious child, most European paintings in the earlier centuries show him only as a small grown-up – a generalisation not invalidated by the numerous medieval representations of the Christ-child and of *putti*, for these had a distinctively religious motive. In literature too, childhood was almost always passed over in silence, as a dull phase prior to entry into society and, especially with girls, prior to sexual maturity. Even memoir-writers commonly passed over their upbringing, and though a few child characters were introduced by such dramatists as Molière, Racine and Voltaire, far more typical in France, even in the earlier-eighteenth century, was the attitude of Marivaux's heroine in *La Vie de Marianne* (1731–41), passing rapidly over her early years, 'since I can well imagine that all their trifling details will bore you'.[8]

A major reason for such attitudes may well have lain in the high death-rate of children – a fact discouraging parents from emotional involvement with their offspring. Even Montaigne, more sympathetic to children than most in the late-sixteenth century, can tell us he has lost 'two or three children' in infancy with a casual inexactness that surprises the modern reader, even after one has recalled that the belief that the child would go to heaven acted to soften the loss. In the seventeenth century some 20% to 30% of babies died in their first year, even without counting, in many cases, those who died in their first few days. Still in the eighteenth century over 40% of children died before the age of six, whilst for those in the Paris foundling hospitals the figure in 1751, for instance, was as high as 68%. We are told that numerous uneducated mothers bore and lost so many children that they did not know the number to which they had given birth or, again, that payment for fostering babies was low largely because few were expected to live for more than a short time.[9]

The prevailing attitudes to children may have been reinforced also by Catholic teaching. Granted, certainly, that there is a tradition in Hebrew and Christian literature which postulates that the child possesses an uncorrupted nature – a view expressed in England, for example, by Vaughan, Traherne and the Cambridge Platonists – all the same and against that, the orthodox and most frequently affirmed teaching, amongst many Protestants also, was derived from the belief in the Fall and asserted that the child is 'conceived and born in sin' – the phrase used in the very opening sentence of the Anglican service of Baptism. Though cleansed by that baptism, he remains deeply corrupt unless redeemed unto salvation. Typical in France was Bérulle, for example, when he declared childhood to be 'the basest and most abject condition of human nature, after that of death'.[10] It is true that Christianity at times took a kindlier view, as witness Christ's injunction quoted in the same service: 'Suffer the little children to come unto me,...for of such is the Kingdom of God.' Yet it is doubtful how far this was emphasised in earlier centuries. Thus, for example, whilst paintings of the childhood of Jesus Himself, depicted with realism and feeling, were abundant in medieval times, this may partly have been, it has been argued, in order to stress how far God had been willing to debase Himself by becoming a child.[11] Paintings of Christ blessing the children, by contrast, seem to have become common only from the seventeenth century – by which time a minority were manifesting greater concern for the child as such. It appears more likely than not as regards France that orthodox Catholicism did serve, prior to that and even later, to confirm the child's lowly status. Certainly religious teachings that were heterodox from the Catholic standpoint led to distinctly different attitudes to the child. One example of this is seen in the impact of Puritanism – in its Protestant forms in England, North America and the Netherlands and, in France, in the Jansenist movement – and an earlier and striking instance is provided within France by the specific and almost clinically isolated case of the Cathar heresy. Within the same village of Montaillou at the same time, between 1294 and 1324, the contrast between Cathars and Catholics is arresting. Whereas the latter had fewer children, the Cathars enjoyed a 'baby-boom', and they also made little use of wet-nurses and seem to have felt more intensely for their children – or at least for their babies. It must surely be likely that this largely uncommon attitude to children at that time was related to the unorthodox Cathar doctrine of metempsychosis – their belief that the soul of some dead person is purified by God before then entering the foetus of some newly conceived human.[12]

Slowly the generally prevailing views gave way to other perceptions. We noted a first illustration in humanist thinkers of the early French Renaissance such as Erasmus, and similarly Rabelais's belief, expressed and illustrated in the ideal of the Abbaye de Thélème in *Gargantua*, is that people who are well-born and well-bred 'have by nature an instinct and spur that impels them to virtuous acts and deflects them from vice'. The new educational system he advocates rests upon this confidence. The medieval approach, as he parodies it, gives little time to study; the young Gargantua passes his day in idle inactivity, eating, wenching, church services and the mumbling of paternosters. The new system, by contrast, regulates his life, from earliest morning to late evening, to ensure his total commitment to his education, but none the less the rigorous discipline involved derives in reality from the premiss that after all there is some hope for the child. It is indeed ironic that Rabelais's optimistic evaluation of the potentialities of the young should have led, but quite logically so, to far more study and far more subjection – and to a good sound thrashing at regular intervals for the boys who would be reared in actual institutions based on this humanist ideal. Montaigne at the reformed Collège de Guyenne was one of them, and in the course of questioning the entire system he tells us that the pupils were forced to work for fourteen or fifteen hours each day and that discipline was a combination 'of violence and force, of horror and cruelty'. Nor was this exceptional in the later-sixteenth century. Charron in *De la sagesse* describes the practice of beating, whipping, abusing and scolding children as being 'almost universal'. One even finds Henri IV complaining that his son was not being whipped enough, as he himself had been and 'having myself profited' from it, and it is striking to learn that when the boy became King Louis XIII on his father's death he continued to be regularly beaten. Partly such treatment may have been to toughen the child for a hard physical life, but even more it was in order to 'beat out the sin' – a view which in England would persist through the age of a John Wesley (who himself stresses this need) and the Victorian period into the use in our own century of corporal punishment for young offenders and for the 'well-born' pupils of our independent schools to this present day.

Yet, however paradoxical it may seem, the strict regime, the long hours of study and the canings sprang from concerns that advanced the cause of the child, even if painfully so. The reformers were thinking of the child as distinctive in its needs and of its upbringing as of great importance. For, secondly, the child has potentialities for both virtue and educated intelligence which should be constantly nurtured and developed, and all the more so if he is of upper-class family and thus destined for high service in church or state.

Such humanistic preoccupations were to be greatly reinforced in the seventeenth century from two quite different directions, the one religious and the other philosophical. The first stemmed from Counter-Reformation puritanism and is well exemplified by the Jansenists' practice at the Ecoles de Port-Royal, analogously in all likelihood with Protestant puritanism elsewhere. Puritan obsession with man's deep sinfulness made it all the more imperative to protect such innocence as the child possessed against the influences of a corrupted world, and the consequences can be illustrated by a single instance. Earlier centuries had had none of what has become our modern concern to shield the young from talk of sex or the sight of sex – and most children slept in their parents' bed, indeed, as well as observing the domestic animals around them. By contrast the nuns of Port-Royal forbade their pupils to sleep together, even when young and especially if of opposite sexes; they insisted upon modest dress and rarely left their charges alone; they produced suitably expurgated versions of books for their studies, such as an edition of the 'Comédies de Térence *rendues très honnêtes*'. Yet here too the severe discipline and the constant study (to which *La Logique de Port-Royal* stands as memorial) sprang from care for the child itself, and it is no coincidence that (say) Pascal's sister, Jacqueline, would refer to children as 'little angels' and 'little souls' or that a sympathiser with Jansenism, Mme de Sévigné, was apparently one of the first to employ the fond diminutive form of address to children. And a little later the Quietist bishop Fénelon, a leading figure in educational thinking with his *Télémaque* (1699) and his *Traité de l'éducation des filles* (1687), would illustrate the same combination, in a somewhat softened form, of puritan awareness of sin and of the need for strict control on the one hand with understanding and tenderness for the child on the other.

Philosophers pressed from a different starting-point but in a similar direction to the Christian moralists. For rationalists like Descartes and Malebranche the child has an unstocked mind, excepting a few 'innate intuitions', and also needs to learn the proper 'method' of reasoning. Whilst that view may encourage the feeling that children in themselves are uninteresting, it also favours the conviction that efficient education can achieve great things – for girls as well as boys, as the Cartesian Poullain de la Barre would argue. The same conclusion followed even more clearly from the empiricism of John Locke and his French admirers. The child is born a 'blank sheet' and all it becomes and learns derives from outside itself. This belief, like the Cartesian, makes the child initially uninteresting but renders its education and the formative impact of social environment all the more decisive. Locke's celebrated *Thoughts Concerning Education* (and the attitudes of a French admirer like Voltaire a little later[13]) thus embody – less guardedly than his predecessors – the convictions that childhood is of high and specific significance and that the 'blank sheet' can be transformed into a reasonable, well-informed and virtuous adult.

These various preconceptions – Christian, Cartesian, Lockian – were of great significance in extending concern and action about child potential and its fulfilment. Many of us today still accept their evaluation of the child, as when, for example, in current controversies about 'nature versus nurture' in educational and family matters we favour the latter against the former. Yet it is noteworthy that all these positions have one central assumption in common. For the Christians the natural in the child has to be resisted and controlled; for the philosophers the natural has to be complemented and trained. On either theory education and broader upbringing are essential *additions* to nature; the natural, uneducated, uncontrolled child will be either sinful or stupid or both. The sympathy of a Fénelon or a John Locke towards children has perhaps obscured the considerable difference between their convictions and a quite different interpretation that was to be advanced by future champions of the child; only in a third phase does the child

New images of the natural

achieve elevation to the status of potential little angel and an apparent liberation.

This further phase in France has to be seen in its context, and here again there is a contrast with England. There new attitudes towards both children and marriage had developed from the mid- (or at least late-) seventeenth century onwards. Increasingly the child was being treated with kindliness and affection, and from that period on, to give one instance, the practice of school floggings had declined. By about 1740 in England, furthermore, one finds literature being written specifically for children and the invention of toys and games for their pleasure. Concurrently, too, writers like Gray and Thomson were presenting childhood as a phase of life that was both distinctive and happy.

> Ah happy hills, ah pleasing shade,
> Ah fields belov'd in vain,
>   Where once my careless childhood stray'd,
> A stranger yet to pain!

– thus Gray, recalling Eton College, well before Blake's *Songs of Innocence* would evoke the child as 'the bird that is born for joy' and praise its imagination, sensitivity and essential innocence as against sterile intellectuality and utilitarian philosophy, and earlier also than the idyllic family groups painted by Joshua Reynolds, Zoffany and Copley and that most angelic of all child portraits, Reynolds's *The Age of Innocence*.

In France the older attitudes persisted for much longer, and so much so that in the eighteenth century there appears to have been an actual decline in feeling for children and family life compared with a little earlier. In the upper classes, we noted, it became unfashionable to seem to care for one's children too much – a reversion to casualness justified allegedly by the claim that to indulge the infant was to weaken him – and this may well explain in part a phenomenon that would shock Rousseau and others: the widespread and increasing employment of wet-nurses to feed and rear their babies. If it explains it only 'in part', that is because there was also a common belief that sexual intercourse would stop or at least spoil the mother's milk. That being so, the mother had to choose between satisfying her

146

husband or her child.[14] By 1715 the use of 'nourrices' was so common that a law was introduced to regulate their recruitment through agencies; later in the century Buffon estimated that one-sixth of all babies were reared by wet-nurses, and by its end only 5 % in Paris were fed by their own mothers, it appears.[15] Many of these foster-mothers took their charges back to their own homes in the countryside, away from parental attention or concern, and not uncommonly they ceased to receive payment from the parents. Weaning came after about one and a half years, but the infant often remained with the 'nourrice' or with a 'séveuse' until the age of three or four, and soon after it would often be sent for education away again from parents it scarcely knew. Some 'nourrices' were kindly; the co-editor of the *Encyclopédie*, d'Alembert, lived on with his 'nourrice' until he was 50, and in other cases the child and the 'nourrice' remained in the parental home. But many others appear to have been callous to the point where the baby quickly died, and there were many stories and beliefs about the moral turpitude of wet-nurses – absorbed, moreover, many thought, along with their milk.

The children of the poor fared even worse in general, perhaps inevitably so. Putting aside the substantial practice of infanticide, poor parents could ill spare time from work or the cost for child-care. In the later-eighteenth century illegitimacy rose, and so did the numbers sent to the foundling hospitals. At Paris no questions were asked: many babies were thus sent from the provinces – say, in bundles of four or five strapped onto donkeys for the slow, often fatal journey, which from Brittany could last a week. Hufton quotes figures for one institution: in 1680 it had 870 children, rising to 5,302 in 1740, 6,018 in 1767, and by 1772 10,634.[16] Of course some children had a happy, indulged upbringing: amongst writers, Diderot at Langres, Marmontel, and Rétif de la Bretonne on his father's farm near Auxerre. But theirs were not poor parents; they escaped the imposed callousness of the over-worked and nearly-starving poor who by 1789 formed one-third of the total population.

Amongst poor and rich alike, in short, the older attitudes persisted in France throughout all or most of the eighteenth century, and if Jansenists and Fénelon had taken a kindlier view, many still stressed the child's essential sinfulness. At the end of the previous century an observer like La Bruyère had described the child in his *Caractères* – and only the French can convey the flavour – as 'hautains, dédaigneux, colères, envieux, curieux, intéressés, paresseux, volages, timides, intempérants, menteurs'. Much the same adjectives continued to be used – for example by the Catholic Abbé Louis de Bonnaire in a work of 1743 that concluded that children 'already have the vices of men', whilst in 1754 the Protestant Formey described them as merely 'stupid and clumsy beasts'.[17] Such is the contrasting background against which one must set the new propaganda on behalf of the child from Rousseau and his fellow-campaigners.

His basic premiss is given in the very first sentence of his educational treatise, *Emile*: 'Everything is good as it leaves the hands of the Author of things' – including, therefore, the child. In practice Locke and other empiricists had anticipated most of the practical recommendations that would be based upon this conviction, but the differences of theory and approach are highly significant. For Locke the child may be innocent in that he is neither indelibly stained by sin nor formed in any way prior to the influences of education and environment, but this is a negative or passive innocence, and without the right influences he may well become corrupt or foolish or both. For Rousseau the innocence is positive and active, verging on a natural goodness that can be developed to maturity if the child is reared in 'natural' ways and protected against 'unnatural' influences. There is a related contrast. Locke's underlying concern was more with the future adult than with the present child in and for itself. Rousseau and his fellows value the child as child, as actually likeable, interesting and distinctive – a supposition declared from *Emile*'s *Préface* onwards. He complains that educationalists are concerned wholly with what the future man should know, 'without considering what children are in a condition to learn'. 'They are for ever seeking for the man in the child, without thinking of what he is before becoming a man.' And he claims the child's natural inclinations are good in at least a potential way: 'Love childhood and look with favour on its games, pleasures and amiable instincts.' Moreover, if one objects by pointing (say) to ill-tempered tantrums in the child, he does not hesitate, any more than other reformers such as Morelly about the same time, to attribute the blame to mistaken upbringing: 'The caprice of children is never the work of nature but of bad discipline.'[18] In addition – and here there is a further contrast with his predecessors – he is specifically concerned that childhood should be a happy and enriching period of life for its own sake as well as for the future: 'Why do you wish to take from these innocent little ones the enjoyment of a period that is slipping from them? Why do you wish to fill with bitterness and suffering these first years that pass so rapidly?'[19] This was a more radically novel approach than is sometimes appreciated today, and it is no coincidence that Rousseau can be rightly seen as a precursor of 'child psychology' in its more optimistic moods. We noted the neglect of childhood in earlier literature; Rousseau, by contrast, was one of the very first French writers to evoke the specific outlook of the child in his writings, so that one scholar of the portrayal of childhood in literature can even conclude: 'At last Rousseau came and everything was transformed.'[20] Julie's children in *La Nouvelle Héloïse* may be somewhat lifelessly portrayed, present in the novel less in their own right than as objects for their mother to love and organise – much as are Emile and Sophie, one may think, for the author's own educational experimentation – but the *Confessions* fully warrant the claim that Rousseau had an original and distinctive understanding of the child's mentality.

A comparable appreciation is found in others who shared his positive sympathy for the natural. In literature this is above all true of Bernardin de Saint-Pierre in his presentation of Paul and Virginie. The novel has often and rightly been singled out as the first in French literature to depict childhood as a special phase in human life. We may think him sentimental by our current standards, but Calvet was surely right in his survey of *L'Enfant dans la littérature française* to conclude of the work: 'Henceforth the child has its place in literature.'[21] Nor is this merely because so extensive a space is given to this evocation within the work; again and again one may be impressed by the accuracy of Saint-Pierre's observations. He certainly over-stresses the children's near-angelic qualities; this was in the service of his thesis that a 'natural' upbringing is superior to what prevailed in current European society. Yet he perceptively captures, for example, the child's impulsiveness, naïvety and emotionalism, shows the interplay between its will to indepen-dence and the awareness of ultimate dependency on adults, and points to signs within the child of the adult in the making. In particular he has been praised, with reason, for his portrayal of the awakening in Virginie of a sexual awareness that she still does not understand, side by side with her childish innocence, and of its impact upon the less mature and hence puzzled Paul. To appreciate Saint-Pierre's originality one need only compare his novel with the new children's literature of the day, albeit it too stemmed from the new concerns, with any of the numerous moralising novels that were being published specifically for them – provided mainly by women writers like Mme Le Prince de Beaumont (her *Magasin des Enfants* was in 1756) and Mme de Genlis. A scholar who has read more of these novels than most of us draws the contrast: whilst they are 'largely unreadable and unimaginative', the 'few' masterpieces in eighteenth-century presentation of childhood are in his judgement Rousseau's *Confessions* and *Paul et Virginie* to which he adds Rétif de la Bretonne's *Monsieur Nicolas*.[22]

A similar awareness is shown by some painters of the time. In the family groupings they executed the children are usually posed and arguably as stiff as in earlier periods; even Mme Vigée-Lebrun does not escape this defect in her painting of Marie-Antoinette and her family. The distinctive innovation lies in others of their paintings which depict the child on its own, caught in some commonplace action or mood, and do so, moreover, in ways that suggest it is attractive and likeable. Some of these portraits undeniably present the boy or, more often, the girl as angelic, as the chocolate-box paragon of Reynolds's *The Age of Innocence*. Greuze provides the clearest examples, to the point of being cloying (and sometimes unpleasantly sensual), as in such works as *Innocence, La Prière du matin, La Colombe Retrouvé, Jeune Fille qui pleure la mort de son oiseau,* and numerous others. Yet even he attends to the child's more ordinary activities: playing with a doll, as in *L'Enfant à la poupée*; disobedient, as in *L'Enfant gâté*; asleep at study, as in *Le Petit Paresseux* and *Un Ecolier endormi sur son livre*; playing with a favourite pet, as in his *Fillette au petit chien*. Often enough, we must shortly note, he and Chardin in particular represent the child at its studying or praying, though even that reflects the same belief as in Rousseau that childhood is of distinctive importance. But, as well, Greuze, Chardin in such portraits as his *Cellar Boy* and *Scullery Maid*, and Fragonard in depicting the mischievous boy in *The Donkey's Stable* acknowledge its less elevated, more human elements.

It is noteworthy that Rousseau shared their perception that the child is not always an angel – and not only when society or its parents have corrupted it. His position has even been interpreted by Snyders as a middle way between the old harshness and the new affection, as less innovative than synthesising.[23] However that may be, he was well-aware that the child – as opposed to the baby and the infant – requires both the learning experience given by physical mishaps and sufferings and the guidance given by discipline. It must also be allowed to learn from its own mistakes in his view: thus, for example, whilst one should not positively punish the child for (say) telling untruths or breaking a window, one should certainly – and rather cheerfully, it almost seems – welcome any uncomfortable consequences that follow for it. And, more broadly, he can declare: 'To suffer is the first thing the child should learn and which he will have the greatest need to know.'[24] Rousseau's general educational system has had considerable influence on later educational and parental practice, either directly or indirectly through such admirers as Pestalozzi, Froebel and Montessori – an influence, oddly enough, more in Britain and America than in France. Yet it is most doubtful if he intended the degree of 'free expression' and 'free development' favoured by some of the present-day theorists who appeal to his ideas: Emile's tutor demands obedience as the one essential prerequisite. In short, for Rousseau and for most of his allies in France in the eighteenth century childhood was an age of natural innocence rather than of natural goodness. This is made all the clearer by two central injunctions that are quite explicit in their works.

First, the need for education remains of great importance – for Emile, in Rousseau's view, during the lengthy training which his tutor is to direct, and seemingly in the eyes of Chardin and Greuze also. One can notice how often they depicted the child living happily within a controlling situation, with study being especially needful – as in Chardin's *La Bonne Education*, *La Gouvernante* or *Jeune homme taillant son crayon*, and, likewise, as in Greuze's *Le Petit Mathématicien*, *La Liseuse* and *Ecolier qui étudie sa leçon*.

Secondly, moral and religious instruction is imperative. Emile listens – for the whole of the *Profession de foi* – to the teaching of the Vicaire Savoyard. Paul and Virginie in Saint-Pierre's novel are inculcated likewise with religious fervour and moral values by their mothers and by Le Vieillard in particular. Of the infant Virginie Marguerite can say: 'She will be virtuous, and she will be happy. I have only known misfortune when I have strayed from virtue.'[25] The implication is clear: happiness above all rests not on following nature, but on following virtue. Rétif de la Bretonne's father, similarly, reads out to the assembled family after the evening meal some improving passages from the Bible and adds his own moral comments. And the painters too stressed the need for church and prayer – as in Chardin's *Bénédicité* and *La Toilette du matin* (made in preparation for going to church), and as in Greuze's *La Prière du matin*.

Their caution in not wholly trusting the natural child is the more noteworthy if one looks a little forward in time to others, often linked with Rousseauism, who seem to have fewer doubts. Young Goethe's Werther would shortly recall the happy, well-behaved children he had met (in his letter of 16 June 1771) and write to a friend in even more glowing terms:

Yes, dear Wilhelm, of all living things on earth, children are closest to my heart. When I watch them, and see in the little creatures the seeds of all the virtues, all the powers, of which they will one day be so much in need; when I perceive in their obstinacy future steadfastness and firmness of character, in their mischievousness good humour...

and so on.[26] Later, writers like Schiller, Wordsworth and Hugo seem equally trustful: Schiller praises the child as 'a sacred object' and for its 'pure, free strength'.[27] For Wordsworth:

> Not in entire forgetfulness,
> And not in utter nakedness,
> But trailing clouds of glory do we come
> From God, who is our home...

Or as Hugo has it in *Les Enfants pauvres*:

> Les enfants sont, avant de naître,
> Des lumières dans le ciel bleu.

Rousseau and his fellows rarely, if ever, achieved such heights of enthusiasm – though it is true that Saint-Pierre in his fourteenth *Etude de la nature* likened children to 'the dews and rains of heaven'. In them all one finds a certain ambivalence about nature in the child as well as in the savage, albeit to a lesser extent. They recognised a tension between the natural and the values of civilisation, parallel to the tension mentioned previously between following emotion or natural impulse and, on the other hand, following reason. These champions of the child deserve great credit, one may think, for encouraging its liberation and increased happiness; they may perhaps deserve credit also for not believing in the natural child too unreservedly. Further evidence of this lies in their emphasis upon the views which the next chapter will survey. For its proper formation the child needs not only education, religion and moral teaching but also – and crucially – the influence of a new notion of family relationships and above all the love and guidance of a new kind of natural woman and mother.

8

HAPPY FAMILIES:
(2) The new Eve

For Rousseau and others the family is basic to the entire social order: 'The most ancient of all societies and the only one that is natural is the society of the family.'[1] And basic to a successful and effective family is the mother. Substitutes, even if female, like the servant, the wet-nurse or the 'séveuse' or nanny after her cannot replace the natural mother herself. Her crucial role begins from the very start of the family's existence, the birth of the child, and in regard to two matters in particular. The reader of *Emile* may be surprised to find that this most celebrated of treatises on education should be preoccupied in its opening pages, and passionately so, with swaddling-clothes and breast-feeding. For Rousseau, however, this was putting first things first, for the reasons we must now see.

Swaddling had been almost universal for centuries. 'Le maillot' was firmly wrapped around the infant, keeping its arms and legs straight, with only the face left uncovered – and so it would stay until some nine months old. The child was kept warm and also relatively inactive whilst its mother worked. Locke had been an early opponent of the unnatural restriction involved, followed later, so far as France is concerned, by the doctor, Andry, in 1741, Buffon in his chapter 'De l'enfance' of 1749, and the *Encyclopédie* article on 'Emmaillotter'. Now Rousseau took up the cause. *Emile* evokes the crying baby tossed in a corner, or hung up from a nail on the wall, or – with 'crimson face' – choked by the swaddling-band. The distortions produced are both physical and psychological: 'Their first feeling is one of suffering and affliction; they find only obstacles to all the movements they need to make; unhappier than a criminal in irons, they make efforts in vain, become angry and cry out.'[2] The practice is 'unnatural' and an affront to liberty, for the free, natural development of the human body is hardly less crucial than mental upbringing. If one looks at Rousseau's tomb at Ermenonville, one finds on one side a number of naked children – jolly, active creatures having a bonfire; what they are burning, it seems, are women's whale-bone corsets and babies' swaddling-clothes. Reflected here was a new interpretation of naturalness on the physical level, alongside the educational. At the same time there was something even more fundamental involved: a re-direction of the mother's preoccupations whose novelty at its inception we perhaps fail to register today. A basic reason for the use of swaddling-clothes had been to free her for other things: her domestic chores, her labour in the fields, and so on. What was central for Rousseau in abandoning them was that the mother in future should centre her attention upon the child – would indeed imperatively have to focus her activities upon it, now that it was freed at last to be active and thus constantly to make demands upon her protective care. As Voltaire might have put it: 'When swaddling did not exist, maternal watchfulness needed to be invented.' All her other tasks now had to take second place – and in Rousseau's view this would be wholly to the good for the creation of the new family. If, as appears, swaddling continued in France well into the nineteenth century amongst the rural working classes, that was because they could not spare the mother from her tasks outside the house; initially, therefore, the abandonment of swaddling-clothes and the notion that woman's place is wholly in the home were luxuries that only the better-off could afford. The earlier disappearance of swaddling in England is perhaps related to its greater economic prosperity, relatively speaking, as well as to other factors.

Secondly, and even more importantly, the new mother must herself feed her baby. In the previous chapter we noted how widespread in France was the practice of employing wet-nurses, as it had been earlier. Michelet recounts that the infant Henri IV had eight wet-nurses and little Louis XIV may have had nine. Of upper-class mothers in the seventeenth century only a few chose to feed their offspring; Cardinal Richelieu's mother was one of them. Fostering increased in the later-seventeenth century, it seems, and thereafter, as we saw, it was ever more frequently adopted by the well-to-do. This is the background for the attack upon it by Rousseau and others, of which the explicit premiss is that it is against nature. In common with others, Toussaint in *Les Moeurs* draws the contrast with animals and prefers their instincts to human reason: 'Brute beasts have no need of our treatises on ethics in order to learn to love their little ones, to feed them and to bring them up.'³ Even more often invoked was the example of the primitive mother – as by Laclos in his essays, *Des femmes et de leur éducation*, where he attacks both fostering and swaddling and refers approvingly to the example of the Negress. He believed that 'happiness exists only in the family' and claimed that to establish it soundly 'milk is the natural bond that unites mother and child'. Rétif de la Bretonne wrote a *comédie larmoyante* entitled *Sa Mère l'allaita* (and how striking that he thought the title would attract). The dramatist Moissy devoted most of his play of 1771, *La Vraie Mère*, to this same theme. Greuze's painting of *Le Repos* was no less committed, and he actually planned a series of pictures about two brothers, *Bazile et Thibault*, which would have contrasted the happy life of the maternally-fed Bazile and poor Thibault who is passed off to a 'nourrice'.⁴ Thibault, aged 30, ends by committing murder and is sentenced to death (by none other than Bazile, now a successful judge). Recognising the ultimate cause, their father kills himself and their mother expires with contrition. One need hardly add that Saint-Pierre held a similar view – though he may perhaps be thought heterodox in that occasionally the mothers of Paul and Virginie exchange their babies for feeding with one another.

What is above all striking in these and parallel instances is the passionate concern, out-doing all issues of educational practice, and the conviction that maternal breast-feeding is crucial. The subject has emotional overtones to this day, of course, but the attitude of Rousseau or Greuze was altogether more intense than that of the average modern mother. One seeks the reason, and it is clearly not, at bottom, a reason of health. True, some believed that the vices of the 'nourrice' would be absorbed with her milk – but sceptics like Brouzet and Vandermonde countered that by noting that most mothers also had vices, and *they* thus concluded in favour of animal milk or artificial feeding.[5] (Against that some contended that animal milk would pass to the infant certain animal characteristics such as hairiness.) The underlying reason was, one may think, more fundamental. What Rousseau and others were primarily asserting was that maternal feeding is the basic way in which 'emotional bonding' can be ensured, the love of mother for child – and of child for its mother also. If attacking swaddling was implicitly saying that the happy family requires the mother's attention to be focussed on the child, what insisting on maternal feeding was saying was that the happy family has to be built on deep, bonded love. By contrast, fostering undermines the good, natural family, as Rousseau stressed. 'Everything follows successively from this first deprivation: the whole moral order changes for the worse; the natural is extinguished in every heart; domestic life assumes a less animated atmosphere; husbands are no longer attached by the moving sight of a growing family.' By comparison, he claims: 'If mothers will deign to feed their children, manners will reform themselves and the feelings of nature will be awakened in every heart.'[6]

It appears that the campaigning of Rousseau and his fellows had its effect, at least with the better-off classes, not excluding Marie-Antoinette. She is reported as declaring: 'I wish to live as a mother, to feed my child and devote myself to its upbringing',[7] and certainly she was keen to be painted by Mme Vigée-Lebrun surrounded by her children, as were other mothers, including the painter herself in self-portraits showing her hugging a loving daughter.

Attention and love are the foundation, but the new family image was to be consolidated most firmly by other contentions of major consequence, arguments about what is truly natural. Of these the most important – and perhaps to this day one of the most persistent, whether one welcomes that or not – concerns what woman 'naturally *is*' and how we may 'liberate' her to be her 'true', 'natural' self. The subject is so central as to require fuller discussion than any other aspect of the new family ideal.

Throughout much of human history woman has been more closely linked with 'nature' than man – in the view of men at least. 'Mother Nature', 'earth mother', the feminine gender in various languages given to the word for nature: those are a few out of countless reflections of the view notoriously summed up in crisp French by Baudelaire, complete with gratuitous insult: 'La femme est naturelle, c'est-à-dire abominable.' And today women's liberationists seek still to refute the special linking – as in a feminist article in 1974 entitled: 'Is female to male as nature is to culture?'[8]

Given the dominance of such an equation, one might well predict, *a priori*, that when nature as a whole was regarded as fallen and evil, woman would be regarded as especially fallen and evil and that when, against that evaluation, others contended that nature is benevolent and even good, they would go on to provide a radically more favourable view of woman also. And so it was: in the eighteenth century there emerged a new notion of 'femininity' which has even been described by Gusdorf as 'a decisive mutation' in the history of civilisation.[9] Certainly the contrast of old and new views is arresting.

The predominant Christian view over the centuries derived from the Genesis story. First, Eve was created by God derivatively out of Adam's rib, but far more decisively it was she who first tasted the forbidden fruit and lured Adam to eat of it too. Through woman, therefore, came the Fall of mankind (and of the whole creation) – that most fatal event in the eyes of even seventeenth-century Europeans from which have followed all death, evil and suffering. And God Himself punished her and her entire sex for this original act of sin: 'I will greatly multiply thy sorrow and thy conception; in sorrow thou shalt bring forth children; and thy desire shall be to thy husband, and he shall rule over thee' (Genesis 3:16). Woman is intended to be subordinate and to suffer, especially in giving birth. Moreover, even more than the male, she is dominated by her fallen nature. In particular she is constantly sexually hungry – and always more so than man until, by her wiles, she has provoked him to an irrational and humiliating desire. The Book of Ecclesiastes (7:26) was one classic Biblical authority among others: 'And I find more bitter than death the woman, whose heart is snares and nets, and her hands as bands: whoso pleaseth God shall escape from her; but the sinner shall be taken by her.' The Bible does not rule out the possibility of a virtuous woman. Proverbs 31:10 offers one instance among others, and so do such women as Martha and Mary, and supremely the Mother of Christ Himself, able to conceive without sexual relations. But for centuries the presupposition was the other way, as was notoriously summed up by Tertullian: 'God's sentence hangs still over all your sex and His punishment weighs down upon you. You are the devil's gateway.' Leviticus 27:3-4 had long ago summed it up: the male is worth 50 shekels, the female 30.

Some protested against this view, naturally enough: the medieval proponents of 'l'amour courtois'; Christine de Pisan; the Marguerite de Navarre side, opposing anti-feminists like Rabelais, in the sixteenth-century 'querelle des femmes'; even more the precursors of feminism in seventeenth-century France. Yet the usual view right down to the eighteenth century (and, indeed, beyond it in many minds) was that woman, by virtue of her very role as begetter of children, is more lustful than man. Burton, to give just one example, can ask in his *Anatomy of Melancholy*: 'Of women's unnatural, unsatiable lust, what country, what village doth not complain?' For the same reason women engage in the black arts far more than men; as two out of many male Christians put it, 'all witchcraft comes from carnal lust, which is in women insatiable'.[10] And the whole notion of woman as endlessly seeking to become pregnant was well captured in the general assumption in the sixteenth century and beyond that women are a prey to the 'medical' complaint of 'wandering womb'. If unsatisfied, the womb wanders around the body and may end up in the brain: hence the excessive emotionalism of women, hence their 'hysteria' – a word coined from the Greek for womb and a condition formerly thought to be confined to females.

This view of woman's nature is light-years away, obviously enough, from the stereotype we connect with Victorian

England. Woman according to that – at least one's own wife and other ladies of good upbringing – is 'the little woman', reluctantly subjecting herself to her husband's distasteful bedtime demands, following the dictate, most famously, of Mrs Ellis in 1845 to 'suffer and be still' and the injunction later to 'close her eyes and think of England'. The gap is startling in two respects especially. In the new image woman is little interested in sexual relations, if at all, and, secondly, in her role as wife and mother she is the guardian of tenderly loving morality. In France in the later-eighteenth century it was the same minority as before who elaborated and propounded this novel re-incarnation of woman.

It has as its background, however, changing scientific and medical ideas as to the differences between the sexes, ideas fully described by Paul Hoffmann's major thesis on *La Femme dans la pensée des lumières* and which need only to be summarised here. The old Christian concept had clearly assumed that woman possesses a distinctively female nature, albeit mostly sinful. The Cartesians, by contrast, argued that sex-differences are purely secondary, bodily and, indeed, mechanist in type: men and women are the same basic human model with a few differences of machinery. Above all, mind and body are quite separate in Descartes' dualistic philosophy, and from that there followed the declaration by one of his followers that 'the mind is without sex'. That in turn led Poullain de la Barre – in his *Egalité des deux sexes* (1673) and in *De l'éducation des dames* (1674) – into strong support of feminism and of female education in particular. Indeed, so enthusiastic was he that he even betrayed his basic premiss on occasion by arguing that woman is *superior* to man – by virtue of her motherhood – and that she incarnates, in a way man does not, the love of the Creator Himself. More often, however, he was asserting that woman should be equal with man since she is in all essential respects – that is, in her mind and soul – identical with man, without any distinctive 'femininity'.

In an earlier chapter we saw that by the end of the eighteenth century 'mechanism' gradually yielded in the sciences to a new 'organicism'. This change became directly relevant to the notion of womanhood. Already, as early as 1708 in his *Theoria medica vera*, the animist G. E. Stahl had argued for the organic unity of soul and body and hence had claimed that woman has 'a sensibility that is as much physical as mental' – and which is 'much superior to that of man', he had added. He also made the assertion which would dominate the thought of Rousseau later: namely, that the reason behind all the ways of feeling and thinking in woman lies in 'the final goal of the female sex', to give birth. Stahl's animism was further developed by such vitalists, around the mid-century, as Bordeu in 1752 and Roussel in 1775 in his *Système physique et moral de la femme*. This work, for example, claims that femininity is a primary characteristic, contends that our spirit controls our bodily mechanism, and (in sharp contrast to Poullain's view that the mind is sexless) ascribes to woman a distinctively female personality – intuitive rather than reasoning, and led by her feelings, not by ideas.

It was this 'organicist' theory that prevailed with the reformers – in the main at least, for a deal of confusion remains in the thought of Diderot, for example. On the one hand he sees the free-loving maidens of Tahiti as natural women and portrays them as healthy and straightforward; on the other hand in his *Rêve de D'Alembert* he can cite the prevalence of 'the vapours' in women as an instance of female bodily 'anarchy'.[11] All the same, the underlying assumption with him, Rousseau and others is that woman is 'woman through and through', in every part of her being; she possesses an objectively special 'female nature' that dominates her whole personality. And since their supposition is that the natural is good rather than evil, they add that woman ought to follow and fulfil that nature.

This same notion of a 'feminine destiny' was being propounded in other ways also. In particular it has been demonstrated by Pierre Fauchery in his extensive thesis on *Le Mythe de la destinée féminine dans le roman européen au dix-huitième siècle* that numerous novels over the century, in France and elsewhere in Europe, were presenting in fictional form this new 'myth', as he believes it to be. He clearly holds the opinion that this was deliberately intended in order to reconcile women, to condition them, to an inferior position: 'One of the major functions of the eighteenth-century novel [he writes] was to promote a certain idea of woman, to elevate the existence of the "natural woman" to the dignity of a myth.'[12] These novels – from, in France, Robert Chasles's *Illustres Françoises* of 1713 to Mme de Staël's *Corinne* of 1807 – were seeking to make woman's continued subordination bearable and, indeed, 'inevitable' for her by presenting it as part of her 'destiny', of her essential being as female.

Fauchery's 860 pages defy summary here, and so do the many other discussions reported by Hoffmann and other scholars. But, put baldly and without qualifications and passing over the 'disputes' that raged about 'woman' as much as about the savage or the child during these years, the upshot was that the old sexy Eve was replaced by a tender, caring, deeply-feeling wife and mother, a creature made and, above all, feeling herself made to cherish her man and her children and to teach them by her example the new morality of sensibility. For her very essence is to love spiritually, not carnally, and far from being more lustful than man, she is essentially modest. Earlier any female sexual reticence had been thought by even a free-thinker like Bayle to be socially conditioned, but by the mid-century others – like Montesquieu, for instance – were claiming that it is innate. Rousseau – almost needless to say – asserts that 'modesty' is indeed natural, that (as his *Lettre à D'Alembert sur les spectacles* puts it) 'every woman without modesty is guilty and depraved', for she tramples under foot 'a feeling that is natural to her sex'.

This image had been anticipated earlier, once again: by Fénelon in his advocacy of better education for girls, by Locke to some extent, and by others. Defoe is typical in claiming that a well-bred, well-educated woman will be 'all softness and sweetness, peace, love, wit and delight'. But in France the full development of the notion only comes at a rather later date.

In the last book of *Emile* Rousseau outlines the education he proposes for Sophie in order to prepare her for marriage to Emile. One should not train her intellect or powers of criticism but seek to preserve her natural feelings and innocence and prepare her to serve her husband and future sons.

> To please males, be useful to them, make oneself loved and honoured by them; to rear them when they are young and care for them when older; to counsel them, console them and make life agreeable and gentle for them: such are the duties of women in every age and what one should teach them from their childhood on.[13]

The specific details of Sophie's education all follow from this basic belief that 'woman is specially made to please man', 'to be agreeable to man instead of provoking him'.[14]

It has been claimed that Rousseau was already somewhat out-dated in his views.[15] Certainly some of the 'philosophes' who held to the 'blank sheet' theory of personality were arguing in favour of an education for girls closer to that provided for boys – to some extent at least. Helvétius offers one example and opposed both Rousseau and Diderot on the subject. Montesquieu too believed in the idea of equality at the theoretical level, though he has been found largely indifferent in practice.[16] D'Holbach seems favourable in the third volume, *Des femmes*, of his *Système social*, and yet thinks women are constitutionally unsuited to abstract thought – because of 'the weakness of their organs' – and he stresses that training of their sensibility should be basic in their moral education. Voltaire, similarly, has been described as 'ambivalent', as one may see in the article on 'Femme' in his *Dictionnaire philosophique*. Of the 'philosophes' Condorcet alone appears unambiguously 'feminist' in our present-day sense:[17] one finds him, for example, expressing doubts as to whether any 'natural difference' between the sexes has been proved and also attacking women's exclusion from political rights in his essay of 1790, *Sur l'admission des femmes aux droits de cité*. For him females are born blank sheets as much as males, and all depends on what society, experience and education write upon them.

But Rousseau and his fellow-campaigners clearly did not hold that view of human personality – at least not about females. From his *Lettre sur les aveugles* onwards Diderot, for example, stresses the influence of physiology, and especially so as regards woman, and in an *Essai sur les femmes* (1772) he can say of her: 'It is from the organ particular to her sex that there stem all her extraordinary ideas.'[18] As one who was at least semi-organicist in his thinking, he opposed Helvétius's position as found in *De l'homme*, and although he conceded in his *Réfutation* of that work that education can achieve 'much' and that girls can be 'better brought up' than at present, Diderot nevertheless believed at bottom that woman is dominated by her nature. He can even declare that nature is cruel to women as much as society. It is thus not surprising to learn that the education he ensured for his own daughter Angélique was conventional and distinctly limited in its range. His belief was that a woman would only be happy if she accepted her biological condition, and he thus above all wanted Angélique to be married and to be a mother. We are told he never regretted educating her primarily for those ends.

The novelist Laclos provides a similar but more fully-developed illustration in his essays, *Des Femmes et de leur éducation* written about 1783 but not published at the time. The contrast he stressed was between woman as he believes she naturally is and woman as she is forced to act in eighteenth-century society, and to ascertain the former he studied her role in such primitive societies as Greenland, Iceland, Korea, Abyssinia and the Congo. He attacked both those who regard the primitive as ignoble and those like Buffon or Voltaire who deny humans can live in the 'state of nature'; he even referred approvingly to the wild girl of Champagne who (like a wild boy near Hanover earlier) had been discovered after years of total isolation from humans, having been reared by wolves, and he also praised the example of the Negress in particular, as we noted. Thus persuaded, he had as his aim to free modern European woman from the depraved social values that he believed had been imposed on her and to allow her to be her true self:

Oh women, come near and listen to me. Let your curiosity, directed for once towards useful objects, contemplate the advantages that nature had given you and that society has stolen from you. Come and learn how, having been born to be a companion for man, you have become his slave.[19]

What is needed for women, he continues, is 'a great revolution', and without it – until their 'slavery' is ended – no really effective education is possible for them. Natural woman is free, he submits, for she has faculties wholly adequate for her needs. Her natural impulses are to feed herself, to receive the approaches of the male, and to nourish her child until it becomes independent. He traces her development, from birth through puberty to her 'point of perfection' and adds that natural woman is superior to socialised woman even as regards the 'two goods without which women count as nothing all other goods' – 'beauty and love'. Even now, to give an example, the painted courtesan, he says, appeals to men less than 'a young and naïve village girl', perfumed only by 'a bath of clear water'. The natural life for woman should be divided between 'the gentle cares of love and of motherhood', rearing her children, and pleasing her man (and a footnote gives his recipe for a facial cosmetic – water apparently not being enough after all).

The education she should receive follows from this notion, even as regards the knowledge Laclos wants her to acquire. 'The elementary books on each branch of knowledge should be included in the library of a young woman who wishes to be pleasing', for then she will be able to talk on matters interesting to men; travel-accounts, novels and plays will help to that end, albeit they are not without their 'dangers'. It is also desirable that she learns to write with 'purity' and 'elegance' and acquires knowledge of at least one foreign language.[20]

Other theorists varied around the same position, as two brief instances may illustrate here. Rétif de la Bretonne has been judged both a 'reactionary' and a 'feminist'; much depends on whether one defines the terms as we do today or within the historical context. What is clear is that he held a vitalist view and accepted biological determinism in woman as much as Rousseau, Diderot and Laclos. In *La Femme dans les trois états* (1773) he asserts that her happiness lies in making a man happy; 'the intended purpose of nature' is that she should 'please'. There is little need to educate her for 'women always remain children' – something shown (Rousseau makes the same point) by the fact that their voices never break.[21] By comparison

Bernardin de Saint-Pierre is more sympathetic and says more about female education, notably in an essay of 1777, 'Comment l'éducation des femmes pourrait contribuer à rendre les hommes meilleurs.' Yet, even so, one meets the same basic conviction: women are still cast in the role of helping 'men' and making them morally 'better'.

It is hardly surprising that these authors should have been greatly criticised in recent years by supporters of women's liberation and equality. S. M. Okin's book on *Women in Western Political Thought* (1979) offers a particularly full instance of the attack upon Rousseau's views; he calls on woman both to inspire passion and to resist it in the cause of marital fidelity, to allure and to be restrained alike: hence the 'tragedies' of both Julie and Sophie.[22] Certainly one may think that Rousseau especially, and Rétif also, more than the others, do fall at times into a 'chauvinism' that goes well beyond the needs of their basic thesis – and, indeed, sometimes betrays that thesis. Whatever one's judgement as to that, however, a few points of special relevance to the general subject need to be added here.

First and most obviously, their 'image' of woman rests centrally upon what they believe to be natural; basic is what they argue to be the essence of 'the natural woman'. Secondly and contrary to the claims of Fauchery and others that they wished only to keep women in a state of subjection, with the implication that this was the whole object of the exercise, it must be reiterated that they in fact attributed a high and crucial purpose to woman. All the 'pleasing' and 'caring', all the undoubted 'subjection' to 'children, kitchen and church', as we may feel, were felt by them to be right not only because they 'come naturally' to woman but also because they relate to her supremely important role as fountain of right feeling and right morality. Rousseau, for instance, denies any public or professional scope to women, for it is against their nature and since (as he puts it) 'dependency is a state natural to women' and 'girls feel themselves made to obey'.[23] But, on the other hand, in Book v of *Emile* he asserts that women are fundamental to the moral regeneration of society, and in the figure of Julie – the great mother–educator – we see Rousseau's ideal of womanhood. One scholar has well stressed what he calls 'the paradox of Sophie and Julie': the contrast between the submissiveness proposed for Sophie and the controlling and far from 'subjected' importance given to Julie, the hero-figure of the novel, not Saint-Preux or Wolmar. Whoever else in *La Nouvelle Héloïse* is down-trodden – such as, arguably, her children, her servants and her peasants – it is certainly not Julie. And the same scholar claims that in fact it was the model of Julie that captured public attention, not the figure of Sophie.[24]

Others advanced this same elevated notion. In part at least Mme de Tourvel in Laclos's *Les Liaisons dangereuses* is 'a spiritual sister of Julie', as Hoffmann especially has stressed.[25] Saint-Pierre likewise idealises woman in the portrayal of the two mothers in *Paul et Virginie* and most emphatically in the *Préambule* he wrote for the novel's 1806 edition: 'Women have contributed more than philosophers to forming and reforming nations.' The first founder of a human society was 'the mother of a family', and though women may not be more perfect than men, it is they who 'civilise the human race'. 'Oh women,... wherever you have enjoyed your natural rights, you have abolished barbaric forms of upbringing, slavery, torture, mutilations, stakes and crosses.' 'Your natural pity gives you both the instinct of innocence and the instinct of true greatness.' 'You are the queens of our opinions and of our moral order.'[26]

Such heady praise leads to a final point. This novel image of woman was created above all by women and by men who in the situation of their time felt themselves to be ardent feminists, who genuinely, even passionately, believed they were liberating women to be their true selves. The contrary 'conspiracy' theory of Fauchery and others seems to be belied by the tone and content of so much that they say, and it is Fauchery himself who notes that the great majority of the European novels he studies were written by women. As Dr Jean Bloch comments, 'it is often the women themselves who are the most conservative'[27] – though one might add also that in their time they were innovators, fighting the old view of lustful womanhood, and that it is only now that, thanks in part to those very eighteenth-century campaigners and their effectiveness, they may today appear conservative and even reactionary. And the evidence seems to be that numerous upper-class women towards the century's end were happy to accept their new status – to breast-feed their children and so on. The Goncourts, in their book on *La Femme au dix-huitième siècle*, noted the frequent attempts even to assume an outward appearance that would express the new spiritualised notion. Some women had themselves bled to make their faces more pale and languid; some adopted hair-styles that surrounded their faces with 'a half-shadow, placing around their features a cloud-like softness'. Their clothes reflected the same aspiration, the Goncourts report. In place of the lavish, bejewelled, artificial gowns of a Mme de Pompadour, typical of the painted society woman Rousseau and his fellows deplored, the new woman adopts 'a fashion that is both virginal and rural and that adorns her with simplicity and veils her in whiteness'.[28]

It may well be, therefore, that Fauchery and similar critics are guilty of judging too much by reference to present-day positions and are failing to evaluate in relation to the historical context. Views which we may now find unacceptable, which today may be restrictive, may have been found liberating in their time. Such is the conclusion of at least one feminist study of *Women in Europe since 1750*, where Patricia Branca, whilst admitting most feminists do not agree, herself claims 'that far from being a major stumbling block, the family has been the stepping stone toward female emancipation'.[29] And even if, to the contrary, one judged that the outcome has been to increase woman's subjection, it would not follow that this was intended by the 'reformers' or was their ulterior motive. Rather, if there is a present-day moral to the story, it would be that women should distrust not only their 'chauvinist' enemies but also other women and their male friends. Almost one adds: with deeply sincere friends (beyond serious doubt) like Laclos and Saint-Pierre, who needs enemies?

However that may be, it is easy to see how deeply relevant to consolidating the new ideal family was this novel concept of woman. She does what is essential not because she is forced to or is economically dependent (though the *Ancien Régime* laws undoubtedly ensured that), but because, in her essential nature, she wishes to.

One figure, however, has not yet entered the charmed domestic circle, for he has been busy with the work of providing and in the public activities of 'the man's world' outside: the father. We markedly lack studies of changing concepts of male-ness and of fatherhood, comparable to those that have proliferated on the woman and mother in recent years. (How, for instance, did we get to the common assumptions that males are naturally aggressive and naturally insensitive?) There appears to have been little discussion in eighteenth-century France about the role or nature of adult males in the way there was about children and women. All the same, most of the campaigners placed emphasis upon the importance, for good or ill, of 'le père de famille'. When, for instance, Greuze represented 'the unhappy family', he depicted a drunken father reeling towards his frightened children and apprehensive wife. Likewise, his friend Baculard d'Arnaud included in *Les Délassements de l'homme sensible* stories entitled *Le Pouvoir de l'amour paternel, L'Amour filial* and *Le Respect filial*, along with others equally reflective of the new ideal such as *La Tendresse conjugale* and *L'Amour fraternel*. Only Saint-Pierre seems to imagine that a family could exist without a father, in the manner of Paul and Virginie's little community run by the two mothers, and even there Le Vieillard is a partial replacement.

'The natural father' – though that phrase does not seem to be used in this sense – has two major characteristics, other than being the economic mainstay of his family. The first is that he naturally and readily feels affection for his children. Des Grieux in *Manon Lescaut* earlier had declared: 'A father's heart is the masterpiece of nature.'[30] Rousseau may not go that far, but one of his arguments for maternal feeding is that the husband's own emotions will be encouraged by it: 'Once women become mothers again, men will soon become fathers and husbands again.'[31] In England the notion of the loving father was already becoming widespread, and yet again Gray's *Elegy* gives us the picture, recalled in retrospect after his death:

For them no more the blazing hearth shall burn,
Or busy housewife ply her evening care;
No children run to lisp their sire's return,
Or climb his knees the envied kiss to share.

In France the affection is present but, though sometimes warmly shown as (say) in Aubry's painting of *L'Amour paternel*, is more often expressed in a reserved way as in Greuze's depictions or the manly greeting of father to grown-up son indicated in Sedaine's play, *Le Philosophe sans le savoir*. Yet emotion does exist, and a good composite image of the family in which Diderot believed, parallel with the picture given by Rousseau in *La Nouvelle Héloïse* of Julie and Wolmar's family-life, is provided by his play, *Le Père de famille* (1758), a moralising and sentimental 'drame bourgeois' at whose first performance in 1761, it is said, there were as many handkerchiefs as spectators. The father is talking to his daughter Cécile (II, 2) and first stresses the marital tie: 'Oh sacred bond of husband and wife, when I think of you my soul is warmed and elevated!' Secondly, he clearly feels affection for his wife, busy at her caring domestic tasks: 'Cécile, remember the life of your mother: is there a sweeter, more gentle life than that of a woman who has spent her day in fulfilling the duties of attentive wife, tender mother, and sympathetic mistress?' Thirdly, there is his own love for his children: 'Oh tender names of sons and daughters, I never pronounce you without thrilling with joy and without emotion!'[32] Indeed, both here and in his other play, *Le Fils naturel*, the father, not the mother, is pre-eminent.

All the same, he proclaims these high sentiments to his daughter at a moment when he is placing emotional pressure upon her to do what he is determined she shall: namely, disavow a young man she loves but whom her father thinks unsuitable for her to marry. Here is the second characteristic of the ideal husband and father: he is depicted as the final authority, as a patriarchal repository of moral approval, as in Greuze's *La Bénédiction paternelle*, and of moral disapproval, as in the same painter's *La Malédiction paternelle*. Like Diderot's Cécile and her brother, who rebel against their father's ban on unsuitable marriages for them, Rousseau's Julie too at first finds

it hard that her father should ban marriage to Saint-Preux whom
she loves and arrange her marriage to Wolmar whom she does
not. Yet she comes to accept that her father had been wiser.[33]
In Diderot's play the problem is differently resolved, but with
a double evasion of the real issue. The father had objected on
grounds of social class; at the end it emerges that his son's
Sophie is not really from the lower classes after all but the niece
of the father's brother-in-law, and he likewise discovers Cécile's
young man is more socially suitable than he had thought. Hence
he agrees to both marriages, but Diderot fails to say what should
otherwise have been decided.

The father of the house likewise holds final authority over
his wife. She is wise, as we have seen, in the ways of morality,
feeling and kindliness but, by her true nature, she is and wishes
to be subordinate to her husband as regards the ways of the
world. We today may well find a paradox here in their ideal of
the natural woman: woman is to be free to be herself at last,
and to be free she needs to depend upon and be obedient to
her husband. Even though one may think that Rousseau and
Diderot sincerely believed in both elements of that paradox, at
the same time it provides another instance of ambivalence
towards the 'natural human' to set alongside the noble savage
and the child. The natural has much to commend it, but so too
have the claims of social conformity and stability, and so one
had better keep ultimate control in more competent hands.

The French reformers also remained reticent, in particular,
in regard to the major change, just touched upon, which, in
England and elsewhere, was working to consolidate the happy
family. This lay in the replacement of the almost universal
acceptance, previously, of 'arranged marriages' by the idea that
one should marry above all for reasons of affection and even
love. In England love seems to have become a significant,
though still not all-determining reason for marriage from the
later- (or even mid-) seventeenth century onwards – first
amongst the urban bourgeoisie, then in the upper landed
classes. No doubt even before that – and perhaps for centuries
and perhaps especially in those classes where less was financially
or socially at stake – fathers did not wantonly go against their

offsprings' affections, but that still did not breach the principle
that there were social, moral and economic reasons for marriage
that might well over-ride romantic feeling. Even in England
the tension was not rapidly resolved in favour of romance, as
is seen (for example) in various eighteenth-century English
novels. Fielding's *Tom Jones* (1749) centres on the clash between
the old financial reasons for marriage and the new reason.
Richardson's *Clarissa* and *Sir Charles Grandison* reflect the same
debate, albeit his young ladies show more spirit than Julie, and,
as Laurence Lerner has claimed in a study of *Love and Marriage*
in literature, Anna Howe and Charlotte are almost vehicles for
feminism as we understand it today.[34]

What of France? Flandrin claims that many French people
by the middle of the eighteenth century were imitating what
they explicitly saw as an English (and welcome) new fashion:
'What Anglomania made fashionable among the French élites
in the eighteenth century [he writes] was married love.'[35]
Certainly Nivelle de La Chaussée in *Le Préjugé à la mode* (1735)
was an earlier advocate of it, as he attacked the contrary fashion.
All the same, more research is needed for France, comparable
to that of Stone and other scholars for England, to ascertain
how far marriages remained primarily non-romantic despite the
exhortations of Voltaire, Turgot and the *Encyclopédie*, for
example, that marriage should be loving and joyful and the
young should choose for themselves.

As for the theoretical attitude of Rousseau in particular, it
has often been claimed that he was in reality attacking 'arranged
marriages' in *La Nouvelle Héloïse*, that he agreed with his
Edouard Bomston (II, 2) and Julie's first protests (III, 18). One
may doubt this. Not only does Julie come to accept the
rightness of her father's choice for her but she even declares
it an error to think 'that love is necessary to form a happy
marriage'; indeed, love is 'ill-suited to marriage, which is a state
of joy and peace', for 'the blind rapture of passionate hearts'
leads to 'mutual self-preoccupation to the neglect of public
and domestic duties'.[36] The significant step forward in the work
is rather that Julie achieves affection for a husband to whom
she was not initially attracted and fulfilment through it and her

family life. But, if this view is right (and others would contest it), Rousseau hesitates to conclude that affection must necessarily precede the marriage or that it should be the decisive factor in one's choice of spouse. Rather he seems to believe it is a highly desirable further 'bonding' within the family, but one which can as well develop during the marriage if each partner has the proper attitude to the other. One can note that his heroine, Julie, is decidedly chary of allowing contacts between the two sexes amongst her domestics: it is 'very important' to avoid 'a dangerous familiarity'.[37] Diderot certainly does not appear any more radical than Rousseau, to judge especially from *Le Père de famille*. He does present the case pleaded by the son and the daughter for following their love, but to read the scene (II, 6) where the subject is debated is to be persuaded that the father's view is favoured. The son asks who is suitable as his wife if not Sophie; the father replies: 'She who by her upbringing, birth, social position and wealth can ensure your happiness and satisfy your hopes.' And he adds – and it is beyond denying that the play presents him as morally admirable: 'I shall never allow you to marry this girl to whom you have become foolishly attached.'[38] The actual outcome, we saw, evades the basic issue, and Diderot was so often 'un esprit de dialogue', reluctant to push any position to its final conclusion. Yet in real life he apparently treated his own well-loved daughter with the same assumption that his 'père de famille' held: that the father had the final authority. Only a small minority may have favoured a different view. One of the mothers in Saint-Pierre's novel had married below her social status for reasons of love; her family thereupon disowned her and she emigrated; the novelist clearly presents their attitude as an instance of civilisation's false values. Likewise, Laclos shows Cécile threatened with the choice between marriage to an older man and a return to the convent. Yet these are isolated cases, and the fair conclusion, even if tentative, is that the French reformers for the most part recognised without accepting the case against arranged marriage, that they valued affection for their ideal family but remained guarded about 'les folles amours'.

If so, they were continuing in a long tradition in France and elsewhere. For centuries the Roman church had distrusted 'profane' as opposed to 'sacred' love and its priests had denounced 'carnal' passion. And their parishioners had agreed with them – at least to judge from popular proverbs like those quoted by Flandrin in *Les Amours paysannes*: 'De fol amour ne vient que mal'; 'Affection aveugle raison'; 'Amour passé, douleur demeure'; and so on.[39] The traditional view is well reflected in even a humanist like Montaigne: 'The friendliness which we show towards our wives is very justifiable; nevertheless, theology does not fail to restrain and limit it all the same.' One should not be carried 'beyond the barriers of reason'.[40] Comparably, French literature over the ages presents 'l'amour-passion' as dangerous: as the fatal poison drunk in the Tristan and Isolde story; as the irresistible force that sweeps Phèdre to her destruction – 'Vénus tout entière à sa proie attachée'. Still by the later-eighteenth century French literature was depicting passion and 'l'amour érotique' with condemnation. The noteworthy change it does reflect, however, is away from the view illustrated by (say) Bossuet in the later-seventeenth century, when he preached that love of one's wife was dangerous since it could turn one away from love of God, and towards a much warmer attitude towards 'l'amour-émotion'. Whereas the period's 'erotic' novels often identify woman as the principal libertine, its 'sentimental' novels show her in her new and tender role.[41]

Two points should be added in conclusion. First, if their approach to marital love seems lukewarm to us today, we should remember how short was the average duration of a marriage even in the later-eighteenth century – probably shorter, it is startling to think, than in present-day America, despite its high divorce rate. Life-expectancy, though rising, was still so low and the age of first marriage was so late in general that the average marriage would last little more than ten years or so, and re-marriage after the death of one's spouse was normal and usually quick – within a year with men, within two to three years with women, on average.[42] (It is not foolish to suggest that modern divorces have proliferated as the period 'till death us do part' has become ever longer on average.) And just as it may be that parents had hesitated to make an emotional investment in children who would probably die in infancy, so too couples may, unconsciously but prudently, have held back from forming too deep an attachment to each other.

Secondly, in order to consolidate the happy family, what was above all desirable was affection between the couple, 'l'amour-émotion', as contrasted with the unpredictable dangers of 'l'amour-passion'. If our eighteenth-century theorists are cautious about abandoning arranged marriages, they do none the less approve of the former – even where they believe it can develop as well during as prior to marriage. But distrust of passion remains, as was argued in the case of Rousseau earlier, and this perhaps explains why all of them, Condorcet alone excepted and he a little later, seem to have been silent about a subject one might have expected them to have discussed: birth-control.

Contraceptive practices could well be considered as desirably consequential upon their new family ideal: they spared the woman from almost continual pregnancy and its dangers (for many women were, without them, bearing a child every twenty-five to thirty months throughout their fertile years); they allowed parental devotion to a smaller number of children, now that these were less likely to die young. Yet one looks in vain for approval of what was apparently becoming more common in later-eighteenth-century France, although its extent is still a matter of historians' debate. Catholic attacks on contraception increased – a reliable indication that its practice was more frequent. Typical was Moheau in his *Recherches et considérations sur la population de la France* (1778): thanks to the 'deadly secrets unknown to any animal other than man', 'Nature is cheated even in the villages.'[43] Yet on this issue an anti-Catholic like Diderot seems in total agreement with Rome, ironically enough. His *Supplément* may seem to approve of total sexual liberty, but it transpires that the Tahitian attitude he presents so favourably bans intercourse at times when the female cannot conceive, and the story of Polly Baker included in one of its versions likewise reflects Diderot's preoccupation with ensuring an amply adequate population.

The silence is the more striking since the adoption of birth-control markedly involved the new views of the natural which in other ways Diderot and his fellows were so original and forceful in expressing. What was required was a leap of imagination and belief greater than we may now appreciate, and in two respects. It had been reasonable enough to conclude, within the long-prevailing assumption that God controls all that happens in His world, that since intercourse does not always lead to pregnancy, God must have willed the conception when it does occur. It followed – and for some Christians to this day does follow – that contraception amounts to an immoral frustration of God's Will. The contrary view, now being carried into practice, rested on the novel belief that the ultimate cause of pregnancy is not super-natural but wholly within the natural realm. Secondly, what was equally involved was the assumption or the assertion that sexual satisfaction is legitimate and desirable even when conception is artificially prevented – the very claim which Diderot appeared to be supporting in his *Supplément*. Both Christians and non-Christians agreed that sexual desire is natural, obviously enough, but the traditionalists saw it as acceptable only or largely as a means to an end beyond itself. The orthodox view is well reflected in the older marriage service of the Church of England. The first of the three reasons for marriage which it gives is for 'the procreation of children'. And the second reason is 'for a remedy against sin, and to avoid fornication; that such persons *as have not the gift of continency* might marry, and keep themselves undefiled' (my italic). Illustrated here is a long-standing Christian attitude to sexual intercourse and enjoyment which the new contraceptive practices were – implicitly rather than consciously, in all probability – rejecting. To the contrary, they presupposed that sexual love is justifiable in itself and may help to unite still further the parents of the happy family.

If our reformers stay silent, they may be convicted of not following the 'logic' implied by their approval of the 'natural', but they were not necessarily misguided – since sexual passion can destroy as well as consolidate a marriage. Rather their silence suggests that, as in the case of the child in his natural state, they refrained from trusting the natural too far. The love-affair of Julie and Saint-Preux may anticipate the heady experiences of Romantic 'amour-passion', and Julie almost seems for her lover, if not for at least one modern reader, a prefiguration of the Romantic *femme fatale*. But Rousseau's heroine turns away and resists her natural inclinations, and the novelist clearly approves. Many of us now value and aspire to the ideal of the deeply-bonded family group which in France they were amongst the first to describe; perhaps we might do worse than to share their cautiousness as well as their hopes.

9

TOWN AND COUNTRY

'God made the country, and man made the town':

thus William Cowper in *The Task*. The contrast is an ancient one, at least as old as Virgil and Horace, and it forms an essential, persisting element in the long pastoral tradition of European thought and culture. Yet for most of its history it seems to have had the status of an agreeable convention and not of a deeply-felt opposition. That generalisation may vary in its validity from writer to writer or painter to painter over the ages, but the overall impression is that the countryside was prized in the main for the enjoyment of tranquil repose, to give a mere respite from the civilised pursuits of urban or courtly life and not to replace them. In chapter 2 we saw that the pastoral tradition was marked by Arcadian dreaming, with little wish or concern for a realistic portrayal of the rural world. Even in the late-seventeenth and early-eighteenth centuries the theories of Rapin and Fontenelle alike, as of others like Pope, were stressing the evocation of 'the Golden Age' or of an escapist existence of 'laziness and love'. Serious commitment, in most educated persons, had long remained firmly in favour of the cultured values and satisfactions of city and court. Attitudes to Paris as expressed in French poetry from the sixteenth to the late-eighteenth century offer one relevant illustration. Pierre Citron, in his book on *La Poésie de Paris*, observes that though there were comparatively few poems about the French capital (largely, one may think, because its attractions were taken for granted), such as there were saw it as a supreme centre of civilisation. A few reservations are made about noise and dirt and moral laxity, but above all it is 'the town of our Kings, the Queen of our towns', and for some observers even after

1750 it still survived as 'a charming abode', 'superb', 'enchanting', 'home of the pleasures and the arts' – so attractive,
declared Casanova, that no other city in the world could dispute
its title as 'la ville par excellence'.[1]

Gradually in the eighteenth century, however, the conventional, essentially playful juxtaposition of town and country
took on greater intensity. As regards literature, for example, the
contrast, instead of being a pleasing and inherited artifice,
assumed the role of a major theme, with deepened implications.
Once again, England was a little earlier than its neighbours –
especially than France, as is evident (say) from the earlier
chapters of Raymond Williams's thorough survey of the whole
subject for Britain in *The Country and the City*. The examples
included Thomson's *Seasons*; Shenstone's *The School Mistress*;
Warton's *The Enthusiast* (with the lines quoted earlier: 'Happy
the first of men, ere yet confined/To smoaky city'); and Gray's
Elegy with its injunction about the country-worker:

> Let not Ambition mock their useful toil,
> Their homely joys, and destiny obscure;
> Nor Grandeur hear with a disdainful smile,
> The short and simple annals of the poor.

Later instances in the century would be from Goldsmith in *The
Deserted Village*, Blake, Cowper, and – most angrily – Crabbe
in *The Village*, and by its end Williams finds a quite new theme
emerging – of nostalgia for a country world that is now in rapid
decline and doomed to be lost.

> Even now the devastation is begun [writes Goldsmith],
> And half the business of destruction done;
> Even now, methinks, as pondering here I stand,
> I see the rural virtues leave the land...

That mood of regret remained largely absent in later-
eighteenth-century France, it seems – and if so for at least one
obvious reason. France changed far more slowly in the direction
of urbanisation and urban industries; even by 1789 over
twenty-two million out of a total population of twenty-seven
million were still peasants – over 80%. All the same, the
changes were under way, even though far less obviously so than

in the home of the agrarian and industrial revolutions across the Channel, and in Europe as a whole the eighteenth century saw a marked growth in the number and size of cities. Georges Rudé gives some useful calculations: in 1700 there were only 13 or 14 European cities above 100,000, whilst by 1800 there were 22; in France in 1700 there were 4 cities above 50,000, whereas by 1789 there were 8, including Paris, which by then had a population of nearly 600,000 (London, by comparison, having nearly one million).[2]

There is another fact one should remember: namely, that what people thought of as a town or city was a much smaller community than we today have in mind. It is striking to note that at the very height of Ancient Greek civilisation the number of free citizens in Athens was only 20,000 and its total population, including slaves and outsiders, only about 100,000. That notion of town-size had been revised by the eighteenth century, but to a lesser extent than we may imagine. Rétif de la Bretonne wrote two novels – *Le Paysan perverti* and *La Paysanne pervertie* – with the sub-title 'ou les Dangers de la ville'. Whilst Paris is the major example described, so also – as the two characters first leave their village home – is the local town of Auxerre, still small today by our standards and much smaller in the 1770s and yet depicted by the novelist as typical of town squalor and vice.

As regards England, the intensified opposition of town and country during the eighteenth century, and notably the spread of urbanisation, have been interpreted as above all the outcome of developing capitalism – the thesis at the centre of Williams's study in particular. 'The division and opposition of city and country, industry and agriculture, in their modern forms, [he claims] are the critical culmination of the division and specialisation of labour which, though it did not begin from capitalism, was developed under it to an extraordinary and transforming degree.' It is beyond this chapter's scope to consider this case, presented in detail, as regards England. One may note the author's own admission that socialism and communism have continued and intensified 'some of the same fundamental processes' and feel with him that this presents 'a genuine historical and political difficulty' for his basic argument.[3] Nevertheless the question here is whether his explanation is applicable for France, whatever may be true for England. One may be doubtful. As regards industrial capitalism, first, its major impact would be in the nineteenth century. Certainly some limited industrialisation occurred during the eighteenth: in silk-manufacturing, mining and a few other ways. Moreover, historians – Hufton, for example – cite evidence of girls leaving their rural homes to find work in the towns (and being promptly seduced there – something that must surely have strengthened rural belief in town immorality), whilst Cobban argues that the 'peasant revolution' was fuelled above all by town depredations against the countryside, notably to cut down the forests.[4] Yet, compared with England, the experience in France was very localised. Agrarian capitalism, secondly, is the major villain for Williams, but here too the French lagged well behind in time. The whole movement of enclosures and the rise of the big country estate as a power-house of exploitation (on which he lays stress) came distinctly later in France, and ironically it did so as a result of the very Physiocratic economic theory that was aiming to *improve* the lot of the French peasant. Those in France like Rousseau and the Physiocrats who were already emphasising the virtues of the country and 'the good earth' in opposition to town ideas were precisely the people who pressed for larger estates, better management of them, improved agricultural policies – and in some part they did so because they believed that in England these novelties had led to greater general prosperity by contrast with French poverty and the small-scale cultivation that was helping to perpetuate it.

In short, the town–country juxtaposition appears to become more fully charged in eighteenth-century France – whatever is true of England and whatever would be true of nineteenth-century France itself – a little before capitalism in either its agrarian or its industrial forms was a really significant factor. Rather, the opposition was developed as yet another expression of the whole re-assessment of nature and the natural we are considering. And it is noteworthy that in France, as compared

with England at this period, it is only a minority that is relevant
– the same minority we have met in previous chapters.
Numerous others, albeit living in the same socio-economic
environment, remained largely indifferent to the contrast, at any
rate as more than a traditional convention.

To avoid misunderstanding, one should add a further point.
It does seem to be the case that the Physiocratic measures served
in the outcome somewhat to worsen the peasants' condition and
to give opportunities for capitalistic exploitation. Behrens, in
her book on *The Ancien Régime*, appears to sum up the matter
with both fairness and realism: 'The concern for the peasant
that developed in the second half of the eighteenth century was
a product both of humanitarianism and of a sense of the
expedient. The latter, however, [she dryly adds] seems to have
been the more powerful.'[5] That the latter would become more
powerful in terms of actual economic consequences seems
undeniable, but at the same time one may contend, first, that
the humanitarianism (and the image of the country that went
with it) came a little earlier than the 'sense of the expedient',
at least in anything worse than a benevolent form, and,
secondly, that it was others and not the minority itself who took
advantage of the would-be humanitarian reforms for their own
interests.

However that may be, we must now ask how the minority
re-interpreted the old comparison and gave to it a range of
richer implications. No doubt the country had always been
linked with the natural and the town with the civilised. Now,
however, the 'pastoral landscapes' were peopled less and less
by stylised shepherds and shepherdesses. Increasingly the aim
was for a more realistic depiction of the actual country-dwellers
– as we saw being urged in the new theories of pastoral poetry
from Saint-Lambert and Blair and as was already being illustrated in practice by Gray's weary ploughman and his kind.
Furthermore, in the process the country-dweller was conscripted
by our minority as a further 'image' of natural man, alongside
the savage, the child, and the new mother. For his admirers he
came to incarnate the new-found sense of a fundamental
harmony between nature and man. We looked earlier at the

various aspects of this harmony in regard to external nature; we must now do so in regard to the comparison between the human inhabitants of the town and those in the countryside.

Three contrasts may be quickly summarised for lack of space. The first is moral: whereas the town corrupts, country life preserves and encourages *virtue*. Secondly, and relatedly, rural life brings *happiness*, whereas the town brings misery and destroys tranquillity of spirit. Thirdly, the difference is *aesthetic*. The town (as Emile says of Paris in paying a relieved farewell to it in Book IV) is a city of 'noise, smoke and mud'; it is dirty, unhealthy, stinking. The country, by contrast, surrounds us with pure air and quietness and all the healing beauties of the natural scene. These oppositions were frequently emphasised, as could be illustrated at length. And there is more than that: alongside these well-recognised notions two further, inter-related juxtapositions call for comment. They concern work and economic theory.

As regards work, there is a contrast prior to the specific distinction that is relevant here. Work in the Book of Genesis is one further outcome of the Fall of man – 'the curse of Adam': 'In the sweat of thy face shalt thou eat bread, till thou return unto the ground' (3: 19). It is true that some Christians had long preached 'the work ethic', that work can have a certain nobility and moral value, and some individuals had often found pride and pleasure in elements of their labour. But what Morelly, Rousseau and other admirers of the natural claimed was that work need be neither a regrettable burden nor, alternatively, valuable only for our moral development but could become inwardly fulfilling to the human spirit. This changing notion of work offers, in fact, a further area of 'contrasts' that would illustrate our total subject no less than those chosen for study in this book, albeit fuller research is required. Existing studies such as David Meakin's *Man and Work* understandably tend to concentrate on nineteenth- and twentieth-century attitudes and the consequences of full industrialisation.[6] Yet a basic revaluation was under way before that – so that by the early-nineteenth century the old 'curse of Adam' resignation was being replaced by the view later captured, for example, in a hymn by Godfrey Thring, markedly at variance with the earlier views:

> Work is sweet, for God has blest
> Honest work with quiet rest.

Here, however, the more pertinent opposition is between rural and urban work. What is increasingly alleged is that work in the towns, and especially in its new industries, is dehumanising, is 'alienating' in the ways which Babeuf would soon explore, well before Marx. Work on the land, by comparison, can be deeply satisfying to the human spirit − a belief found in Morelly's *Code de la nature* (1755) and that persisted well into the nineteenth century, for example with utopians like the Saint-Simonian intellectuals who withdrew to Ménilmontant to dig and lay bricks from 5 a.m. each day and like other idealists who emigrated to North America to till usually unsuitable land they had bought unseen.[7] As for the later-eighteenth century, Rousseau yet again offers the best example − and notably in the wine-harvest scene in *La Nouvelle Héloïse* (v, 7). We see how contented the peasants are, and at the end of the day each goes to his bed 'happy after a day spent in work, gaiety and innocence and that he would not be sorry to begin again the next day, the day after that and for all his life'. Saint-Preux, in this letter, criticises exploitation of country-workers by avaricious owners, but without that, he claims, 'the work of the countryside is agreeable to contemplate'. It was man's original vocation, in the time of the 'patriarchs'; 'it recalls a pleasing notion to one's mind, and to one's heart all the charms of the Golden Age'. He can even add that when one observes the workers' 'joy' and the 'abundance' they produce in association with 'Providence', 'one would like oneself to put one's hand to the work and share in the rustic labour and the happiness one sees linked with it'.[8] (He does not actually do so, however.)

At the same time as such views of country work were being expressed in these idealising terms, they were also being elaborated in the language of economic theory by the Physiocrat group, notably from *L'Ami des Hommes* (1757) onwards, written by Mirabeau, father of the revolutionary, and in the work of Quesnay. One may perhaps doubt whether 'the French Physiocrats are at once the most exciting and the most contemporary group of economists in the whole history of economic thought' – as has been claimed during the recent renewal of academic interest in their ideas.[9] At the most one may note in regard to current revivals of 'laissez-faire' economics in some Western countries that the term itself was first coined by the most influential disciple of Physiocracy, Turgot. But the meaning he intended by it underlines the way in which its brief rise and influence illustrate our general subject. For him the injunction of 'laissez-faire' rested on the conviction that we should trust and follow the processes of 'nature'. The original claim was not that the forces of capitalism should have freedom to operate for the general good, whatever economic casualties might result on the way. Notwithstanding the actual historical outcome – and that was without doubt a dramatic consolidation of capitalism – the rise of 'laissez-faire' began from a trust in the beneficence of the laws of nature, not of man. One need be no economic historian to appreciate the consequent relevance here of Physiocracy's basic notions – of which a summary outline must suffice.

True economic value lies in cultivation of the earth; agriculture is the supreme form of work, not only because it provides for our primary need for food but also because it alone produces a 'disposable surplus', unlike commerce or manufacturing. The agriculturalists are thus termed by this theory 'the productive class', whereas all other workers are 'the sterile class' – the very distinction between rural and industrial work already referred to. Not that 'sterile work' is useless despite that adjective; it provides us with many goods that we wish to have. All the same, it is the level of *agricultural* production that mainly determines the general level of economic prosperity in a society. The greater the agricultural surplus, the better-off the society: from this principle there followed the detailed Physiocratic proposals that the French government, from 1761 on and especially under Turgot, put into practice. The creation of larger estates in place of countless small-holdings; better management

by active, instead of absentee, landlords; more investment in
new methods by the new class of 'fermiers'; the replacement
of obsolete and inhibitive forms of taxation by a single tax on
land rent; the rejection of existing Mercantilist institutions and
practices and the introduction of free trade in corn above all;
the encouragement of more scientific breeding of animals and
plants – drawing on those new ideas about reproduction and
inheritance which we noted in chapter 4 in regard to the Ruhe
family's six fingers: all these and other measures were designed
to make agriculture more productive and thereby to make more
prosperous the peasantry in particular and the whole population
as well. It did not turn out like that for the peasantry, as
mentioned earlier, and the impact of the Physiocrats was also
to be short-lived: in 1776 Turgot fell from power, and in the
same year Adam Smith, albeit influenced by Physiocracy, put
forward a different theory of economic value in his *Wealth of
Nations* that would further hasten its demise.

For a brief period, however, their well-intentioned views
expressed in the theoretical language of economics rested on
the same belief we have seen in earlier chapters in the reliability
of nature. The consequences are clear for them: the economic
primacy of country over town; the central role of the peasantry
– so that one of their most famous slogans read 'Poor Peasants,
Poor Kingdom'; the need, to cite one of their 'General Maxims
for the Economic Government of an Agricultural Kingdom',
to follow the 'general laws of the natural order'. And it is
noteworthy that if at bottom they believed nature to be good,
most of them did so because they believed it had been created
by God. Mirabeau, for example, was an opponent of the
atheistic 'philosophes' and, though critical of priests, a supporter
of religion. Quesnay too (of peasant stock, incidentally) saw his
task as to restore God's plan for man and nature, and one of
his first writings was an essay arguing belief in the immortality
of the soul. Trusting God, one can also trust nature – the word
'Physiocracy', coined a little late, in 1767, actually means the
'rule of nature'; one can 'laisser faire', confident in Him and
His world.

It is only a pity, one may think, that *human* nature turned out in some cases to be rather less trustworthy: in those who exploited the new measures in favour of large estates, or those like the Société Malisset who hoarded grain to force the prices up, for example. There was an undeniable gap between what the Physiocrats and their allies sincerely and seriously meant to ensure and what actually resulted from the combined consequences of their economic measures and the opportunism of others. Yet for a while their confidence in nature as economic agent was deeply-held and was shared by most of the enthusiasts for the natural who were concurrently praising country life and work. Diderot was a Physiocrat supporter. Rétif de la Bretonne quotes with approval the dying declaration of his father: 'The art that is most worthy of man is agriculture: all the others are reliant upon it.'[10] Bernardin de Saint-Pierre even argues that agriculture 'preserves manners and religion'. As for Rousseau, he may not have accepted all the Physiocratic ideas: one can note that his *Discours sur l'inégalité* blames agriculture as well as metal-working for producing societies and the deterioration that resulted. Yet he clearly shared their general sympathy for country attitudes, as we noted, and in more detailed ways also his standpoint is similar – as in the description in *La Nouvelle Héloïse* of Wolmar's model estate and his enlightened agricultural methods (v, 2) and, again, in a contrast he draws between the two sides of Lake Geneva (IV, 17). The land on the two shores is of equal quality, but one side, suffering from having an absentee owner, is a neglected semi-wilderness with only a few poverty-stricken peasants amidst 'a spectacle of misery'. The other side, which is well-managed, offers by contrast 'a delightful picture': 'the land, everywhere cultivated and everywhere fruitful, offers the assured fruit of their labours to the ploughman, the herdsman and the vine-grower'.[11]

This economic faith in the land contributes a final element to the composite contrast of country with town. To summarise, whilst the town is its antithesis in every respect, the country is the home of a life that is moral, happy, fulfilled and prosperous and that is lived amidst the beauties of nature and in harmony and collaboration with it. This idyllic concept has increasing attractions, it seems, for twentieth-century urban man, but it was the late-eighteenth-century adherents of nature who presented it for the first time in a detailed, appealing manner that was also far less playful than in the older pastoral tradition.

Numerous further examples could be given if space allowed, all of them reinforcing the ideal and the contrast. Rétif de la Bretonne's evocation of happy and prosperous peasant life on his natal farm in *La Vie de mon père* and *Monsieur Nicolas*; the equivalent picture in a tropical setting in the idyllic community of *Paul et Virginie*, so soon to be destroyed by civilised urban wickedness as seen in Virginie's aunt, the priest, the slave-owner and the governor; Delille's long poem hymning *L'Homme des Champs*, even claiming that love of countryside leads to love of virtue:

Qui fait aimer les champs fait aimer la vertu–

these are a few French instances of a European-wide comparison between what Goldsmith in his preface to *The Vicar of Wakefield* termed 'the simplicity of his country fire-side' and, by contrast, 'high life'. To stand for all the literary examples, one may quote, for the last time here, Goethe's *Werther*, praising the 'simple and innocent pleasure' of the peasant – 'whose table is covered with food of his own rearing, and who not only enjoys his meal, but remembers with delight the happy days and sunny mornings when he planted it, the soft evenings when he watered it and the pleasure he had in watching its daily growth'.[12] As to music, Rousseau's *Le Devin du village* provides one obvious example amongst others. The young lover Colin is briefly tempted by city glitter and courtly sophistication, but returns with happiness to his beloved Colette in their village:

Adieux, châteaux, grandeurs, richesse,
Votre éclat ne me tente plus...[13]

French painters offer fewer illustrations than such English contemporaries as Gainsborough, Stubbs, Constable and others. There are relatively few pictures comparable to (say) Stubbs's *Haymakers* and *Reapers*, or, as regards the French tradition, to the seventeenth-century depictions of humble life by Louis Le Naïn and by the engraver Jacques Callot. This may in part have followed from the restraints exerted by the establishment disdain in classicist France for landscape-painting as a whole; it may also reflect the wishes of their mainly court and town patrons. All the same there is more evidence than might at first appear that some artists at least felt a sincere appreciation of country life and people. It is noteworthy how often the moralising depictions of the good family life by Chardin and Greuze are within rural and village settings – as with *La Toilette matinale*, *Bénédicité*, *L'Accordée de village*, and others. Moreover, the former especially liked to paint such humble workers as *The Cook*, *The Cellar Boy*, *The Scullery Maid*, a *Woman Cleaning Turnips* or a *Woman Drawing Water from a Tank*. A comparably sympathetic realism is found in Fragonard also – such paintings of country figures as in *The Washerwoman*, *The Gardener* and *The Donkey's Stable* – truthful portrayals that are surely far less artificial than, earlier, Boucher's portrayal of *The Flower Gatherers*. It may also be, though more research seems needed for a reliable evaluation, that less 'official' artists were at work, perhaps away from the urban centres, and were giving a wider description of rural existence. Oudry's depiction of *La Ferme* and Louis Watteau de Lille's *Le Repas à la Ferme*, for example, suggest a transcending of the more idyllic treatment seen in (say) Boucher's *Landscape with Watermill*, *Evening Landscape*, *The Mill* and *The Bridge*.

Two unavoidable questions nevertheless remain in regard to the favourable evocations – by writers, painters and others – of rural as contrasted with urban life that have been surveyed. First, did its proponents believe it – or, more exactly, in what form did they believe it? Secondly, how deeply did they believe it?

As to the first of these questions, some scholars – mainly Marxist-inclined – have contended that the belief was at best skin-deep and at worst merely pretended for ulterior purposes. One firmly-argued example of this view is offered by John Barrell's book on late-eighteenth-century English landscape-painting, *The Dark Side of the Landscape*. Others would add that what he alleges of painters at one period in England is also far more widely applicable: his arguments may thus serve here to indicate a general analysis that cannot be ignored. Barrell's thesis – summarised and thus unavoidably simplified – is that the paintings of rural life by Gainsborough, Stubbs, Constable and even (though only sometimes and with mitigating merits) Morland were *concealing* as much as *revealing* the hard realities of the peasant's lot. There is certainly greater realism than in earlier 'ideal landscapes', he agrees, but the realism does not go too far; indeed the peasantry is often placed in the background or middle distance of the painting, so that the rustics are almost merged with their surroundings. Above all, he claims, these painters were offering to their upper-class clientele a re-assuring, even complacent picture of the peasants' condition – and also, by depicting them at work far more often than at leisure, were providing 'prescription' as much as description.[14] Barrell interestingly notes the frequency of the harvest as a feature of late-eighteenth-century paintings, but whereas some might interpret that as reflecting increasing awareness of nature's abundant fertility, for him the painters are taking the chance to depict with approval yet more back-breaking toil.

The question for us (as with Williams) is whether this argument, be it right or wrong for England, is applicable to France. It seems very likely that many of the upper classes were indeed re-assured by the literature, art and music that depicted the rural workers as prosperous and as enjoying their hard labours. That does not necessarily imply conscious or intended complacency on their part: we all have a marked ability unconsciously to ignore or over-look facts that are before our eyes. Some of the nobility, in Paris or at court, may thus genuinely have believed – as Louis XVI is said to have done – that the peasantry was happy. But, even if so, it still remains highly probable that the country idyll of Rousseau and his fellows did re-assure them in their gross mis-apprehension. Again, one should not assume that the ladies like Marie-Antoinette who played at being shepherdesses and milkmaids were insincere: what little evidence one has suggests she thoroughly enjoyed getting away from the court to her hamlet. Yet, all the same, her and many others' unawareness or neglect of peasant hardships may be due in part to the Rousseauist vision or may have been confirmed in their minds by it. To take a minor case, Rousseau's *Le Devin du village* had a considerable success at both the court and the Paris Opéra; it even made him as much money, he says, as *Emile*. To explain its popularity one may conjecture that his contemporaries appreciated the music itself more than we may. But it could also be that its presentation of village life was not unwelcome to the well-born audience; certainly their enjoyment was not disturbed by any jarring social criticism. In the rural world of this operetta work is going on, as well as love, the villagers wish to stay in the country, in their 'proper station', rejecting the false appeal of the town, and their life is presented as happy and even gay.

All the same, there is an obvious distinction to be made between how the audience was affected or chose to be affected and what was intended by the writer, painter or musician himself, and our questions are concerned with the latter and with 'how it seemed at the time' in *their* minds. On that, first of all, one can recall those declarations by theorists of pastoral poetry that were cited in chapter 2. The poet, said Saint-Lambert, should not depict 'unhappy peasants, who are interesting only for their misfortunes'; Blair, amongst others in Britain, likewise wished to have excluded 'mean, servile and laborious' shepherds and asked the poet to present 'the pastoral life somewhat embellished and beautified, at least seen on its fairest side only'. This may well seem to confirm an accusation of concealment instead of truthfulness. Yet the very fact that these poets inform their readers in advance of the 'embellishing' bias of their pastoral portrayals must surely destroy any notion that the concealment was intended for nefarious ends, and their very references to 'unhappy peasants' and 'mean, servile and laborious' shepherds surely shows they were not ignorant of rural hardships. (Some prints of peasant life show the same awareness.) What we have here, rather, is in the first place the constraint of an aesthetic tradition. These poets do want more realistic pastoral writing, related to the present, moreover, but they still feel the obligation that their poems should 'please'. In *Les Saisons* Saint-Lambert included *notes in prose* in which, for example, he influentially attacked slavery, but such radical comment was, significantly, excluded from the poetry itself. The prose literature of the period is filled with social and moral criticism, but then prose in France was free of inherited conventions and expectations whereas poetry or drama were still in the shadow of classicism.

That aesthetic argument may be valid for poets or painters, however, but cannot be utilised as regards 'prosateurs' like Rousseau, as just noted. An historian's examination has established that, at the date of Rousseau's comparison between the two shores of Lake Geneva, the side which he described as fertile was in reality as impoverished as the other bank.[15] Was Rousseau, then, deliberately falsifying facts he must have known, in outline at least, having himself lived in the area? Comparably, in *Emile* he declares that 'the peasants are boorish, coarse and blundering', and in his *Contrat social* he says of 'le peuple' as a whole that they 'cannot even bear that one should do anything about their ills in order to remedy them, like those stupid and frightened sick persons who tremble at the sight of the doctor'. Some may say that these are moments of indiscreet candour in which Rousseau gives his 'true', underlying view that the peasantry is stupid and that one may thus conclude that his depiction of peasant goodness and happiness amounted to wilful deception.

Such a conclusion seems in all probability to be largely mistaken. First, to read the relevant passages of Rousseau, Rétif de la Bretonne and others or to look at the paintings of Chardin, Oudry or even Fragonard is to be persuaded, from the very quality and detail of their works, that they were deeply sincere and serious. They were convinced, or thought they were convinced,[16] that the country was far preferable to the town in all the ways earlier referred to. – Or, rather, with the majority of them, that the country was *potentially* far preferable. For, secondly, their evocations of the country were presenting neither a picture of some Arcadian and now irretrievable *past* nor a realistic description of the actual, inadequate *present*, but a propaganda sketch or even vision of some *future* possibility. Their slogan, one may submit, was not 'back to nature as it *was*' or, even, 'as it *is*' but 'forward to nature as it *could be*'. In some respects they clearly found 'nature as it is' to be already preferable to the urban environment, but in their minds the country's full potentialities for virtue and happiness remained to be realised in the future as much as did the prosperity to be achieved through agricultural reforms of the Physiocratic kind. It would be obviously wrong to interpret (say) Wolmar's letter describing those reforms as aiming to present the normal *realities* of 1761. Only within the previous ten years in France had the first advocacy of Physiocratic methods begun: the *Encyclopédie* article of 1751 on 'Agriculture'; Mirabeau's *L'Ami des Hommes*; the starting in Brittany in 1757 of the very first of what would be many agricultural societies; government measures in 1761 itself; and so on. This letter was a part of the wider campaign, evoking what could and should be done in the future, and it may well be claimed that the same interpretation applies to substantial parts of the whole country 'image'. What we have is vision added to and even transcending reality.

Our first question may thus be answered by submitting that its proponents did indeed believe in it but that they did so only partially as representing present truth; their full conviction lay in the hope that it could become a future reality.[17] The second question thus remains applicable: it concerns how *deeply* they believed in the country image, but to this the answer seems more double-sided.

In the first place, their view of the town or city was not quite as condemnatory as they commonly implied. One may see this by looking at their reactions to Paris in particular, and Rousseau is the first obvious instance to take. His first visit was in 1731; despite his prior dreams of splendid avenues and palaces, he found 'dirty, stinking little streets, wretched, blackened houses, an atmosphere of filth, poverty and beggars'. Yet his second visit in 1742 revealed a more brilliant side to Paris life, and his reaction then has been summed up by one scholar as 'very ambivalent, a powerful aversion finally overcoming his initial fascination'.[18] That was in real life; by contrast, such writings for moral and social purposes as *Emile* and *La Nouvelle Héloïse* (II, 14–21) describe Paris in most unfavourable ways. It is 'this vast desert', with 'the most deplorable misery', alongside 'the most sumptuous opulence'; it provides an outstanding example of outward appearance at odds with inner truth: such are some of Saint-Preux's impressions. 'Towns are the abyss of the human race': thus Book I of *Emile*, and the young man's own farewell to Paris is to the city of 'noise, smoke and mud, where women no longer believe in honour nor men in virtue'. And yet, notwithstanding such condemnations, Rousseau chose to reside in Paris for the last seven years or so of his life and even before that he had conceded its attractions, notably and perhaps significantly in his still unpublished *Confessions* as opposed to his propaganda works. If any love for manners and morals exists in Europe (Book XI can even claim), it is found in Paris – and it is also noteworthy that Emile's education is not felt to be complete without a visit to develop his good taste, even though he dislikes the city, as we have seen.

Comparable examples of ambiguity about the city are found in other admirers of nature and the country life. Rétif de la Bretonne's hero Edmond, in *Le Paysan perverti*, finds it dirty and corrupt but comes, as did Rétif himself, to enjoy its freedom and to cherish it. Elsewhere Paris is described as 'the home at one and the same time of delights and horrors', is 'the refuge of Reason, of true Philosophy and of Manners, as well as the home-land of Taste and of the Arts'. And Rétif's father, in *La Vie de mon père*, is quoted as adding his approval of it as 'the refuge of all the oppressed and the consolation of the human race' – praise which Edmond reiterates in hymning 'this delightful home of liberty'.[19]

Sébastien Mercier likewise presents a two-sided view in his *Tableau de Paris* (in twelve volumes, 1782–8): Paris is 'a monstrosity and a wonder'. He is above all critical and thinks it 'almost impossible to be happy in Paris'; the preface to the whole work ends with the advice to flee from the city. And yet one part of him is clearly attracted – by its 'unlimited greatness', its 'monstrous wealth', its 'scandalous luxury'. His reactions, although expressed in a critical tone, arrive at a balance-sheet that reveals that not all is bad: 'I have more often met...hideous poverty than honest affluence, and sorrow and anxiety more than joy and gaiety.'[20]

Bernardin de Saint-Pierre's *Etudes de la nature* gives another instance in the chapter on Paris. He declares that its 'pleasures' rest on 'the poverty of its people'; the frivolity and decline of Venice show the way Paris too might go. He wishes to have only one city in all of France and for the provinces to contain only hamlets and villages. Yet, despite this, he too lived in Paris during the period Rousseau was there – and was one of his very few faithful friends – and in his chapter Saint-Pierre praises Paris for the freedom it gives to live there 'obscure and free', 'poor without being scorned': it is 'the shelter and the refuge of the wretched'. He even declares: 'I love Paris; after the countryside – of the kind which I like – I prefer Paris to everything that I have observed in the world.'[21]

Other illustrations could be cited, but these may suffice to establish that for these admirers of nature the city both repels and attracts. This is not surprising: many of us, reared in the *British* provinces, still have a love–hate relationship with London. What is more interesting to consider is the tension that underlies or that explains their ambivalence and perhaps ours. That tension is surely between the attractions of nature – which from the eighteenth century onwards have become increasingly appealing – and, on the other hand, the attractions of civilisation and culture. We have met this tension and the resultant division of mind in some previous chapters. Diderot and others admire aspects of 'the noble savage', but they also admire reason and science and the values of the Enlightenment. Rousseau and others think the child is innocent and even good – but one had better make certain by giving it a thorough education and instilling sound religious and moral views. The 'natural woman' is the fountain of love and care and of good ethical training for her children – but she needs to be correctly educated (like Rousseau's Sophie and Diderot's actual daughter) in order to ensure that she becomes a devoted wife and mother, and she also needs to be under the final control of her wiser husband.

What of the peasant? In theory he is good and happy by virtue of living amidst nature and following country ways, but in practice one discovers a second respect in which ambivalence is expressed, alongside the mixed response to the city we have just noticed. Like the noble savage, the child and the woman, the peasant too is one of 'nature's children' and requires guidance and supervision. He does not greatly need education, and Rousseau notoriously claims in *Emile* that 'the poor child has no need of education'. His explicit justification for this would be that the poor child is not in danger of corruption by the values of upper-class parents, by the 'civilised' notions against which the tutor has to protect poor little rich Emile. It may be (as some scholars have argued)[22] that Rousseau was an unconscious snob, or again one could think that this view shows he disliked the peasantry and that it was wrong earlier in this chapter to dismiss that charge as largely unjustified. In all likelihood, however, what really explains his attitude lies elsewhere – lies in what seems to be undeniable: that the country vision he and others were presenting was basically *paternalistic*. Greuze's peasant families need to go to church, to pray, to acquire good moral values, and so also do most of the peasants evoked by other enthusiasts of the time. Moreover – and above all – they need wise guidance from their betters. Rousseau's *La Nouvelle Héloïse* gives ample evidence of this attitude. There is no doubt that Wolmar and Julie control the model estate, and in that idyllic wine-harvest scene there is a very revealing incident. One of the happy peasants gets drunk; nothing is said at the time, amidst the general merriment, but Rousseau tells us (with obvious approval and no awareness of what he is exposing) that the next morning the miscreant was dismissed from the estate, 'sans rémission'. The paternalism is made quite explicit in wider ways also. Julie's chief maxim, we learn, is 'in no way to favour changes in social station but to work towards making everyone happy in his existing station'. If everyone's talents were to be developed, furthermore, there would no longer be enough workers to till the land and to grow our food. Nor would they be as happy if they were educated: 'Those who are destined to live in a state of rural simplicity have no need, in order to be happy, that their faculties should be developed.' The injunction that follows is evident: 'Do not educate the child of a villager, for it is not advisable for him to be educated.'[23]

Comparably, the idyllic world of Rétif de la Bretonne's upbringing rests upon the wise leadership of his father, maintaining the old values, reading each evening to his numerous children some improving passages from Holy Scripture, keeping a clear eye on the workers at his farm. Emmanuel Le Roy Ladurie, in his chapters in Duby's *Histoire de la France rurale*, makes especial use of Rétif's work and illustrates from it a range of contemporary attitudes. What he finds — and what Rétif evokes with apparent approval — is above all a world of duties and controls. There is the mother, preoccupied and exhausted in providing food. ('The duties of the mother of a family are crushing; they are summed up in a single word: food.') There is the new bride, now dressed in black — a dress she will retain until she or her husband dies — and who will never dance again. There is the strict regulation of domestic responsibilities as between dealing with the animals or with their 'products' or with vines and corn. Above all there is what Ladurie calls 'the model of the authoritarian father, a patriarch hard to his sons and even more to his daughters'.[24] In this instance the control comes from within the rural society itself — a contrast with Rousseau's fictional estate where Wolmar and his wife come from outside in a social sense. In both cases, however, the ideal finally rests upon paternalism.

There is no adequate ground for alleging — this chapter has submitted — that Rousseau and his fellow-campaigners were other than entirely sincere in elevating the country-dweller as a further embodiment of 'the natural human', alongside savage, child and woman, or that their whole pastoral vision was other than a deeply-held ideal. It may certainly be true that their idealisation was a privilege in which they could indulge only because they themselves were outside the harsher travails of rural existence: one need only turn to the popular literature of the day, sold by hawkers around the countryside, as studied by Robert Mandrou, Geneviève Bollème and others, in order to discern the differences between its representations of the countryside and theirs.[25] Yet that need only make one cautious, and not dismissive, of their pastoral 'image of the natural'. None the less, the conclusion one can hardly avoid is that they did not take their trust in the natural too far. The peasant is innocent rather than positively reliable or good; he requires, almost day by day, the benevolent direction of cultivated enlightenment. If the contrast of town and country mirrors the tension between civilisation and nature, what is believed in the last resort is that, for all the merits of the natural and rural, civilised persons like Rousseau and his Julie had better keep a firm, albeit naturally well-intentioned, upper hand.

UNFINISHED BUSINESS

In this limited, compressed survey of a vast subject much has had to be neglected or mentioned too rapidly. Even though the preceding chapters may be thought to have ranged over-widely, numerous other culturally indicative areas could have been considered. 'The mere smell of cooking can evoke a whole civilisation': thus Fernand Braudel in a splendid sentence – which other historians of mentalities also have helped to justify as well as he.[1] Food will remain unconsidered here except, shortly, in relation to vegetarian campaigning, but a few different subjects call for mention even at this late stage – and not least to confirm how extensive and detailed were the reverberations of change.

Perhaps the salient omission has been in relation to a third distinctive part of the natural world, alongside its external scenes and human beings: the realm of the animals. We did note that the pastoral landscape was commonly completed by the presence of not only good peasants but also contented domestic animals like cows, sheep and horses, serving in poems and paintings alike as supplementary 'carriers' of the pastoral message. Again, we saw the growing use at this time (albeit more frequently in England than in France perhaps) of poetic apostrophes to nature, usually addressed to birds such as sky-larks and cuckoos, and also that the angelic children in Greuze's paintings often manifest their sensibility by grieving over a dead bird or cuddling a lamb, much as Paul and Virginie too love their dog. Yet again we found the sense of 'wild sublimity' being represented or reinforced by such wilder animals as Blake's tiger, Stubbs's lions and David's rearing charger, spurred up the high mountain pass by an inspired leader in the guise of Napoleon, in a triple assertion of the mood. These and other instances certainly reflect the way in which the new-found sympathy for nature was extended to animals, but over and beyond their adoption in such ways there lies a distinctive and important theme in intellectual and cultural history. Yet its absence so far is not only for reasons of space: here again France was for the most part distinctly later than some other countries in embracing the new attitudes. Whereas Keith Thomas writing of England prior to 1800 has provided a major study of the theme, rich in evidence, even he might have found it difficult with the French. Further research might show the contrary, but what remains the fullest survey, Hester Hastings's *Man and Beast in French Thought of the Eighteenth Century* of 1936, is not encouraging – and as regards the previous century, George Boas's work on 'the happy beast' reveals how much that theme was merely an inherited convention in French thought.[2]

All the same, what little can be said here (to avoid a total blank within the broader picture) suggests that the limited evidence comes mainly from precisely the same writers and others we have met in earlier chapters. Thus, those whom Hastings lists as unusually sympathetic to animals at this time include Rousseau, Bernardin de Saint-Pierre, Saint-Lambert, Delille, Rétif de la Bretonne, Mercier, Roucher, author of *Les Mois* and pioneer in appreciation of mountain landscapes, and Beaurieu, author of *L'Elève de la nature*, written in praise of natural man. 'The definite change in man's attitude toward animals comes in the eighteenth century', she claims,[3] and it is they above all whom she cites in justification.

They were not the first to take a kindlier view; they had been long anticipated, for instance, by Montaigne in his essay 'De la cruauté' and by La Fontaine. None the less, Hastings concludes that even in the first half of the eighteenth century pity for animals was 'striking' by its 'absence', apart from a few exceptions like the Abbé Pluche in his *Spectacle de la nature*. In Britain by that date – to draw the contrast – it was widespread, and Thomas finds vegetarian moral views being expressed as early as the mid-seventeenth century.[4]

Gradually, however, from around 1750, change is found in

France as well, albeit still minimal and sporadic, and – most relevantly here – it reveals clear parallels with what has been found in relation to other aspects of our subject. The reaction was, underlyingly, against traditional church beliefs (albeit many individual Christians had held kindlier views)[5]: in the 'dominion' given by God to man over fish, fowl and every living thing (Genesis 1:28) and in the permission given in His blessing of Noah: 'the fear of you and the dread of you shall be upon every beast of the earth...Every moving thing that liveth shall be meat for you' (Genesis 9:2–3). But, even more, by the mid-eighteenth century the reaction was against the mechanistic assertion of Descartes and his followers that animals are unfeeling automata. Throughout the later-eighteenth-century years there was a running debate centred on whether and in what way, as against that view, animals may have souls. Voltaire, d'Alembert, Grimm and even Réaumur remain uncertain but seem sceptical, albeit not approving of cruelty. Buffon moves away from the old theory more emphatically, and the major studies he wrote, in collaboration with such helpers as Montbéliard, on animals and birds, spread appreciation, as did their splendid colour-plates. Yet despite his undoubted sympathies and their influence on others he remained theoretically cautious (as on certain scientific issues, we saw): animals are largely machines, albeit with some capacity for feeling, though not for thought. By comparison, contemporaries like Maupertuis, Condillac, Charles Bonnet and the Physiocrat Quesnay were now claiming that animals do possess souls of a kind, although only Bonnet thought them capable of immortality.

Feeling for animals by the later-eighteenth century was certainly not confined to such somewhat doctrinal arguments. Increasingly, it was contended that animals are not only useful to man but possess a beauty which – just like that of external landscapes – illustrates the goodness of the Creator. Some – above all Bonnet – added that animals also have moral qualities we should admire. Devotion to man is shown by the horse and the dog – in *Paul et Virginie* actually named Fidèle, 'faithful' like our own English Fido. The lion illustrates the virtues of nobility, magnanimity and bravery – more so than the tiger which (analogously with the Maori or Hawaiian savages) apparently had a more equivocal reputation. The donkey reveals the qualities of patience, humility and sobriety, and indeed there was an especial 'rehabilitation' of the ass, led by Pluche and Buffon (and which is perhaps reflected also in Fragonard's sympathetic portrayal in *The Donkey's Stable*). It was Buffon again who stressed the mutual attraction between a man and his horse or his dog, and Saint-Lambert likewise evoked the love and confidence between man and birds. The animals owned by Rétif de la Bretonne's father readily respond, similarly, to his kindness to them; one of his dogs even pines with guilt after mistakenly attacking his master. In every case one is observing expressions of a sense of harmony between man and animal that is co-extensive with the sense of harmony with external nature.

From such heightened appreciations there followed the beginnings of unambiguous campaigning against cruelty to animals. Grimm and Maupertuis were early in protesting against it, and somewhat later Mercier attacked their undue confinement in the over-crowded conditions of Paris. Bernardin de Saint-Pierre argued in his first *Etude* that animals should be allowed to live freely where nature has placed them, and in the tenth *Etude* he opposed vivisection. Hunting too was criticised, notably by Delille in *L'Homme des champs* – though that is by 1800, and Hastings finds very few other objections to it – perhaps comprehensibly in a far more agrarian economy than England's.[6] There was even a didactic campaign against animal abuse in the new books written specifically for children – in Mme de Genlis's *Adèle et Théodore* (1782), for example – even though less so than in comparable English books.

In particular one finds the first stirrings of vegetarian conviction. Rousseau was a leading advocate. A note to his *Discours sur l'inégalité* remarks that man has teeth and intestines appropriate for a vegetable diet and alleges that if primitive men had not departed from it, they could more easily have remained in their original peaceable 'state of nature'. Book II of *Emile* re-asserted his position. 'One of the proofs that the taste of meat is not natural to man is the indifference which children feel towards it' and their preference for such foods as milk products and fruit. Moreover, cruelty to animals leads on to cruelty to one's fellow-men: 'Great meat-eaters are in general more cruel and fierce than other men' (well-illustrated by the English, he adds).[7] His Julie is hardly less convinced. Although she greatly enjoys her meals, 'she likes neither meat nor stews'; 'excellent vegetables, eggs, cream, and fruits were her normal food'.[8] She does much appreciate fish – a predilection which Rousseau observes prevents her from being a full disciple of Pythagoras – but even there her attitude is kindly: we read of an incident where she tells her children to put back the fishes they have caught. Those wishing to defend her might also note that the distinction between fish and meat remains with some vegetarians to this day – and certainly it is found again in Saint-Pierre's small community, which also eats fish but not meat.

Nevertheless, only a few in France seem to have been converted – and one should also recall that in any case the majority lived on vegetable foods out of economic necessity. Buffon and Helvétius, for example, were even openly critical, Saint-Pierre himself was a vegetarian for some years, as were Roucher and – to judge from his *Malheur et pitié* (1801) – Delille. Yet Hastings concludes that Jean Antoine Gleizes, the major vegetarian campaigner of the day in her view, significantly won more responsiveness in England and Germany than in France. She acknowledges too that 'the eighteenth century discovered animals too late to celebrate them in *belles lettres*' and that it was only in the following century that 'animal literature becomes an important genre in France'.[9] It may be that some of the less vocal amongst the better-off were ahead of the writers and artists – hungry as ever for a 'square meal' – but, pending a French Keith Thomas, the 'time-lag' behind England is suggested even by the dates at which official movements in favour of animals were started. The first English law to prevent cruelty was the Martin Act of 1822, and the R.S.P.C.A. was founded in 1824; in France the first comparable event was the Loi Grammont of 1850.

It is not only such new attitudes to animals that show similarities with what has been described in previous chapters; so too do shifting views on a variety of other subjects. Some of these have already been referred to in passing: for example, explanations of mental abnormality and, consequentially, different treatments for it; notions about work and the contrast between its rural and urban forms; preferences in dress fashions, moving from Mme de Pompadour's ornate extravagances to Mme Récamier's neo-Grecian simplicity; theories about the causes of the plague. Yet further areas of evidence would warrant examination, as a few instances may briefly suggest.

The problems posed by death and destruction in the natural order were also provoked by the occurrence of gross abnormalities, 'freaks of nature', amongst plants, animals and, above all, humans. The existence of these 'monstres', in the French term, was diversely accounted for. Many had earlier held that the Devil was responsible for them, but even orthodox Christians, if they rejected that, felt some concern about this apparent illustration of the so-called 'problem of evil'. This was especially the case where they held the preformationist theory, as sketched in chapter 4: if God pre-forms all that exists, He must surely be responsible for such 'monstres'. Some – Boyle, Malebranche, Leibniz, for instance – thought that they are the result of 'accidents' permitted by God, but that still leaves the question of why He should allow the 'accidents' to happen. Others argued, as had Montaigne (II, 30) over a century before, that 'monstres' are not really so in the eyes of God but are merely thought so by foolish mankind. Some even went onto the offensive and praised them as marvels, as when a distinguished scientist Duverney commented upon Siamese twins born in Vitry in 1706: 'the inspection of this Monster reveals the richness of the Creator's mechanical skills'.[10] Others again, however, thought that one could only absolve God in a different way: by abandoning the idea of preformation, of nature as passive, and in effect blaming a nature which was now to be thought of as active. The problem of 'monstres' was thus, almost adroitly, transferred to those who alleged the beneficence of nature – exactly as with the phenomena of death and destruction. In the case of Diderot in particular it would become a source of embarrassment and uncertainty; the existence of such 'moral' monsters as sadists may be blamed on social conditioning, but otherwise (as a specific study of this theme in his thought concludes) 'the issue of monsters reveals the vulnerable side to his materialism' and accounts for a continuing 'paradox' in his system.[11]

Another quite different area of illustration is found in the history of architecture. This has been mentioned previously only at the domestic level – in relation to the new family concept (and the corridor and bedroom door) or as regards occasional buildings like the artificial 'hamlets' at Chantilly and Versailles. Yet the new appreciations of the Gothic, from the 1740s in England, derived from claims that its style was more 'natural' than the Classical and that a Gothic interior is the equivalent of an external landscape or informal garden. Gothic architecture (as Lovejoy argued in a classic essay years ago) was felt to be 'characterised by a kind of wildness and irregularity'.[12] His argument demands development as regards France, but one is not surprised, at a later date, to read Sébastien Mercier's appreciation of Notre-Dame de Paris or to find Bernardin de Saint-Pierre praising the Gothic in his *Harmonies de la nature* by invoking an analogy with a forest of tropical palms: 'the lofty arches foreshadowed, like the tops of palm-trees, an airy and celestial prospect that fills us with a religious sentiment'.

Music (to allude to a final example) has been as rarely cited here as architecture, excepting only for references to one of its more minor compositions, Rousseau's *Le Devin du village*. Yet surrounding even that slight pastoral operetta there was a highly significant controversy, the 'querelle des Bouffons', between supporters of French and of Italian opera, of Rameau and of 'opera buffa' like Pergolesi's *La Serva padrona*.[13] Rousseau's own *Lettre sur la musique française*, published in 1753 but probably written by October 1752, the very month in which *Le Devin* was first performed at Fontainebleau, did much to provoke the ensuing debate, and it centred on the notion, precisely, of 'natural music'. For Rameau, in such theoretical works as his *Traité de l'harmonie* (1722) and *Nouveau système de*

musique théorique (1726), music is certainly based on 'nature' –
but interpreted as the 'nature' revealed by mathematics. Music
is founded on the timeless realities of numbers, and harmony
is its fundamental element. He even claimed that primitive man
had derived mathematics *from* music and tried hard to persuade
the Académie des Sciences to accept music as 'a physico-
mathematical science' (and himself to its membership), though
without success. Rousseau, already a teacher of music and
composer of *Les Muses galantes* (1747), came to admire Italian
music during a period in Venice, working at the French
Embassy; after his 'conversion' to the values of 'the natural'
and his first expression of it in the *Discours sur les sciences et les
arts* (1750), he would next apply those values in defence of the
Italian style of opera. He too wants music to be 'natural', but
against Rameau's stress on mathematics and harmony, he
contends that it is melody which is fundamental and that
melodies are explicable as the products of varying climates,
conditions and above all languages – that is, as consequences
of the realities of human living as opposed to mathematical
abstractions. The Italian language is favourable to melody,
whereas French is not, and hence French music is only a kind
of 'modulated plain-chant', driven to substitute for pleasing
melodies 'artificial and unnatural beauties', to over-burden
itself with 'modulations that are frequent and regular but cold
and graceless'.[14] His fiery brochure, which provoked numerous
replies, including Rameau's own *Observations* (1754), reflects his
commitment to other notions of the natural as well, as does *Le
Devin* itself – notions that would be re-asserted later, notably
in *La Nouvelle Héloïse* in letters stressing melody and criticising
the Paris opera. But behind them all – the relevant point for
us – there lies an outlook that is opposed to the more theoretical
sciences and that is formed by concern for 'the living', even
by insights (it has been argued) drawn from the developing life
sciences themselves.[15] And certainly it seems more than
coincidence that in the 'querelle' itself it was Rameau who was
supported by defenders of the older scientific attitudes –
d'Alembert and Voltaire, for example – and Rousseau by such
proponents of the later, more 'organic' or 'organicist' approach

as Diderot. Yet this was only an incident in a continuing debate about the 'natural' in music. It is a nice irony to find Gluck, some twenty years later, both criticising *Italian* opera and also praising *Le Devin* in his *Lettre-dédicace d'Orphée* (1774): 'I saw with satisfaction that the accent of nature is the universal language.'

The instances outlined in this chapter so far could undoubtedly sustain further research – which might modify or overturn the interpretations just proposed. They all represent 'unfinished business' from the viewpoint of this book's general subject. Yet they are relatively specific, encouragingly so; and the same would be true of the detailed studies that are needed of the more neglected individual writers, painters and others whom we have encountered, and of their role and place within the broader movement. This would certainly not be the case, however, with much vaster areas that remain to be noticed.

The centre of attention has been France. Only occasional references have been made to other countries, especially to England and Germany, partly in order to illustrate that French developments were only one national instance of a much wider European phenomenon and partly for comparative reasons to which we shall return. Shortcomings in those references no doubt exist; they are due above all to authorial ignorance of the relevant primary sources, and yet also, to some extent, to what seems to be an absence of general studies of the subject in regard to those other countries. Some mostly very recent works have helped to remedy that as regards England in particular; though their authors would be the first to stress their intended delimitations, the amply-researched books from such scholars as McManners, Stone and Thomas (to name only British examples) illuminatingly over-flow their specific themes. Yet, as they might well agree, much remains to be examined on the general subject of this present book, and that seems even truer – failing further authorial ignorance – of Germany and Italy, amongst other countries. To give a specific instance, are the paintings of wild nature, referred to earlier, by Salvator Rosa and by Zuccarelli and Diziani later no more than surprising exceptions, or were they created within the context of a more widespread sympathy for 'the sublime'? Scotland and Switzerland in particular appear to have received less attention than they demand, and especially if Van Tieghem was correct in contending that they were amongst the first of the European countries to move towards the new perceptions and attitudes.[16] Were Haller, Saussure and other Swiss just isolated figures, or were they the best-remembered examples of broader cultural transitions, and what was the situation within Scotland of such as Allan Ramsey earlier and Macpherson later in the century? In both instances it seems difficult, *a priori*, to believe they were lone eccentrics and to a limited extent we know that they were not. We know, for example, of the eighteenth-century 'discovery' of the appeal of the Highlands and the resulting rise in tourism – but much else remains for investigation. Both countries offer, moreover, cultural situations of an unusual kind, for in the eighteenth century both were fairly sharply divided in two major ways: between Catholic and Protestant and between (in the case of Switzerland) French- and German-speaking cultures and (in the case of Scotland) Lowland and Highland cultures. The distinctions and contrasts that might be revealed could well prove decidedly informative, not least for those seeking the factors behind cultural relativities.

And of all the countries where such examination seems required the outstanding case concerns the Low Countries in the seventeenth century – almost wholly omitted in earlier chapters, and by intention until this point in the argument. The reasons behind its especial relevance must be outlined. Again and again we have noticed 'time-gaps' as between England earlier and Germany not far behind and, by contrast, the distinctly later dates in France at which the evidences of change were manifest, and this has appeared to be the case in regard to almost every 'cultural indicator' – from the liking for informal landscapes and gardens and for mountains and the sea to better treatment of children and the rejection of arranged marriages. Only in the distinctly international realms of science and exploration does the generalisation appear to be belied. If we are ever to discern more clearly the causes behind cultural change, a promising starting-point may well lie in the practice of what could be termed '*comparative* cultural studies' – studies, that is to say, which contrast the emergence of similar cultural phenomena in one country as compared with another, each with their different social, economic, religious, intellectual and other environments. It may be here that attention to 'time-gaps' could lead to useful discriminations. If so, then as concerns the present subject we are in need – or some of us are, at any rate – of much greater knowledge about seventeenth-century Dutch literature, thought and general culture as well as about its art. The new attitudes to children have been found by Stone and others in Dutch as well as English settlers in North America, but far more arresting is the evidence of Dutch painting. It repeatedly suggests the prevalence of several of the novel appreciations we have studied – amongst many ordinary citizens, moreover – at a date that is, to generalise, decades ahead of England and well over a century ahead of France.

Quite early in the seventeenth century Dutch art was already depicting the everyday and commonplace. In a Protestant land, with undecorated churches, religious subjects were little in demand, whereas, to a quite unusual extent, the owners of ordinary homesteads wished paintings for their walls. The outcome in the first place was, in one scholar's words, 'an unprecedented humanization of art', manifested in the desire for themes related to the lives and environment of the majority.[17] Examples are numerous: representations of humble family existence, as from Rembrandt, Pieter de Hooch, Vermeer and others including, in Flemish art, Rubens; scenes of peasant life, as from Brouwer and Hobbema in particular; more specifically, sympathetic portrayals of the child, as from Rembrandt and Franz Hals especially. Even animals – domestic and wild alike – are not neglected, as evidenced by works from Rembrandt, Van de Velde and Paulus Potter, to which Rubens's *Lion Hunt* should be added. And there was distinctly more than that, for, secondly, there was a flowering of landscape-painting of a diversity that France, certainly, would not know until very much later. Here the Flemish landscapists had priority, but already by 1610 to 1620 landscapes – and seascapes too – were being painted in Haarlem. Over the century the genre thrived, as witness, most notably, Salomon van Ruysdael, Jan van Goyen, and above all Jacob van Ruisdael. It was the last-named especially, and Everdingen also, who took as subjects not only domesticated landscapes but also scenes of 'wild sublimity' – forests, steep mountain-sides, rushing torrents – and nor was the stormy sea ignored by him, or by a less-remembered artist like Jan Porcellis in his *Stormy Sea*. Other aspects of apparently more alien nature were depicted as well, and with a sense of human affinity being conveyed: night-time, particularly in the nocturnal scenes from Aert van der Neer; and, supremely, winter, as rendered with such enjoyment by Hobbema, albeit the range of mood in Dutch winter paintings, one authority concludes, 'extends from serenity to gloom'.[18] Nor was 'exotic' nature entirely absent: one finds not only paintings of Tyrolean, Scandinavian, Italian and other European scenes but even the Brazilian landscapes of Franz Post.

Such a list and all it suggests – not least since the artists were working for so much broader a clientele than elsewhere – leaves one with a salient question, for it implies a 'time-gap' in the diffusion of new attitudes on most aspects of our subject that seems far beyond discussion.

If the enquiry could well be extended in space, to other countries, it could no less be extended in time. The theme of nature in seventeenth- and earlier-eighteenth-century French thought and culture has been treated in various studies that are noted in the bibliographies, but to look forward to the nineteenth century and beyond would be even more pertinent. In particular two separate and contrasting facts about the nineteenth-century scene impose themselves.

First, the Romantics, in literature, art and other forms, greatly expanded the currency of the new notions – to the point where they have sometimes been credited with originating them – and thereafter others too developed them. One of the earliest, Chateaubriand, has been quoted previously on certain themes, and he is rightly regarded as a leading figure, in this as in other respects. Even so short a text as *Atala*, written in the eighteenth

century's final years, illustrates his high relevance. It evokes
external nature, both Edenic and wild, stresses our human
affinities with it, and expresses (as at greater length in *Le Génie
du christianisme*) the religious trust which appreciation of its
beauties reinforced in him. Furthermore, the story was originally
planned as part of an 'epic of natural man', and here too it
reiterated his predecessors' views by its praise of the simple life
led by 'le père Aubry' (and, in *René*, by the Ossianic bard) and
by the savages (within whose huts the author claimed to have
first drafted it), of what in *René* he would call 'the innocence
of country manners'. And indeed he also resembles the
eighteenth-century innovators even in his admixture of caution
about following the natural to the extreme and in his emphasis,
not least as a Catholic, upon the over-riding claims of religious
truth. Lamartine, Hugo and others clearly followed, be it in
their portrayals of child and family life or of rustic contentment
or in their evocations of the natural world in all its moods. The
Romantic generation re-experienced and gave added intensity
to what it inherited.

Yet, secondly, some of the Romantics would re-assess even
external nature, especially in the light of Lamarckian science:
going almost as far as only such lone figures as de Sade had
previously gone. Far from being beneficent, harmonious and
idyllic, nature for Vigny and Sainte-Beuve's Amaury illustrates
a savage struggle for survival, as 'red in tooth and claw' as
Leconte de Lisle, like Tennyson, would depict it a little later.
The nineteenth century would also bring the re-assertion of
pessimism about human nature, a fresh emphasis upon its
sinfulness – coming most evidently in France from the restored
forces of Catholicism, and in Britain from the impact of
'Victorian' puritan Protestantism. And there is far more than
that – revealed by so many features of nineteenth-century life
in both those countries and elsewhere. In France the condition
of the peasants worsened over the decades after 1800. Slavery,
we noted, had been briefly abolished in 1794 but was restored
by Napoleon in 1802. Following his new legal code women too
were even further under subjection than during the *Ancien
Régime*. Children were put into factory labour from around the

age of eight – with a life-expectancy thereafter, on one calculation, of one and a half years – and though some, like Chateaubriand, Hugo and Baudelaire, attacked this cruel exploitation, it persisted in the French industrial towns as much as in Dickensian London. Even those allowed to stay at school were subject to all the rigours and restored beatings of the school-master and, when at home, to the discipline of a stern, withdrawn, 'Victorian', father. Thanks to the industrial revolution, town life too became steadily more appalling, notwithstanding the appeals to country virtues of such, in France, as George Sand.

The nineteenth-century realities, thus briefly pointed to, may well lead one to fear that novel attitudes and ideas, even if increasing lip-service be paid to them, make little real difference to what actually happens. Some will propose a Marxist explanation as to that or at least adopt Hegel's sombre saying that 'the owl of Minerva flies only at midnight'. Others will still hope that 'ideas will out' – and from the vantage-point of the present day one can at least note how warmly accepted, especially amongst the younger generations, are many of the erstwhile originalities of Rousseau and his fellows. But for much of the nineteenth century (and well into the twentieth also) the counter-currents were strongly running, and the resulting oppositions render the period all the more fascinating for study of our subject. Glacken ended his survey in *Traces on the Rhodian Shore* at 1800; a successor would find a great deal more to examine.

That successor would also be forced to consider one of the most persistent but intractable of all the inter-actions involved in men's relationship with the natural – a conflict that clearly helps to explain the nineteenth-century situation. This book has largely concerned those who felt 'sympathetic' towards nature and wished to 'collaborate' with it; but it is abundantly clear that such attitudes have often been qualified or defeated by the conflicting wish to 'exploit', to modify it for utilitarian ends. This long-standing tension – visible today at every planning enquiry for a new power-station or motorway and in many other still more threatening ways – has been a fundamental element in the development of the modern world, obviously enough. It is, in the words of Keith Thomas, 'one of the contradictions upon which modern civilization may be said to rest', and the conflicts have been greatly sharpened since the eighteenth century.[19]

On the one hand, technological, scientific and economic developments, for example, have made it ever easier to impose human will upon the natural; on the other hand more appreciative evaluations of it from that time onwards have heightened opposition to its exploitation, and the more so with every destructive incursion upon it. Thomas further comments that 'a mixture of compromise and concealment has so far prevented this conflict from having to be fully resolved'. Perhaps the hard question, however, is whether it ever could be resolved, and behind that may lie a truth, even if an unwelcome one. It is entirely arguable that the new sympathies for nature were attainable, that they became imaginatively feasible, only when nature had to some degree been 'tamed' by exploitive, utilitarian achievements, bringing with them a measure of security within what had previously been a constantly menacing, wholly uncontrollable environment. Two instances – the first minor, the other major – may serve to illustrate this. For Defoe, we saw, Westmorland was 'the wildest, most barren and frightful' area he had ever passed over; the train-traveller over that same wildness is freed to appreciate its outstanding landscapes – thanks to the exploitive activities of the nineteenth-century railway builders. Far more important an example relates to the long delay in Christian times before our own warmer notions of family relationships emerged. McManners, notably, seeks to explain it in a distinctive way:

The historian does not have to account for the rise of the marriage of free choice, the improving status of women, the centring of family life on the children, so much as to account for the delay and distortion of these manifestations of devotion under the pressure of adverse social conditions.[20]

And the more favourable conditions he adduces include lower mortality, more ease and comfort, greater assurance for the future, and improved education. The fact (as he might agree) is surely that most of these resulted from an attitude to the natural which was far less 'collaborative' than resistant, unaccepting, seeking to control and change.

It may thus be – though this is unfinished business with a vengeance – that the oppositions are unavoidable and permanent (and would be in any human society), that at best they can be rendered creative tensions rather than destructive conflicts (albeit predictions as to all the future consequences will often be difficult). This would seem to be the view accepted in Glacken's work, for it amply illustrates the perennial interplay over the centuries between 'the force and strength of natural conditions' and 'man as a modifier of nature'. René Dubos, writing of *The Wooing of Earth*, recognises in detail the same phenomenon and terms it 'environmental ambivalence'; although a noted conservationist, he accepts that man has never lived in harmony with nature by leaving it undisciplined and he defends what he calls 'the humanization of the Earth'.[21]

It could well be that the late-eighteenth-century French 'sympathisers' would not have rejected such a claim – and were, indeed, implicitly supporting it. Even their admiration for external nature was not unconditional. They deeply and sincerely responded to the natural world, but most of them, like Rousseau, much preferred the pastoral mountain-slopes to the harsh Saussurian peaks. Moreover, their appreciations were from within an environment of civilised life; only a much later generation would come to feel that 'sleeping rough' is an essential element in the 'return to nature'. Their ambivalence about the natural in its human representations was even clearer. In every case we have taken – children, women thus interpreted, peasants and savages – even the most eloquent enthusiasts did not finally feel able to dispense with additions to nature in the form of education, morality and religious teaching or of enlightened control by father, husband, squire or good colonial administrator. The tensions so often noted within their attitudes reflect their acknowledgement that the ideal for them, at bottom, lay in a *marriage* of nature and culture, of (say) the values of the country and the benefits of the town or the better qualities of 'noble savage' and civilised man alike. For the most part they did not have to face the grosser conflicts between 'collaboration' and 'exploitation' – but their ambiguous reactions to Paris, noted in chapter 9, suggest that in the end, for all their innovative desires, they remained in favour of compromise.

The reader of this final chapter may reasonably be wondering, not unlike its author, whether any of the 'business' with which this book has been concerned has progressed beyond being 'unfinished'. Some conclusions, though they could never be definitive on so complex a subject, seem relatively firm, whilst others are more tentative, far closer to what could be called 'implications'. Those who have read thus far deserve to hear both for their judgement.

The first aim was to survey afresh a specific movement in later-eighteenth-century France: the rise of an intensified 'feeling for nature' that had previously been described by such scholars as Daniel Mornet, Gustave Charlier and Paul Van Tieghem, valuably so but seeming to warrant re-examination in the light of later scholarship. It was apparent that for most observers its significance has been assessed from two viewpoints. The first concerns its relationship to the intellectual originalities of Enlightenment thought; it has been seen either as a 'translation' of the *philosophes*' ideas into literary and emotional terms or, alternatively, as in Lenoble's words a 'reaction of affectivity', a protest against the abstractness of those ideas. Secondly, it has been interpreted in relation to the rise of the Romantic movement, especially by those interested in cultural 'evolutions'; it has often been identified, indeed, with 'pre-Romanticism' and viewed as preparing the way for the more major movement that would follow. It is probably accurate to add that, whichever perspective has been adopted, it has been judged (one or two 'giants' like Rousseau excepted) as of more limited importance than either the Enlightenment properly speaking or Romanticism in its early-nineteenth-century prime.

Such assessments may be justified, but both perspectives have been quite deliberately set aside here in order to examine the movement in relation to an obviously central theme in all human history, since, try as we might, we could never escape from nature, this side of the grave at least. And seen in this context the movement and its sometimes eccentric participants have taken on, it seems, a distinctly greater significance and originality than has normally been acknowledged. It has been argued that what was occurring was, in the first place, far wider than a change of 'sensibility' alone, far more than a matter of feeling sentimental about (say) landscapes or children. What was involved – well beyond that – was the gradual formation of new 'images', in the senses defined, of new ways of 'seeing' and 'representing', derived from factors as diverse as scientific observations and theories, reports from overseas explorers, economic and social pressures, critical reactions to accepted Christian teachings, and so on. What was involved, secondly and crucially, was a questioning of hitherto largely-assumed and generally-accepted evaluations of both the world around us and the natural (as we try to guess it) within us, and a novel assertion of harmony between them. 'Contrasts' with what preceded have led to the claim that this was a time of quite fundamental novelty in the development of many European attitudes. The eighteenth century in France has most often been described as an age when great and important abstract nouns flew thick and fast – liberty, equality, justice and others – and that is a no doubt fully-justified account. Yet – setting the abstractions aside, but with no denial of all they have achieved for human advance – the eighteenth century also brought a ferment of change in quite other ways, less theoretical, closer to the everyday, extensively ramifying in its effects. For it greatly modified – either then or over a longer time-span – people's views on matters, both major and minor, as diverse as the scenery, gardens or paintings they enjoy, how to feed, dress and rear their children, on what primary grounds to choose and behave towards their spouse, where and how to bury their deceased, and numerous others, amounting, taken together, to far more than the details in isolation. What, cumulatively, was happening – and perhaps largely without the participants being aware of its enormity – was the replacement of the old view of man's situation within the world and his relationship to it by another view which, by and large, still prevails, for good or ill, to the present day. A final, collective 'contrast' may help one to measure the distance between the two.

In traditional Christian teaching the natural world is fallen, spiritually irrelevant, uninteresting outside the limited range of daily preoccupations, and fearful in its wilder forms (as when even in the later-seventeenth century the villagers of Chamonix beseeched their bishop at Annecy to exorcise the glaciers of Mont Blanc). Earthquakes, volcanoes, even the seas and mountains, are the 'ruins' of a debased creation. And man above all is fallen and depraved, still labouring under God's curse in the Garden of Eden: women are 'the devil's gateway', fated to suffer in childbirth and to be subordinate to men; men are fated to work in the sweat of their brow; even children are 'conceived and born in sin'. More broadly, too, men's earthly condition is over-shadowed by 'the miseries of this sinful world', to be endured as a transitory testing-time before the dread assignment to Heaven or to Hell.

This book has been looking at the period in France, albeit later than in some other places, when – notwithstanding earlier anticipations, notably during the Renaissance – a first significant minority was abandoning that general view and replacing it by very different evaluations. In the first place, thanks to a virtual explosion of observations of the natural world – scientific, geographical and purely personal all combined – there was an unmistakeable enlargement of awareness of it, of appreciation of its variety, beauty and wonder. Quite simply, more people enjoyed it more, and the minority at least was led increasingly to a deep sense of affinity between man and nature, of a harmony that is psychological, aesthetic, even economic and moral. With many people this may have amounted to little more than a renewal of the old Classical pastoralism, but with a few at least the responsiveness extended from the picturesque to embrace the sublime and the wildnesses of nature. Even death, for some of them, was re-interpreted: separation from nature was replaced by absorption into nature; 'God's best undertaker', covering our remains with her flowers, even offers a new version of eternal life through her processes of continual renewal, her prospects of timeless time. As the same people wondered about human nature, they became more cautious – one's decisions as to that matter far more directly than whether one responds to sea-views or garden-vistas. Yet, here again, a surely most significant difference from what had preceded is evident: towards a growing belief that humans, far from being 'born in sin', are naturally innocent or even good. The child, attractive and interesting in himself and rich in future promise; woman in her true nature – loving spiritually rather than passionately, devoted to her happy family and her affectionate husband; primitive man, a few exceptions apart, living contentedly by following the healthy impulses of his own nature; the peasant, fulfilled and morally sane as he works in harmony with nature's good earth: such examples all suggest that corruption comes not from Adam's fall but from pressures – social, educational, religious and the like – that have, precisely, betrayed the natural. If man will collaborate with it, allow it to flow through him, as it were, even in the extremer cases of the inspired bard or creative genius, then – so the argument went – our life can be happy and enriched through our relations with our fellow-humans as much as with external nature. Even if one's final hope remains in the world-to-come (as for most of the minority it still did), all the same this world is not unavoidably a 'vale of tears' and of 'miseries': it can be enjoyed instead of being endured.

Both the thinkers who expressed such views in the language of 'ideas' and those who embodied them in the looser but perhaps more vivid language of 'images' may have been mistaken or deluded, of course, as they sketched this appealing picture. It must be remembered that many Christians to the present day (and followers of some other religions also) hold at bottom to the traditional view – from many Catholics at one end of the Christian spectrum to many Protestant fundamentalists at the other. Yet that view is surely poles apart from what countless *other* Christians – let alone non-Christians – believe today. One may even wonder whether, around the whole issue of the status of the natural, the polarisation is not now so marked that there are almost *two* Christianities – seeking

reconciliation, no doubt, as in doctrinal commissions or attempts
to define (say) an agreed Christian teaching on sex, but for now
still seeking. If that is even partially true, it relates to one further
conclusion this study has sought to illustrate. Some interpreters
have seen the whole movement under discussion as above all
secularising and anti-Christian, and in some intended way,
moreover, and they have claimed that its very goal was to
establish nature as a rival divinity. This may be severely
doubted – and no matter what one may think about some of
the longer-term consequences that have followed. Certainly
Diderot and some others were unbelievers, opposed to all forms
of Christianity, but others – from Rousseau to Bernardin de
Saint-Pierre and Chateaubriand – were no less certainly not. In
their thinking, first, the old barriers between 'secular' and
'religious' were being eroded: their attempt (whether one
judges it successful or not) was rather to unite them than to
reject one for the other. For, secondly, as they saw it, their
re-interpretations of the natural did not conflict with Christian
faith in what they believed to be its essentials – at odds on that
with both Catholics and some Protestant churches though they
undoubtedly were. In their minds, we saw, nature's beauties and
marvels served to add faith in God's goodness to the earlier
respect for His efficiency as designer. Similarly, the scenes of
'wild sublimity' were most often felt to speak (in Cowper's
words) of 'the power and majesty of God'. Even in the country
burial-ground one could trust in God and in nature alike, with
no need to choose between them. Nor did they accept that their
'rehabilitation of human nature' was unavoidably contrary to
Christian belief. They certainly rejected any doctrine that man
is *totally* corrupt and were, rather, implicitly stressing the belief
that man is made 'in the image of God'. But, conversely, they
did not concur in the claim of some in their time and ours that,
by his own efforts alone, man is totally perfectible: even their
trust in the 'individual conscience' rested on the premiss that
God speaks through it.

Two centuries after them countless people, beyond denial,
broadly accept their views of nature and the natural. Indeed,
it will be clear to the reader that at the present day these are

being re-affirmed, whether explicitly or not, in a variety of quite specific commitments, as a few examples may illustrate. Ecological and environmental concern; rejection of racism and any notion of the inherent inferiority – God's curse – of coloured peoples; campaigns for species-preservation and 'animal liberation'; advocacy of vegetarian and 'organic' foods, of 'natural health' and 'alternative medicine'; the wish for 'natural child-birth' – away from Eve's age-long distress and fear; attitudes to children, on one side of our educational debates at any rate, that favour 'free development' (and an end to those beatings of earlier days); above all perhaps – going well beyond the eighteenth-century minority – appeals to 'natural morality': such convictions as these have been fuelled today (it is abundantly obvious) by numerous other factors related to the sharpening oppositions between 'exploitation' and 'collaboration'. Yet at the same time all of them, and much else in contemporary thinking, are inter-related in a distinctive way: all of them – for the most part as unconnected at first sight as liking landscapes and liking children – are within the 'image-context', as it could be called, whose creation we have seen in its beginnings. The 'new images of the natural' developed by Rousseau, Diderot and their fellows and by their equivalents in other countries amounted, cumulatively and added to more abstractly-intellectual arguments, to an extensive re-evaluation of the world and of human life that was greatly more radical and far more recent in European thought (since the Ancients, at least) than may sometimes be appreciated. It is thus hardly surprising if many of its implications are still in dispute; whilst some may judge that the eighteenth-century innovators have a good deal to answer for and others that a good deal they achieved deserves salute, it seems clear, on either view, that they initiated and have bequeathed to us all – and not only to research scholars – an impressively great deal of 'unfinished business'.

BIBLIOGRAPHIES

The bibliographies of secondary works that follow are intended as a guide to further reading and are deliberately selective. They are in general limited as follows:

(i) The focus of selection is on developments in France; studies of European and of national movements other than French are included only where of distinctive interest or special relevance.

(ii) Studies of individual writers, painters and others are deliberately excluded; bibliographies on Diderot, Rousseau and their contemporaries are easily accessible and any sufficient listing would be beyond the space available; the few exceptions below and in the Notes are obviously not intended, even collectively, as an adequate reading list on the individual concerned. For that the English general reader might turn first, as regards thinkers and literary writers, to D. Mahaffey, *A Concise Bibliography of French Literature* (London and New York, Bowker, 1975), and for more specialist details to D. C. Cabeen, *A Critical Bibliography of French Literature*, vol. 4: *The Eighteenth Century*, ed. G. R. Havens and D. F. Bond (Syracuse U.P., 1951) and its *Supplement*, ed. R. A. Brooks (1968). In addition, many of the studies cited below contain useful bibliographies.

The place of publication, where not given, is Paris; periodical abbreviations are given at the head of the Notes (p. 232).

1. *General*

The development of the idea of nature from the Ancients to modern times is authoritatively surveyed in C. J. Glacken, *Traces on the Rhodian Shore: Nature and Culture in Western Thought* (Berkeley, U. of California P., 1967) and R. Lenoble, *Histoire de l'idée de nature* (Albin Michel, 1969). Cf. also R. Lenoble, 'L'évolution de l'idée de "nature" du XVIᵉ au XVIIIᵉ siècle', *Revue de métaphysique et de morale*, 58 (1953), 108–29, for a relevant summary of his interpretation.

On the idea of nature in eighteenth-century France the outstanding authority is J. Ehrard, *L'Idée de nature en France dans la première moitié du XVIIIᵉ siècle* (2 vols., Service d'Edition et de Vente des Publications de l'Education Nationale, 1963), but numerous other studies of Enlightenment thought are hardly less pertinent. Of these notable examples in English are E. Cassirer, *The Philosophy of the Enlightenment* (Princeton U.P., 1951); L. G. Crocker, *An Age of Crisis: Man and World in Eighteenth-Century French Thought* (Baltimore,

Bibliographies

Johns Hopkins U.P., 1959) and *Nature and Culture: Ethical Thought in the French Enlightenment* (Baltimore, Johns Hopkins U.P., 1963); P. Gay, *The Enlightenment: An Interpretation* (2 vols., London, Weidenfeld and Nicolson, 1967–70); and I. O. Wade, *The Structure and Form of the French Enlightenment* (2 vols., Princeton U.P., 1977). In French major works include S. Goyard-Fabre, *La Philosophie des lumières en France* (Klincksieck, 1972); G. Gusdorf, *Dieu, La Nature, L'Homme au siècle des lumières* (Payot, 1972) and *Naissance de la conscience romantique au siècle des lumières* (Payot, 1976); R. Mauzi, *L'Idée du bonheur au XVIIIe siècle* (Colin, 1960); and R. Mercier, *La Réhabilitation de la nature humaine (1700–1750)* (Villemonble, Editions 'La Balance', 1960). Other works of relevance include R. G. Collingwood, *The Idea of Nature* (Oxford, Clarendon Press, 1945) for a general philosophical discussion; B. Tocanne, *L'Idée de nature en France dans la seconde moitié du XVIIe siècle* (Klincksieck, 1978), helpful as background and as contrast with later developments; and B. Willey, *The Eighteenth-Century Background: Studies on the Idea of Nature* (London, Chatto and Windus, 1940), albeit mainly dealing with English writers.

The so-named 'feeling for nature' in later-eighteenth century France is still most authoritatively described in D. Mornet, *Le Sentiment de la nature en France de J.-J. Rousseau à Bernardin de Saint-Pierre* (Hachette, 1907). Other substantial treatments include G. Charlier, *Le Sentiment de la nature chez les romantiques français (1762–1830)* (Brussels, Académie Royale de Belgique, 1912); Paul Van Tieghem, *Le Sentiment de la nature dans le préromantisme européen* (Nizet, 1960); and, for a useful but less systematic gathering of evidence, C. Dédéyan, *Rousseau et la sensibilité littéraire à la fin du XVIIIe siècle* (Société d'Edition d'enseignement supérieur, 1966). Since the theme of nature is commonly linked with Romanticism and its precursors, cf. also A. Monglond, *Le Préromantisme français* (2 vols., Grenoble, Arthaud, 1930); D. Mornet, *Le Romantisme en France au XVIIIe siècle*, 2nd edn (Hachette, 1925); P. Trahard, *Les Maîtres de la sensibilité française* (4 vols., Boivin, 1931–3); and Paul Van Tieghem, *Le Préromantisme* (2 vols., SFELT, 1948). The feeling for nature in France at periods prior to the later-eighteenth century is surveyed in G. Atkinson, *Le Sentiment de la nature, 1690–1740* (Droz, 1960) and G. L. McCann, *Le Sentiment de la nature dans la première moitié du XVIIe siècle* (New York, Burt Franklin, 1972).

Numerous historical works are valuable, both to provide essential background and for their treatment of cultural developments wider than those in literature and philosophy alone (to which most of the studies above are limited). Of these, cf. in particular, C. B. A. Behrens, *The Ancien Régime* (London, Thames and Hudson, 1967); F. Braudel, *Civilisation matérielle et capitalisme, XVe–XVIIIe siècles* (Colin, 1967); P. Chaunu, *La Civilisation de l'Europe des lumières* (Arthaud, 1971); A. Cobban (ed.), *The Eighteenth Century: Europe in the Age of the Enlightenment* (London, Thames and Hudson, 1969); N. Hampson, *The Enlightenment* (Harmondsworth, Penguin Books, 1968); O. H. Hufton, *The Poor of Eighteenth-Century France, 1750–1789* (Oxford, Clarendon Press, 1974); R. Mandrou, *La France aux XVIIe et XVIIIe siècles* (Presses Universitaires de France, 1970); R. Mousnier, E. Labrousse and M. Bouloiseau, *Le Dix-Huitième Siècle, révolution intellectuelle, technique et*

Bibliographies

politique (Presses Universitaires de France, 1955); and A. Soboul, *La Société française dans la 2ᵉ moitié du XVIIIᵉ siècle* (Centre de Documentation Universitaire, 1969). Relevant essays are in E. R. Wasserman (ed.), *Aspects of the Eighteenth Century* (Baltimore, Johns Hopkins U.P., and London, Oxford U.P., 1965). Other historical works are highly relevant to specific subjects and will be noted under 4, 6 and 7 below.

Numerous studies of French literature cast useful light on several aspects of the subject. Recent general literary histories include R. Niklaus, *A Literary History of France: The Eighteenth Century* (London, Benn, 1970); and two volumes in the series on *Littérature Française* edited by C. Pichois and published by Arthaud: R. Mauzi and S. Menant, *Le XVIIIᵉ Siècle: II – 1750–1778* (1977) and B. Didier, *Le XVIIIᵉ Siècle: III – 1778–1820* (1976) (with full bibliographies). Certain more specific studies are referred to in the Notes where especially relevant. On French art, good general works in English are P. Conisbee, *Painting in Eighteenth-Century France* (Oxford, Phaidon Press, 1981); M. Levey, *Rococo to Revolution* (London, Thames and Hudson, 1966); and J. Thuillier and A. Châtelet, *French Painting from Le Nain to Fragonard* (Geneva, Skira, 1964). The Goncourts' older, more partial but still evocative book has been translated as E. and J. de Goncourt, *French XVIIIth Century Painters* (London, Phaidon Press, 1948). An especially incisive study, even though only partially relevant here, is N. Bryson, *Word and Image: French Painting of the Ancien Régime* (Cambridge U.P., 1981). Amongst works in French, especially useful are P. Francastel, *Histoire de la peinture française*, vol. 1 (Paris and Brussels, Elsevier, 1955) and L. Hautecoeur, *Littérature et peinture en France du XVIIᵉ au XXᵉ siècle*, 2nd edn (Colin, 1963). Histories of aesthetic doctrines provide pertinent background as well as illustrations of particular topics. They include J. Chouillet, *L'Esthétique des lumières* (Presses Universitaires de France, 1974); W. Folkierski, *Entre le classicisme et le romantisme* (Champion, 1969); A. Fontaine, *Les Doctrines d'art en France de Poussin à Diderot* (H. Laurens, 1909); and T. M. Mustoxidi, *Histoire de l'esthétique française, 1700–1900* (Champion, 1920). A recent probing study in English, but only occasionally relevant here (notably on 'the sublime') is M. Hobson, *The Object of Art: the Theory of Illusion in Eighteenth-Century France* (Cambridge U.P., 1982). I am conscious that music is neglected for lack of space. The interested reader might turn first to general works such as P. Daval, *La Musique en France au XVIIIᵉ siècle* (Payot, 1961) and G. Snyders, *Le Goût musical en France aux XVIIᵉ et XVIIIᵉ siècles* (Vrin, 1968).

2. Pastoral landscapes and wild sublimity

Especially valuable are the works on the 'feeling for nature' listed under 1 above. On the rise of relevant aesthetic concepts, cf. especially C. Hussey, *The Picturesque*, 2nd edn (London, Cass, 1967); S. H. Monk, *The Sublime* (New York, Modern Language Association of America, 1935), though its discussion is largely confined to England; A. O. Lovejoy, '"Nature" as aesthetic norm', in his *Essays in the History of Ideas* (Baltimore, Johns Hopkins U.P., 1948), pp. 69–77; and the works on aesthetics listed under 1 above. K. Clark, *Landscape into Art* (London, John Murray, 1949) considers, albeit rather briefly, the aesthetics of landscape-painting but is mainly concerned with nineteenth-century English works.

Classic studies on their themes, also centred on England, are M. H. Nicolson, *Mountain Gloom and Mountain Glory* (New York, Norton, 1963) and M. Reynolds, *The Treatment of Nature in English Poetry between Pope and Wordsworth* (Chicago U.P., 1909). Equally authoritative – and valuable for France also – is J. E. Congleton, *Theories of Pastoral Poetry in England, 1684–1798* (New York, Haskell House, 1968). On appreciation of mountain scenery a major study is C. E. Engel, *La Littérature alpestre en France et en Angleterre aux XVIIIe et XIXe siècles* (Chambéry, Dardel, 1930), and for the later period there is also C. Lacoste-Veysseyre, *Les Alpes romantiques: le thème des Alpes dans la littérature française de 1800 à 1850* (2 vols., Geneva, Slatkine Reprints, 1981). Also relevant are Paul Van Tieghem, *Ossian en France* (2 vols., Rieder, 1917) and C. Hibbert, *The Grand Tour* (London, Weidenfeld and Nicolson, 1969). Van Tieghem's essay on 'Les Idylles de Gessner et le rêve pastoral', in *Le Préromantisme*, vol. 2, is less useful on its theme, other than as a study of 'influences' in France from England and Germany. Directly relevant for particular authors are C. M. Vance, *The Extravagant Shepherd: a study of the pastoral vision in Rousseau's 'Nouvelle Héloïse'*, St. Volt., 105 (1973); J. J. Simon, *Bernardin de Saint-Pierre ou le Triomphe de Flore* (Nizet, 1967); and E. Guitton, *Delille et la poésie de la nature de 1750 à 1820* (Klincksieck, 1974), to which may be added essays, notably by R. Mauzi and J. Ehrard, in a collective volume, *Delille est-il mort?* (Clermont-Ferrand, Bussac, 1968), and P. Auserve, 'Delille préromantique', in P. Viallaneix (ed.), *Le Préromantisme* (Klincksieck, 1975), pp. 114–28.

Interesting exhibition catalogues, though inevitably somewhat limited, include *Les Joies de la Nature au XVIIIe siècle* (Bibliothèque Nationale, 1971); *French Landscape Drawings and Sketches of the Eighteenth Century* (London, British Museum Publications, 1977); *Jardins en France, 1760–1820* (Caisse Nationale des Monuments Historiques, 1977); and *Grandes et Petites Heures du Parc Monceau* (Musée Cernuschi, 1981).

The history of landscape-gardening is increasingly well covered by reliable studies, both general and particular. Most directly useful are D. Wiebenson, *The Picturesque Garden in France* (Princeton U.P., 1978) and W. H. Adams, *The French Garden, 1500–1800* (London, Scolar Press, 1979), especially ch. 5. Wider studies of value include E. de Ganay, *Les Jardins de France et leur décor* (Larousse, 1949); M. Charageat, *L'Art des jardins* (Presses Universitaires de France, 1962); and, amongst the most wide-ranging of general surveys, L. Hautecoeur, *Les Jardins des dieux et des hommes* (Hachette, 1959) and C. Thacker, *The History of Gardens* (London, Croom Helm, 1979). Concerned more with England but of relevance are J. D. Hunt, *The Figure in the Landscape: Poetry, Painting and Gardening during the Eighteenth Century* (Baltimore and London, Johns Hopkins U.P., 1976); E. Malins, *English Landscaping and Literature, 1660–1840* (London, Oxford U.P., 1966); C. Hussey, *English Gardens and Landscapes, 1700–1750* (London, Country Life, 1967); and J. D. Hunt and P. Willis, *The Genius of the Place: The English Landscape Garden,*

1620–1820 (London, Elek, 1975). France appears to be less well served by such cross-disciplinary studies.

Although a few social historians are now paying more attention, all too little study seems to have been given – as with the history of leisure in general – to the history of seaside appreciation and resorts as a branch of cultural history. Interesting general surveys include S. Howell, *The Seaside* (London, Studio Vista, 1974); R. Cameron, *The Golden Riviera* (London, Weidenfeld and Nicolson, 1975); and C. Graves, *Royal Riviera* (London, Heinemann, 1951). In French there are P. Boussel, *Histoire des vacances* (Berger-Levrault, 1961) and Guy de Frondeville, *Les Visiteurs de la mer* (Le Centurion, 1956), and also pertinent is an older study, C. Maxwell, *The English Traveller in France, 1698–1815* (London, Routledge, 1932).

I regret that C. Thacker, *The Wildness Pleases* (London and Canberra, Croom Helm, 1983) appeared too late for me to be able to profit from it here. Its evidence is drawn from England, Germany and other countries as well as France; I have been able to do no more than refer to a little of it in the Notes below.

3. *Sciences of nature*

Good general histories of science are A. R. Hall, *The Scientific Revolution, 1500–1800* (London, Longmans, 1962) and R. Taton (ed.), *The Beginnings of Modern Science from 1450 to 1800* (London, Thames and Hudson, 1964). A short, helpful introduction, though centred on England, is G. S. Rousseau, 'Science', in P. Rogers (ed.), *The Context of English Literature: The Eighteenth Century* (London, Methuen, 1978); on France specifically cf. Wade, *The Structure and Form of the French Enlightenment*, vol. 1, pp. 516–82. Other discussions are in A. N. Whitehead, *Science and the Modern World* (Cambridge U.P., 1945); C. C. Gillespie, *The Edge of Objectivity* (Princeton U.P., 1960); and, the classic study on its theme, A. O. Lovejoy, *The Great Chain of Being* (Cambridge, Mass., Harvard U.P., 1936). A major and wide-ranging collaborative work on the historiography of eighteenth-century science is G. S. Rousseau and R. Porter (eds.), *The Ferment of Knowledge* (Cambridge U.P., 1980), well worth consulting on each particular science.

On the life sciences the fundamental study is J. Roger, *Les Sciences de la vie dans la pensée française du XVIIIᵉ siècle* (Armand Colin, 1963). Other helpful works include Gusdorf, *Dieu, La Nature, L'Homme au siècle des lumières* (cf. 1 above), part 2; D. Mornet, *Les Sciences de la nature au XVIIIᵉ siècle* (Armand Colin, 1911), albeit inevitably somewhat dated; and (slighter) E. Guyénot, *Les Sciences de la vie aux XVIIᵉ et XVIIIᵉ siècles: l'idée d'évolution* (Albin Michel, 1941). Valuable essays on particular themes are in B. Glass *et al.* (eds.), *Forerunners of Darwin, 1745–1859* (Baltimore, Johns Hopkins U.P., 1959) – notably by A. O. Lovejoy, L. Crocker, B. Glass and F. C. Haber. The movement from 'mechanism' to 'organicism' is persuasively described in C. Kiernan, *The Enlightenment and Science in Eighteenth-Century France*, 2nd edn, *St. Volt.*, 59A (1973). Links with materialism are considered by L. C. Rosenfield, *From Beast-machine to Machine-man* (London, Oxford U.P., 1940) and A. Vartanian, 'Trembley's polyp, La Mettrie, and 18th-century French materialism', *Journal of the History of Ideas*, 11 (1950), 259–86. On ideas drawn from geology, cf. especially F. D. Adams, *The Birth and the Development of the Geological Sciences* (Baltimore, Williams and Wilkins, 1938); and also (though it is mainly on the nineteenth century) C. C. Gillespie, *Genesis and Geology* (New York, Harper and Row, 1959). A readable survey on its subject is S. Toulmin and J. Goodfield, *The Discovery of Time* (London, Hutchinson, 1965); cf. also F. C. Haber, 'Fossils and the idea of a process of time in natural history', in B. Glass *et al.* (eds.), pp. 222ff., and Haber, *The Age of the World* (Baltimore, Johns Hopkins U.P., 1959), especially ch. 3.

On individuals, an introduction to Buffon's work for English readers is O. E. Fellows and S. F. Milliken, *Buffon* (New York, Twayne, 1972) but Roger, *Les Sciences de la vie*, part 3, ch. 2; A. O. Lovejoy, 'Buffon and the Problem of Species', in B. Glass *et al.* (eds.), pp. 84ff.; and the substantial introductions by J. Piveteau and J. Roger respectively to the Buffon editions given at the head of the Notes provide more detailed discussion on aspects relevant to this chapter. Of numerous works alluding to Diderot and science, cf. especially J. Mayer, *Diderot homme de science* (Rennes, Imprimerie Bretonne, 1959); Roger, pp. 585ff.; L. G. Crocker, *Diderot's Chaotic Order* (Princeton U.P., 1974); and A. Vartanian, *Diderot and Descartes* (Princeton U.P., 1953). On the conflict with D'Alembert, cf. T. L. Hankins, *Jean D'Alembert: Science and the Enlightenment* (Oxford, Clarendon Press, 1970) and also, more generally, R. Grimsley, *Jean D'Alembert* (Oxford, Clarendon Press, 1963).

4. *Death and destruction*

In recent decades attitudes to death in eighteenth-century France have been very fully studied in several authoritative works. Of these the most directly helpful for our subject are R. Favre, *La Mort dans la littérature et la pensée françaises au siècle des lumières* (Lyon, Presses Universitaires, 1978) and J. McManners, *Death and the Enlightenment* (Oxford, Clarendon Press, 1981), an outstanding scholarly synthesis which draws also, as the author stresses, on other important books. Noteworthy amongst these are two works by P. Ariès; the later and more major is *L'Homme devant la mort* (Editions du Seuil, 1977), also translated as *The Hour of Our Death* (London, Allen Lane, 1981); rather less detailed but none the less stimulating is *Essais sur l'histoire de la mort en Occident du moyen âge à nos jours* (Editions du Seuil, 1975), also translated as *Western Attitudes toward Death* (Baltimore, Johns Hopkins U.P., 1974). Other notable scholarship is in F. Lebrun, *Les Hommes et la mort en Anjou aux XVIIe et XVIIIe siècles* (Paris and The Hague, Mouton, 1971), a moving and close study; and M. Vovelle, *Mourir autrefois: Attitudes collectives devant la mort aux XVIIe et XVIIIe siècles* (Gallimard-Julliard, 1974) (with numerous illustrative extracts) and Vovelle's major work on *Piété baroque et déchristianisation en Provence au XVIIIe siècle* (Plon, 1973).

Later-eighteenth century responses to ruins, tombs and memorials are discussed in some of the works above, notably in McManners and Favre, but in addition there are specific studies as regards literature: R. Mortier, *La*

Bibliographies

Poétique des ruines en France (Geneva, Droz, 1974); Paul Van Tieghem, *La Poésie de la nuit et des tombeaux en Europe* (Geneva, Slatkine Reprints, 1970; original edn, 1921); and a short but still useful article, R. Michéa, 'Le "Plaisir des Tombeaux" au XVIIIe siècle', *Revue de littérature comparée*, 18 (1938), 287–311.

The wider theme of nature's destructiveness is, in a single chapter, only briefly considered, I am aware: perceptions of volcanoes alone as expressed in French thought, literature and art at the period would form a research subject of distinctive interest and relevance, reflecting many debates of the age. For a lively account of the most traumatic natural disaster at the time, cf. T. D. Kendrick, *The Lisbon Earthquake* (London, Methuen, 1956), and for its intellectual tremors in France, cf., amongst other works, W. H. Barber, *Leibniz in France* (Oxford, Clarendon Press, 1955) and R. Pomeau, *La Religion de Voltaire* (Nizet, 1956).

5. Transoceanic perspectives

There are several substantial accounts of transoceanic explorations and reactions to them in the eighteenth century. For journeys over the Pacific Ocean cf. in particular J. Dunmore, *French Explorers in the Pacific*, vol. 1: *The Eighteenth Century* (Oxford, Clarendon Press, 1965); B. Smith, *European Vision and the South Pacific* (Oxford, Clarendon Press, 1960); and A. Sharp, *The Discovery of the Pacific Islands* (Oxford, Clarendon Press, 1960), as well as such primary sources as L. A. Bougainville, *Voyage autour du monde* (1771) and J. Hawkesworth, *An Account of the Voyages...in the Southern Hemispheres* (1773). On explorations in the Americas a lively and well-illustrated account is H. Honour, *The New Golden Land* (London, Allen Lane, 1975); a still very useful study is G. Chinard, *L'Amérique et le rêve exotique dans la littérature française aux XVIIe et XVIIIe siècles* (Droz, 1934), as for the seventeenth century is G. Atkinson, *Les Relations de voyages du XVIIe siècle* (Champion, 1924). Interesting but less substantial is D. Echeverria, *Mirage in the West: A History of the French Image of American Society to 1815* (New York, Octagon Books, 1966). For Africa the outstanding work is R. Mercier, *L'Afrique noire dans la littérature française: Les premières images (xviie–xviiie siècles)* (Dakar, Publications de la section de langues et littératures, 1962); cf. also W. B. Cohen, *The French Encounter with Africans: white response to blacks, 1530–1880* (Bloomington and London, Indiana U.P., 1980).

There are further valuable studies of the impact of the explorations on ideas in France and elsewhere in Europe. Of these, a major work is M. Duchet, *Anthropologie et histoire au siècle des lumières* (François Maspero, 1971), and equally important – but relating to America alone – is A. Gerbi, *The Dispute of the New World* (Pittsburgh, U. of Pittsburgh Press, 1973) (original Italian ed., 1955). The same press published a stimulating collective work, E. Dudley and M. E. Novak (eds.), *The Wild Man Within* (1972); its essays range from the Middle Ages on, and for the eighteenth century cf. those by M. E. Novak and G. Symcox. The notion of the noble savage is surveyed in a classic study, H. N. Fairchild, *The Noble Savage: a study in Romantic Naturalism* (New York, Columbia U.P., 1928). In addition cf. R. Gonnard, *La Légende du bon sauvage*

Bibliographies

(Editions politiques, économiques et sociales, 1946), a rather slight survey; A. O. Lovejoy and G. Boas, *Primitivism and Related Ideas in Antiquity* (Baltimore, Johns Hopkins U.P., 1935), relevant as background; A. Sinclair, *The Savage: a history of misunderstanding* (London, Weidenfeld and Nicolson, 1977); and an excellent essay by J. Franco, 'The Noble Savage', in D. Daiches and A. Thorlby (eds.), *The Modern World: I – Hopes*, vol. 3 of *Literature and Western Civilisation* (London, Aldus Books, 1975), pp. 565–94. On the abolitionist movement, cf. E. D. Seeber, *Anti-Slavery Opinion in France during the second half of the Eighteenth Century* (Baltimore, Johns Hopkins U.P., 1939) and C. L. Lokke, *France and the Colonial Question* (New York, Columbia U.P., 1932), as well as Mercier, *L'Afrique noire* above.

Relevant studies on specific topics include M. Alexander, *Omai: Noble Savage* (London, Collins and Harvill Press, 1977); Y. Giraud, 'De l'exploration à l'utopie: Notes sur la formation du mythe de Tahiti', *French Studies*, 31 (1977), 26–41; Y. Benot, *Diderot: de l'athéisme à l'anticolonialisme* (François Maspero, 1970); W. Keit (ed.), *Captain Cook: Image and Impact* (Melbourne, Hawthorne Press, 1972); and M. Holloway, *Heavens on Earth: Utopian Communities in America, 1660–1880* (London, Turnstile Press, 1951).

6. *Happy families:* (1) *The age of innocence and* (2) *The new Eve*

Very considerable attention has been given to family history over the past twenty years and more; a high degree of selectivity is thus necessary in the bibliography below, broadly divided between studies of the family as a whole, of the child and of woman.

The first major study of concepts of family life in France in our period – and which has prompted much later research – was P. Ariès, *L'Enfant et la vie familiale sous l'Ancien Régime* (Plon, 1960), also translated as *Centuries of Childhood: A Social History of Family Life* (New York, Random House, 1965). Cf. also P. Ariès's *Histoire des populations françaises et de leurs attitudes devant la vie depuis le XVIIIᵉ siècle* (Editions Self, 1948), part 2. As regards France in particular later substantial works include J. L. Flandrin, *Familles: parenté, maison, sexualité dans l'ancienne société* (Hachette, 1976), also translated as *Families in former times* (Cambridge U.P., 1979); G. Snyders, *La Pédagogie en France aux XVIIᵉ et XVIIIᵉ siècles* (Presses Universitaires de France, 1965), much wider than its title suggests; and D. Hunt, *Parents and Children in History* (London, Basic Books, 1970), this being a re-statement of Ariès's evidence in particular from a psycho-history viewpoint. Much relevant information as regards 'lower-class' attitudes is found in J. L. Flandrin, *Les Amours Paysannes* (*XVIᵉ–XIXᵉ siècles*) (Gallimard-Julliard, 1975) and Hufton, *The Poor of Eighteenth-Century France, 1750–1789* in particular, and there is also a more uneven collective number of *Dix-huitième siècle*, 12 (1980), 7–232, on 'Les Représentations de la vie sexuelle au 18ᵉ siècle.' For the nineteenth-century aftermath the English reader could begin from T. Zeldin, *France, 1848–1945*, vol. 1: *Ambition, Love and Politics* (Oxford, Clarendon Press, 1973), part II.

Works related above all to English and American evidence but also referring to France include L. Stone, *The Family, Sex and Marriage in England*,

1500–1800 (London, Weidenfeld and Nicolson, 1977) and E. Shorter, *The Making of the Modern Family* (London, Collins, 1976), a readable but less detailed work than Stone's. A special aspect of the French experience is dealt with in R. Phillips, *Family Breakdown in Late Eighteenth-Century France: Divorces in Rouen, 1792–1803* (Oxford, Clarendon Press, 1981); cf. the same author's useful summary of similar title in *Social History*, 2 (1976), 197–218. Several other studies on family history are mainly confined to Britain. They include, most notably, P. Laslett, *The World We Have Lost*, 2nd edn (London, Methuen, 1971).

The child is, obviously enough, considered in the studies above, but other works are specifically focussed upon it. They include R. Mercier, *L'Enfant dans la société du XVIIIᵉ siècle (avant l'"Emile")* (Dakar, Publications de la section de langues et littératures, 1961), a major scholarly study of particular relevance to France; G. Boas, *The Cult of Childhood* (London, Warburg Institute, 1966), an outline survey over several centuries; and L. de Mause, *The History of Childhood* (New York, Harper and Row, 1979). On the history of education in France, cf. Snyders, *La Pédagogie*, as above, and R. Chartier *et al.* (eds.), *L'Education en France du XVIᵉ au XVIIIᵉ siècle* (Société d'Editions d'Enseignement Supérieur, 1976). As regards the presentation of the child in literature, cf. especially P. Coveney, *The Image of Childhood* (Harmondsworth, Penguin Books, 1967), a revised edition of his *Poor Monkey* (London, Rockcliff, 1957), mainly but not wholly centred on English literature; R. Kuhn, *The Child in Western Literature* (Hanover and London, U.P. of New England, 1982), largely concerned with nineteenth- and twentieth-century writers, however; J. Calvet, *L'Enfant dans la littérature française* (2 vols., Lanore, 1930), vol. 1; *The Child's Part, Yale French Studies*, 43 (1969) (with essays of varying relevance); and P. Hazard, *Les Livres, les enfants et les hommes* (Flammarion, 1932), though it and Calvet's work now seem somewhat slight in the light of later books. An interesting study of the rise of children's literature in France is A. L. P. Kempton, 'Education and the child in 18th-century French fiction', *St. Volt.*, 124 (1974), 299–362; cf. also K. S. Wilkins, 'Children's literature in 18th-century France', *St. Volt.*, 176 (1971), 429–44. As regards England, cf. the essay by J. H. Plumb in N. McKendrick, J. Brewer and J. H. Plumb (eds.), *The Birth of a Consumer Society: The Commercialisation of Eighteenth-Century England* (London, Europa Publications, 1982), ch. 7.

Changing concepts of woman have been much studied in recent decades. As regards France, major works are P. Hoffmann, *La Femme dans la pensée des lumières* (Ophrys, 1977), which also has very full bibliographies; a most interesting and wide-ranging *Festschrift* collection of essays, E. Jacobs *et al.* (eds.), *Woman and Society in Eighteenth-Century France: Essays in honour of J. S. Spink* (London, Athlone Press, 1979); and P. Fauchery, *Le Mythe de la destinée féminine dans le roman européen du XVIIIᵉ siècle* (Armand Colin, 1972). For a general but older history, cf. L. Abensour, *La Femme et le féminisme avant la Révolution* (Geneva, Slatkine Reprints, 1977) and also M. Albistur and D. Armogathe, *Histoire du féminisme du moyen âge à nos jours* (Editions des femmes, 1977). Of numerous other treatments one may especially note

P. Branca, *Women in Europe since 1750* (London, Croom Helm, 1978) and M. and J. H. Bloch, 'Women and the dialectics of nature in eighteenth-century French thought', in C. MacCormack and M. Strathern (eds.), *Nature, Culture and Gender* (Cambridge U.P., 1980), pp. 25–41. For the context, cf. in particular I. Maclean, *Woman Triumphant: Feminism in French Literature, 1610–1652* (Oxford, Clarendon Press, 1977) and also E. T. Dubois, 'The education of women in seventeenth-century France', *French Studies*, 32 (1978), 1–19. E. and J. de Goncourt, *La Femme au XVIIIe siècle*, new edn (Charpentier, 1887) presents a slight but marginally suggestive argument that woman was predominant in the high society of the time. Rousseau in particular has been much attacked for his view of woman; cf. especially S. M. Okin, *Women in Western Political Thought* (Princeton U.P., 1979), part III. An excellent article, amongst many other studies of his view on love, is M. Macklem, 'Rousseau and the Romantic ethic', *French Studies*, 4 (1950), pp. 322ff., and a useful, recent discussion of *La Nouvelle Héloïse* is T. Tanner, *Adultery in the Novel: Contract and Transgression* (Baltimore and London, Johns Hopkins U.P., 1979), ch. 2.

7. Town and country

The actual condition of the peasantry in eighteenth-century France is well surveyed in several works, in addition to the more general histories of France noted under 1 above. These include G. Duby and A. Wallon (eds.), *Histoire de la France rurale: L'Age classique des paysans, 1340–1789* (4 vols., Seuil, 1975–6), vol. 2, part 3, by E. Le Roy Ladurie, 'De la crise ultime à la vraie croissance, 1660–1789'; I. Woloch (ed.), *The Peasantry in the Old Régime: Conditions and Protests* (Huntington, N.Y., Krieger, 1977), essays by several historians of mainly *Annales* affiliation and with interesting illustrations; and G. Walter, *Histoire des paysans en France* (Flammarion, 1963), pp. 301–91 (on the eighteenth century). On views of the city, cf. a symposium volume, P. Fritz and D. Williams (eds.), *City and Society in the Eighteenth Century* (Toronto, Hakkert, 1973); P. Citron, *La Poésie de Paris dans la littérature française* (2 vols., Editions de Minuit, 1961), vol. 1; and also G. Rudé, *Paris and London in the Eighteenth Century: Studies in Popular Protest* (London, Collins, 1970). A study of some relevance as one illustration is J. M. Fahmy, *Voltaire et Paris*, *St. Volt.*, 195 (1981).

The fullest discussion of the town and country contrast in literature is R. Williams, *The Country and the City* (London, Chatto and Windus, 1973), but this mainly concerns Britain. France is less well served, but cf. the work by C. M. Vance under 2 above (limited to Rousseau, however), and also the works under 1 above concerning the 'feeling for nature' in later-eighteenth-century France, most of which give some treatment of literary representations of rural life as well as of external nature. I am indebted in this chapter to R. M. Renyi's unpublished dissertation on 'Pastoral form or propaganda? The significance of the peasant in French culture, 1750–1789', submitted for the degree of M.A. in the Graduate School of European Cultural History of the University of Warwick in 1982. His study is in part discussing the applicability to France of the thesis about English painting developed in

Bibliographies

J. Barrell's stimulating but controversial book, *The Dark Side of the Landscape: The rural poor in English painting, 1730–1840* (Cambridge U.P., 1980). Historians of French art in the eighteenth century seem to have neglected the subject.

On the Physiocrats basic studies are G. Weulersse, *Le Mouvement physiocratique en France de 1756 à 1770* (2 vols., Mouton, 1968) and *La Physiocratie à la fin du règne de Louis XV (1770–1774)* (Presses Universitaires de France, 1959), but a very useful introduction, with essays and translated extracts, is R. L. Meek, *The Economics of Physiocracy* (Cambridge, Mass., Harvard U.P., 1963), and also relevant is E. Fox-Genovese, *The Origins of Physiocracy* (Ithaca and London, Cornell U.P., 1976).

A major, richly-researched study, K. Thomas, *Man and the Natural World: Changing Attitudes in England, 1500–1800* (London, Allen Lane, 1983), was published only at a very late stage in my own work. I have been able to do no more than allude to it in my final chapter, especially as regards men's views of the animals – the subject at the centre of Thomas's attention – but it contains much other relevant evidence, not least for a comparison of English and French developments and especially in relation to my own earlier chapters.

NOTES

The place of publication, unless given, is Paris.

References to primary printed sources, where publication details are not given, are to the following editions:

J. H. Bernardin de Saint-Pierre, *Les Etudes de la nature*, 2 vols. (Napoléon Chaix, 1865); *Paul et Virginie* (Garnier, 1964).

G. L. L. de Buffon, *Oeuvres philosophiques* ('Corpus général des philosophes français, auteurs modernes', vol. 41, 1, Presses Universitaires de France, 1954); *Les Epoques de la nature*, critical edition (Mémoires du Muséum National d'Histoire Naturelle, vol. 10, Editions du Muséum, 1962).

J. Delille, *Oeuvres*, 2nd edn (Lefèvre, 1833).

D. Diderot, *Oeuvres esthétiques* (Garnier, 1968); *Oeuvres philosophiques* (Garnier, 1961); *Oeuvres romanesques* (Garnier, 1962); *Salons*, 2nd edn (Oxford, Clarendon Press, 1975– : vol. 1, 1975; vol. 2, 1979; vol. 3, 1983); *Correspondance* (16 vols., Les Editions de Minuit, 1955–70).

P. C. de Laclos, *Oeuvres complètes* (Bibliothèque de la Pléiade, Gallimard, 1979) (abbreviated as *O.C.*).

J.-J. Rousseau, *Oeuvres complètes* (4 vols., Bibliothèque de la Pléiade, Gallimard, 1959–69) (abbreviated as *O.C.*).

J. F. de Saint-Lambert, *Poésies*, new edn (Bure, 1826).

References to periodicals are given in full except – as also in the Bibliographies – for the *Revue d'histoire littéraire de la France* (*R.H.L.F.*) and *Studies on Voltaire and the Eighteenth Century* (*St. Volt.*). References are in general limited to French sources within the 1750–1800 period; although, at the Press's suggestion, I have translated French prose quotations, references are to the French text.

1. *Contrasts*

1. J. Ehrard, *L'Idée de nature en France dans la première moitié du XVIIIe siècle* (Service d'Edition et de Vente des Publications de l'Education Nationale, 1963), vol. 1, p. 12.
2. S. Goyard-Fabre, *La Philosophie des lumières en France* (Klincksieck, 1972), p. 134.
3. Ehrard, vol. 2, p. 788; as he succinctly puts it, 'le plus sûr moyen de *naturaliser la morale* était de *moraliser la nature*'.
4. Ehrard, vol. 2, p. 741.
5. R. Lenoble, *Histoire de 'idée de nature* (Albin Michel, 1969), p. 342.

6. A. O. Lovejoy, *Essays in the History of Ideas* (Baltimore, Johns Hopkins U.P., 1948), pp. 69–77.
7. E. H. Gombrich, *Ideals and Idols* (Oxford, Phaidon Press, 1979), p. 11. For an extensive illustration, relevant to this book and especially to chapter 4, and a discussion of 'metaphor' and its epistemological status, cf. J. Schlanger, *Les Métaphores de l'organisme* (Vrin, 1971).
8. Cf. G. Gusdorf, *Dieu, La Nature, L'Homme au siècle des lumières* (Payot, 1972), pp. 502–3, and on Pinel G. S. Rousseau, 'Psychology', in G. S. Rousseau and R. Porter (eds.), *The Ferment of Knowledge* (Cambridge U.P., 1980), pp. 153–60. Far more detailed discussions of the wider subject are J. Starobinski, *Histoire du traitement de la mélancolie des origines à 1960* (Geneva, Geigy, 1960) and M. Foucault, *Histoire de la folie à l'âge classique* (Plon, 1961).

2. *Pastoral landscapes*

1. D. Mornet, *Le Sentiment de la nature en France de J-J. Rousseau à Bernardin de Saint-Pierre* (Hachette, 1907), p. 443.
2. Cited in Mornet, pp. 44 and 46.
3. M. Reynolds, *The Treatment of Nature in English Poetry between Pope and Wordsworth* (Chicago U.P., 1909), p. 328.
4. Rousseau, *Correspondance complète*, ed. R. A. Leigh, vol. 9 (Geneva, Institut et Musée Voltaire and Madison, U. of Wisconsin Press, 1969), pp. 349–50.
5. J. E. Congleton, *Theories of Pastoral Poetry in England, 1684–1798* (New York, Haskell House, 1968), p. 113, citing Mackail.
6. Saint-Lambert, *Poésies*, pp. 1–23.
7. Congleton, p. 295.
8. Cf. P. Conisbee, *Painting in Eighteenth-Century France* (Oxford, Phaidon Press, 1981), especially ch. 6.
9. K. Clark, *Landscape into Art* (London, John Murray, 1949), p. 1. The notion of 'the natural' in eighteenth-century French art carries other meanings, obviously enough, as well as depiction of external nature. Though not relevant here, their inter-relations would repay fuller study.
10. C. Hussey, *The Picturesque*, 2nd edn (London, Cass, 1967), p. 5.
11. On Saint-Pierre's period at the Jardin des Plantes cf. two detailed articles by Lieutenant-Colonel Largemain in *R.H.L.F.*, 4 (1897), 246–81, and 6 (1899), 120–32.
12. Cf. C. Thacker, *The Wildness Pleases* (London and Canberra, Croom Helm, 1983), p. 10.
13. A. Blanc, 'Le Jardin de Julie', *Dix-Huitième Siècle*, 14 (1982), 357–76.
14. Rousseau, *O.C.*, vol. 2, p. 471.
15. E. de Ganay, *Les Jardins de France et leur décor* (Larousse, 1949).
16. L. Stone, *The Family, Sex and Marriage in England, 1500–1800* (London, Weidenfeld and Nicolson, 1977), p. 395; cf. Thacker, p. 32.
17. S. S. B. Taylor, 'Rousseau's romanticism', in S. Harvey *et al.* (eds.), *Reappraisals of Rousseau: Studies in honour of R. A. Leigh* (Manchester U.P., 1980), p. 10.

18. Rousseau, *Lettres à M. de Malesherbes*, ed. G. Rudler (London, Allen and Unwin, 1928), pp. 41–2.
19. C. E. Engel, *La Littérature alpestre en France et en Angleterre aux XVIIIe et XIXe siècles* (Chambéry, Dardel, 1930), p. 41.

3. *Wild sublimity*

1. M. H. Nicolson, *Mountain Gloom and Mountain Glory* (New York, Norton, 1963), p. 3. Like all other students of the rise of mountain appreciation in England, I am indebted to this work.
2. Cf. Nicolson, p. 233. On 'the Burnet controversy', cf. chs. 2, 5 and 6 and B. Willey, *The Eighteenth-Century Background: Studies on the Idea of Nature* (London, Chatto and Windus, 1940), ch. 2.
3. Burke, *A Philosophical Enquiry into the Origin of our Ideas of the Sublime and Beautiful*, ed. J. T. Boulton (London, Routledge and Kegan Paul, 1958), p. 39.
4. Nicolson, pp. 29–30, note 39, and cf. p. 143.
5. Cited by Nicolson, pp. 30, 305 and xii.
6. T. Gray, *Correspondence*, 2nd edn (3 vols., Oxford, Clarendon Press, 1971), vol. 1, p. 128.
7. Nicolson, p. 352.
8. Paul Van Tieghem, *Le Sentiment de la nature dans le préromantisme européen* (Nizet, 1960), p. 159.
9. Rousseau, *O.C.*, vol. 2, pp. 77 and 518.
10. C. E. Engel, *La Littérature alpestre en France et en Angleterre aux XVIIIe et XIXe siècles* (Chambéry, Dardel, 1930), p. 41.
11. H. B. de Saussure, *Voyages dans les Alpes*, 2nd edn (8 vols., Neuchâtel, Louis Fauche-Borel, 1796–1803), vol. 4, pp. 389–90 (ch. 52).
12. Engel, p. 35. A similar conclusion is reached by C. Lacoste-Veysseyre, *Les Alpes romantiques: le thème des Alpes dans la littérature française de 1800 à 1850* (2 vols., Geneva, Slatkine Reprints, 1981); a few scientists and travellers apart, she finds little appreciation of the Alps by French writers (cf. vol. 1, pp. 17–42). She concludes that even Marmontel's *La Bergère des Alpes* is centrally a story of human feeling, and, again, notes that, though Florian had visited the Chamonix valley, his *Claudine* praises God for having made mountain storms, 'ces belles horreurs', so infrequent.
13. Mme Roland cited by D. Mornet, *Le Sentiment de la nature en France de J-J. Rousseau à Bernardin de Saint-Pierre* (Hachette, 1907), p. 55. All the same, one can note how few travel-accounts were published in French: cf. the bibliographies of works prior to 1800 in Engel, pp. 253ff. and Lacoste-Veysseyre, vol. 2, pp. 859–60.
14. Goethe, *Werther*, translated by B. Q. Morgan (London, John Calder, 1976), p. 69.
15. Mme de Staël cited by Engel, p. 133; Chateaubriand, *Oeuvres complètes*, new edn, vol. 6 (Nendeln/Liechtenstein, Klaus Reprint, 1975), pp. 341–51 and especially p. 347.
16. Cited by Mornet, *Le Sentiment de la nature en France*, p. 199.

17. Burial inscriptions, like hymns and service-books, are somewhat neglected by historians. In St Mary's Church, Tenby, there is a splendid memorial to one such 'dipper' which itself deserves to be preserved from oblivion: 'This tablet was raised by a few Ladies and Gentlemen, to preserve from oblivion the Memory of Peggy Davies. Bathing woman 42 years to the Ladies who visited Tenby: Her good humour, respectful attention, and Gratitude made her employers Friends: On the 29th of Sept' 1809 In the Water She was seized with Apoplexy and expired, Aged 82.'

18. Cited by S. Howell, *The Seaside* (London, Studio Vista, 1974), p. 14. Brighton acknowledged its debt in 1951 with a week's celebration of the bi-centenary of the work's publication and with a plaque on the Royal Albion Hotel, which itself replaced Russell's own house.

19. Cf. Howell, p. 55; even so Smollett entered the sea in a sedan chair.

20. Cited by Howell, p. 44.

21. Van Tieghem, p. 211.

22. Cited by Van Tieghem, p. 209, the second assertion being preserved at the opening of his *Voyage*.

23. Saint-Pierre, *Paul et Virginie*, p. 200.

24. Mornet, *Le Sentiment de la nature en France*, p. 336.

25. Diderot, *Salons*, vol. 3, p. 165.

26. Saint-Lambert, *Poésies*, p. 11.

27. Cited by D. Mornet, *Le Romantisme en France au XVIIIe siècle*, 2nd edn (Hachette, 1925), pp. 46–7.

28. Cf. M. Butler, *Romantics, Rebels and Reactionaries: English literature and its background, 1760–1830* (Oxford U.P., 1981), p. 23 and *passim*, and also H. Trevor-Roper, 'The invention of tradition: The Highland tradition of Scotland', in E. Hobsbawm and T. Ranger (eds.), *The Invention of Tradition* (Cambridge U.P., 1983), pp. 15–41.

29. E. J. Hobsbawm, *Bandits* (London, Weidenfeld and Nicolson, 1969), p. 109.

30. Cf. 'Le Cheminement d'un héros', in A. Berchtold *et al.*, *Quel Tell?* (Lausanne, Payot, 1973), pp. 181–321.

31. Diderot, *Oeuvres esthétiques*, p. 261.

32. Goethe, *Werther*, p. 24.

33. Hawkesworth cited by Thacker, p. 170. Cf. also Paul Van Tieghem, *Le Préromantisme* (2 vols., SFELT, 1948), vol. 1, 'La Découverte de la mythologie et de l'ancienne poésie scandinaves.'

34. Diderot, *Oeuvres esthétiques*, pp. 97 and 135.

35. Ramond cited by Mornet, *Le Sentiment de la nature en France*, p. 280; Rousseau, *O.C.*, vol. 2, p. 79.

36. For an outline of changing interpretations of Spinoza's relation to religion, cf. D. G. Charlton, *Secular Religions in France, 1815–1870* (London, Oxford U.P., 1963), pp. 119–21.

37. Goethe, *Werther*, pp. 15, 69, 70 and 23.

38. *Werther*, p. 107.

39. Van Tieghem, *Le Préromantisme*, vol. 1, p. 261.

4. *Sciences of nature*

1. D. Mornet, 'Les Enseignements des bibliothèques privées, 1750–1780', *R.H.L.F.*, 17 (1910), 449–92, and *Les Sciences de la nature au XVIIIe siècle* (Armand Colin, 1911), pp. 248–9.
2. Diderot, *Oeuvres philosophiques*, p. 180.
3. C. Kiernan, *The Enlightenment and Science in Eighteenth-Century France*, 2nd edn, *St. Volt.*, 59A (1973), 13.
4. Cited by J. Roger, *Les Sciences de la vie dans la pensée française du XVIIIe siècle* (Armand Colin, 1963), p. 395. Throughout this section I am greatly indebted to this work.
5. Cf. A. Vartanian, 'Trembley's polyp, La Mettrie, and 18th-century French materialism', *Journal of the History of Ideas*, 11 (1950), 259–86, and also L. C. Rosenfield, *From Beast-machine to Machine-man* (London, Oxford U.P., 1940).
6. Cf. especially Roger, part 3, ch. 2, and essays in B. Glass *et al.* (eds.), *Forerunners of Darwin, 1745–1859* (Baltimore, Johns Hopkins U.P., 1959).
7. Buffon, *Oeuvres philosophiques*, pp. 287A–289B.
8. As well as Roger, cf. the discussion by A. Lovejoy, 'Buffon and the problem of species', in B. Glass *et al.* (eds.), pp. 84ff.
9. L. Crocker, *Diderot's Chaotic Order* (Princeton U.P., 1974), pp. 30 and 21.
10. R. Taton (ed.), *The Beginnings of Modern Science* (London, Thames and Hudson, 1964), p. 501.
11. Cf. J. Ehrard, 'Opinions médicales en France au 18e siècle: la peste et l'idée de contagion', *Annales: économies, sociétés, civilisations*, 12 (1957), 46–59.
12. For a detailed discussion at length, cf. J. Schlanger, *Les Métaphores de l'organisme* (Vrin, 1971). A shorter collective treatment, especially of links with aesthetics, is G. S. Rousseau (ed.), *Organic Form: the Life of an Idea* (London, Routledge and Kegan Paul, 1972).
13. I. Berlin, *Vico and Herder* (London, Hogarth Press, 1976), p. 147, note 1. More broadly, cf. H. B. Nisbet, *Herder and the Philosophy and History of Science* (Cambridge, Modern Humanities Research Association, 1970).
14. Buffon, *Oeuvres philosophiques*, p. 31A.
15. Cited by I. O. Wade, *The Structure and Form of the French Enlightenment* (2 vols., Princeton U.P., 1977), vol. 1, pp. 530 and 534.
16. Buffon, *Les Epoques de la nature*, p. 4.

5. *Death and destruction*

1. Cf. H. Vyverberg, *Historical Pessimism in the French Enlightenment* (Cambridge, Mass., Harvard U.P., 1958).
2. Cf. M. Vovelle, *Mourir autrefois: Attitudes collectives devant la mort au XVIIe et XVIIIe siècles* (Gallimard-Julliard, 1974), ch. 8, and F. Lebrun, *Les Hommes et la mort en Anjou aux XVIIe et XVIIIe siècles* (Paris and The Hague, Mouton, 1971), p. 489.
3. L. Stone, *The Family, Sex and Marriage in England, 1500–1800* (London,

Weidenfeld and Nicolson, 1977), part 4, in particular, notes its expressions in relation to death and burial.

4. Cited by T. D. Kendrick, *The Lisbon Earthquake* (London, Methuen, 1956), p. 1, and cf. p. 151.

5. Cf. Lebrun, pp. 494–5 and *passim*, and R. Favre, *La Mort...au siècle des lumières* (Lyon, Presses Universitaires, 1978), ch. 3. J. McManners, *Death and the Enlightenment* (Oxford, Clarendon Press, 1981), presents a rather gentler picture, and Favre, p. 546, acknowledges numerous kindly exceptions.

6. Hume, *Dialogues concerning Natural Religion*, 2nd edn (London, Nelson, 1947), p. 211; Diderot, *Oeuvres philosophiques*, p. 123; Buffon, *Oeuvres philosophiques*, p. 304B.

7. Cf. Favre, pp. 390–400 in particular.

8. J. G. Herder, *Ideen zur Philosophie der Geschichte der Menschheit* (2 vols., Berlin and Weimar, Aufbau-Verlag, 1965), vol. 1, book 1, ch. 3; Rousseau, *O.C.*, vol. 4, pp. 1059–75.

9. Diderot, *Oeuvres esthétiques*, pp. 98 and 195.

10. Diderot, *Oeuvres romanesques*, pp. 387ff. and 866.

11. Cf. his essay on 'How the Ancients represented death', in Lessing, *Selected Prose Works*, translated E. C. Beasley and H. Zimmern (London, George Bell, 1879), p. 225. I am indebted to Dr J. R. Williams for drawing my attention to this work.

12. *Oeuvres de Prévost* (Presses Universitaires de Grenoble, 1978), p. 439.

13. Chateaubriand, *Atala* (Textes Littéraires Français, Geneva, Droz, 1973), pp. 130–1.

14. Rétif de la Bretonne cited by McManners, p. 350; Delille, *Oeuvres*, p. 27.

15. On the Père-Lachaise, cf. P. Ariès, *L'Homme devant la mort* (Editions du Seuil, 1977), p. 524. As a comparable American example he refers to Mount Auburn in Massachusetts and also notes (p. 334) that even in the mid-seventeenth century colonists in Virginia often chose to be buried amid nature, on the plantations or in a churchyard.

16. Favre, p. 446, and R. Mortier, *La Poétique des ruines en France*, p. 142. By contrast Paul Van Tieghem (*Le Préromantisme*, 2 vols., SFELT, 1948, vol. 2, p. 156) takes a lighter-hearted view of the age's poetry of tombs, linking it with 'la mélancolie rêveuse et tendre, un peu molle, exempte d'idées trop sérieuses et trop sombres'.

17. Diderot, *Salons*, vol. 3, p. 228.

18. Saint-Pierre also argues that unless we died, new humans could not be born into the world for lack of space. That in turn would transform the configuration of the two sexes and all the relationships of conjugal, filial and paternal love on which the whole system of our happiness, in his view, is based (*Les Etudes de la nature*, vol. 1, p. 75).

19. Saint-Pierre, *Les Etudes de la nature*, vol. 2, pp. 244–54.

20. Chateaubriand, *Le Génie du christianisme*, part 3, book 5, ch. 3, in *Essai sur les révolutions; Génie du christianisme* (Bibliothèque de la Pléiade, Gallimard, 1978), p. 882.

21. Mme de Staël, *Corinne*, book 8, ch. 4; cf. also *De l'Allemagne*, IV, 9, 'De la contemplation de la nature'.

22. There is one striking and significant exception to this linking of ruins and nature: Volney's *Les Ruines* (1791). His concern was primarily political and hence with the *man-made* ruins that would illustrate his criticisms and support his radical progressivism. Other than in abstract terms 'the natural' seems of little interest to him. Cf. Mortier, ch. 10, and B. Rigby, 'Volney's rationalist apocalypse', in F. Barker *et al.* (eds.), *1789: Reading, Writing, Revolution* (University of Essex, 1982), pp. 22–37.
23. The one partial exception known to me is Favre, ch. 8.
24. Diderot, *Correspondance*, vol. 2, pp. 283–4.
25. Cited by Favre, p. 354.
26. Cf. Favre, pp. 452–3.
27. Rousseau, *O.C.*, vol. 4, p. 1068.
28. For a statement of his view of death, cf. D'Holbach, *Système de la nature*, new edn (2 vols., Hildesheim, Georg Olms, 1966), vol. 1, ch. 13.
29. Cited by Favre, p. 499.
30. Saint-Pierre, *Paul et Virginie*, p. 220.
31. Diderot, *Correspondance*, vol. 2, p. 284.
32. Cited by Favre, p. 511.
33. Diderot, *Correspondance*, vol. 3, p. 56, and *Salons*, vol. 3, p. 228.
34. Lebrun, p. 495.

6. Transoceanic perspectives

1. M. Duchet, *Anthropologie et histoire au siècle des lumières* (François Maspero, 1971), pp. 483ff.
2. Bougainville, *Voyage autour du monde* (Collection 10/18, Union Générale d'éditions, 1966), p. 186.
3. J. Dunmore, *French Explorers in the Pacific*, vol. 1: *The Eighteenth Century* (Oxford, Clarendon Press, 1965), p. 79.
4. Bougainville, pp. 195 and 209.
5. Bougainville, pp. 212–13 and 195.
6. Bougainville, p. 195.
7. Cf. M. Alexander, *Omai: Noble Savage* (London, Collins and Harvill Press, 1977), pp. 17ff., and H. N. Fairchild, *The Noble Savage: a study in Romantic Naturalism* (New York, Columbia U.P., 1928), pp. 106–7.
8. G. Howard, *Castle Howard*, new edn (n.p., n.d.), p. 15. I am grateful to Dr H. G. Hall for drawing my attention to this work.
9. Cited in Bougainville, p. 392.
10. C. F. P. Fesche, *La Nouvelle Cythère* (Ducharte et van Buggenhoudt, 1929), p. xxx.
11. For a comprehensive list of paintings and drawings cf. B. Smith, *European Vision and the South Pacific* (Oxford, Clarendon Press, 1960), pp. 258ff.
12. On Omai himself cf. Alexander, and on the production p. 128 and Smith, p. 81.
13. A most useful survey is given in Y. Giraud, 'De l'exploration à l'utopie: Notes sur la formation du mythe de Tahiti', *French Studies*, 31 (1977), 26–41.

14. Rousseau, *O.C.*, vol. 2, p. 413; cf. p. 441. On one noteworthy link, cf. C. Thacker, '"O Tinian! O Juan Fernandez!"': Rousseau's "Elysée" and Anson's desert islands', *Garden History*, 5 (1977), 41–7.

15. Columbus cited in Fairchild, p. 9.

16. Shakespeare's juxtaposition of Caliban and Prospero is one instance of the ambivalent reactions of the time – as of earlier periods also, on which cf. R. Bernheimer, *Wild Men in the Middle Ages* (Cambridge, Mass., Harvard U.P., 1952).

17. Cartier cited in D. Echeverria, *Mirage in the West: A History of the French Image of American Society to 1815* (New York, Octagon Books, 1966), p. 6; Leo cited in R. Mercier, *L'Afrique noire dans la littérature française: Les premières images (xviie–xviiie siècles)* (Dakar, Publications de la section des langues et littératures, 1962), p. 15; Paracelsus cited in E. Dudley and M. E. Novak (eds.), *The Wild Man Within* (Pittsburgh, U. of Pittsburgh Press, 1972), p. 264.

18. Cited in G. Atkinson, *Les Relations de voyages du XVIIe siècle* (Champion, 1924), p. 68.

19. The quotations in this paragraph are cited in Mercier, pp. 44, 61 and 101.

20. Cf. M. E. Novak, 'The wild man comes to tea', and G. Symcox, 'The wild man's return', in Dudley and Novak (eds.), pp. 183–222 and 223–47.

21. M. Arnould, *La Mort du Capitaine Cook*, pantomime en 4 actes (Lagrange, 1788).

22. Cf. A. Gerbi, *The Dispute of the New World* (Pittsburgh, U. of Pittsburgh Press, 1973), pp. 4 and 47.

23. Cf. Gerbi, p. 330.

24. Cf. Echeverria, p. 14. The latter perception forms a main theme of his study.

25. Gerbi, pp. 170ff.

26. A. O. Lovejoy, 'The supposed primitivism of Rousseau's "Discourse on Inequality"', in *Essays in the History of Ideas* (Baltimore, Johns Hopkins U.P., 1948), pp. 16 and 22.

27. Rousseau, *O.C.*, vol. 3, pp. 141–3, 153–4 and 162.

28. Cf. Y. Benot, *Diderot: de l'athéisme à l'anticolonialisme* (François Maspero, 1970) and Duchet, pp. 407ff.

29. A. O. Aldridge, 'The state of Nature: an undiscovered country in the history of ideas', *St. Volt.*, 98 (1971), 16.

30. Diderot, *Oeuvres* (Bibliothèque de la Pléiade, Gallimard, 1951), pp. 1024–5.

31. H. Dieckmann, in Diderot, *Supplément au Voyage de Bougainville*, p.p. H. Dieckmann (Geneva, Droz, and Lille, Giard, 1955), p. lii; S. Warner, 'Diderot's *Supplément* and late Enlightenment thought', *St. Volt.*, 86 (1971), 244–5.

32. Duchet, pp. 11 and 18. For a rather different view, cf. P. Gay, *The Enlightenment: An Interpretation* (2 vols., London, Weidenfeld and Nicolson, 1967–70), vol. 2, pp. 410–23. An analogous but questionable view is found in Hayden White, *Tropics of Discourse: Essays in Cultural Criticism* (Baltimore and London, Johns Hopkins U.P., 1978), ch. 8: 'The

noble savage theme as fetish', pp. 183–96. The savage both appeals and repels – to summarise – by his violation of European taboos on nakedness, sexual promiscuity, lawlessness, community of property and cannibalism. Any indulgent feelings towards him, however, only emerged after he had already been subordinated to the European. Moreover, any praise aimed 'not to dignify the native, rather to undermine the idea of nobility itself'; elevation of the '*noble*' savage served the radicals' ideological needs 'perfectly, for it at once undermined the nobility's claim to a special human status and extended that status to the whole of humanity'. White believes this true of France also, where the term is 'le *bon* sauvage', and even though, he claims, the radicals intended only to confer higher status on the bourgeoisie (pp. 191 and 194).

33. H. Honour, *The New Golden Land* (London, Allen Lane, 1975), p. 132.
34. Saint-Lambert, *Poésies*, p. 260. Cf. also the 'Document annexe' in Duchet, pp. 177ff.
35. Mercier, pp. 169–71.
36. Saint-Pierre, *Paul et Virginie*, p. 96.
37. Chateaubriand, *Le Génie du christianisme*, part IV, book 2, ch. 5, in *Essai sur les révolutions; Génie du christianisme* (Bibliothèque de la Pléiade, Gallimard, 1978), pp. 930–1.
38. *Paul et Virginie*, p. 229.

7. *Happy families: (1) The age of innocence*

1. J. McManners, *Death and the Enlightenment* (Oxford, Clarendon Press, 1981), p. 440.
2. P. Ariès, *L'Enfant et la vie familiale sous l'Ancien Régime* (Plon, 1960), p. 461.
3. D. Herlihy, 'Medieval children', in R. E. Sullivan *et al.* (eds.), *The Walter Prescott Webb Memorial Lectures; Essays on Medieval Civilization* (Austin and London, U. of Texas P., 1978), pp. 109–41, and specifically p. 130. Amongst other studies of the child during the Middle Ages, cf. L. Demaître, 'The idea of childhood and child care in medical writings of the Middle Ages', *Journal of Psychohistory*, 4 (1977), 461–90; H. Goldberg, 'The literary portrait of the child in Castilian medieval literature', *Kentucky Romance Quarterly*, 27 (1980), 11–27; and a collective and wide-ranging volume, *L'Enfant au moyen-âge* (Champion, 1980). I am very much indebted to Dr Linda M. Paterson both for these and other references and for her own stimulating discussion of them.
4. Herlihy, pp. 114–17 and, citing St Augustine, p. 120.
5. L. Stone, *The Family, Sex and Marriage in England, 1500–1800* (London, Weidenfeld and Nicolson, 1977), p. 395. For the view that the bedroom door may have been adopted for puritanical reasons – in particular to separate parents when in bed from their children – cf. J. L. Flandrin, *Familles: parenté, maison, sexualité dans l'ancienne société* (Hachette, 1976), pp. 91ff. and especially pp. 93 and 109.
6. Stone, p. 323.

7. Diderot, *Salons*, vol. 2, p. 155.
8. Marivaux, *Romans* (Bibliothèque de la Pléiade, Gallimard, 1949), p. 88.
9. Cf. Flandrin, p. 57; R. Mercier, *L'Enfant dans la société du XVIIIe siècle (avant l'"Emile")* (Dakar, Publications de la section de langues et littératures, 1961), p. 28; O. H. Hufton, *The Poor of Eighteenth-Century France, 1750–1789* (Oxford, Clarendon Press, 1974), p. 326; and McManners, pp. 5–10.
10. Cited by G. Snyders, *La Pédagogie en France aux XVIIe et XVIIIe siècles* (Presses Universitaires de France, 1965), p. 194.
11. P. Ariès, *Histoire des populations françaises et de leurs attitudes devant la vie depuis le XVIIIe siècle* (Editions Self, 1948), p. 472.
12. Cf. E. Le Roy Ladurie, *Montaillou, village occitan de 1294 à 1324* (Gallimard, 1975), ch. 13. It is the more surprising that he should severely criticise Ariès (p. 307) – albeit accepting part of his thesis – since such evidence, drawn from his own study, clearly illustrates that the Cathars were quite unlike their Catholic neighbours in this respect. The contrasts at Montaillou confirm Ariès's argument rather than weakening it.
13. On Voltaire cf. Snyders, pp. 276 and 281.
14. Cf. Stone, p. 398.
15. Cf. McManners, p. 10.
16. Hufton, *passim*, and specifically p. 344.
17. Cited by R. Mercier, *La Réhabilitation de la nature humaine* (Villemonble, Editions 'La Balance', 1960), p. 336.
18. Rousseau, *O.C.*, vol. 4, pp. 242, 302 and 364; cf. also p. 322: 'Posons pour maxime incontestable que les premiers mouvements de la nature sont toujours droits; il n'y a point de perversité originelle dans le coeur humain.'
19. Rousseau, *O.C.*, vol. 4, p. 302.
20. J. Calvet, *L'Enfant dans la littérature française* (2 vols., Lanore, 1930), vol. 1, p. 66.
21. Calvet, vol. 1, p. 74.
22. A. P. L. Kempton, 'Education and the child in 18th-century French fiction', *St. Volt.*, 124 (1974), 333 and 362.
23. Snyders, p. 270 and cf. also pp. 417ff.
24. Rousseau, *O.C.*, vol. 4, p. 300.
25. Saint-Pierre, *Paul et Virginie*, p. 85.
26. Goethe, *Werther*, translated by B. Q. Morgan (London, John Calder, 1976), p. 42.
27. Schiller, *On the Naïve and Sentimental in Literature*, translation of *Uber naïve und sentimentalische Dichtung* by H. Watanabe-O'Kelly (Manchester, Carcanet New Press, 1981), p. 23.

8. *Happy families: (2) The new Eve*

1. Rousseau, *O.C.*, vol. 3, p. 352 (*Du Contrat social*, 1, 2).
2. Rousseau, *O.C.*, vol. 4, p. 254.

3. Cited by R. Mercier, *La Réhabilitation de la nature humaine* (*1700–1750*) (Villemonble, Editions 'La Balance', 1960), p. 398.

4. Cf. A. Brookner, *Greuze* (London, Elek, 1972), Appendix.

5. Cf. R. Mercier, *L'Enfant dans la société du XVIIIᵉ siècle* (*avant l'"Emile"*) (Dakar, Publications de la section de langues et littératures, 1961), p. 85.

6. Rousseau, *O.C.*, vol. 4, pp. 257–8. It has been argued that Rousseau only adopted his view on breast-feeding as an afterthought; cf. T. Zeldin, *France, 1848–1945*, vol. 1: *Ambition, Love and Politics* (Oxford, Clarendon Press, 1973), p. 317. Even so, however, it would not follow that, after his 'conversion', he was any less sincere.

7. Cited by J. McManners, *Death and the Enlightenment* (Oxford, Clarendon Press, 1981), p. 54.

8. By S. B. Ortner, in M. Z. Rosaldo and L. Lamphere, *Women, Culture and Society* (Stanford U.P., 1974), pp. 67–87.

9. G. Gusdorf, preface to P. Hoffmann, *La Femme dans la pensée des lumières* (Ophrys, 1977), p. 12.

10. Cited by B. Easlea, *Witch-Hunting, Magic and the New Philosophy* (Sussex, Harvester Press, and New Jersey, Humanities Press, 1980), p. 8, amongst numerous other examples. A short, vivid evocation of the old view is given by N. Z. Davis, *Society and Culture in Early Modern France* (London, Duckworth, 1975), pp. 124–51.

11. Diderot, *Oeuvres philosophiques*, pp. 346–8. This view was widespread, as Hoffmann fully illustrates (pp. 175–99); he also sympathetically highlights Diderot's 'ambiguity' and 'contradictions' (pp. 488–536).

12. P. Fauchery, *Le Mythe de la destinée féminine dans le roman européen au XVIIIᵉ siècle* (Armand Colin, 1972), p. 832.

13. Rousseau, *O.C.*, vol. 4, p. 703.

14. Rousseau, *O.C.*, vol. 4, p. 693.

15. Cf. J. H. Bloch, 'Women and the reform of the nation', in E. Jacobs *et al.* (eds.), *Woman and Society in Eighteenth-Century France: Essays in honour of J. S. Spink* (London, Athlone Press, 1979), and also Mercier, *L'Enfant dans la société du XVIIIᵉ siècle*, of which a major conclusion is that Rousseau's ideas had all been advanced before him (p. 185).

16. Cf. S. Mason, 'The riddle of Roxane', in Jacobs *et al.*, notably p. 40, where 'archaic dimensions' are attributed to his attitude to woman.

17. Cf. in particular the discussion in E. J. Gardner, 'The *philosophes* and women: sensationalism and sentiment', in Jacobs *et al.*

18. Diderot, *Oeuvres* (Bibliothèque de la Pléiade, Gallimard, 1951), p. 985. On his view on woman, cf. the essays by E. Jacobs and R. Niklaus, in Jacobs *et al.*

19. Laclos, *O.C.*, p. 390; cf. pp. 389–443.

20. Laclos, *O.C.*, pp. 436–7. On his views on female education cf. also L. Versini, *Laclos et la tradition* (Klincksieck, 1968), pp. 521ff.

21. Cf. in particular the argument in D. Fletcher, 'Restif de la Bretonne and woman's estate', in Jacobs *et al.*

22. S. M. Okin, *Women in Western Political Thought* (Princeton U.P., 1979), pp. 99–196.

23. Rousseau, *O.C.*, vol. 4, p. 710.
24. P. D. Jimack, 'The paradox of Sophie and Julie', in Jacobs *et al.*
25. Hoffmann, p. 553. It has been argued, indeed, that all three women characters, Cécile and Merteuil as well as Tourvel, 'command sympathy because all are the prisoners of sexual inequality'; cf. H. Mason, *French Writers and their Society, 1715–1800* (London, Macmillan, 1982), p. 206.
26. Saint-Pierre, *Paul et Virginie*, pp. 57–63. His concept of woman here, as well as references within the novel itself, make it the more surprising that Virginie's refusal to remove her clothes in order to escape drowning should have been interpreted by some critics as indicating that the author saw female 'modesty' as a false value derived from European society. On this, cf. an incisive article by P. Robinson, 'Virginie's fatal modesty', *British Journal of Eighteenth-Century Studies*, 5 (1982), 35–48, and also Saint-Pierre's own section, 'Du sentiment de l'amour' in his *Etudes de la nature*.
27. Bloch, in Jacobs *et al.*, p. 13.
28. E. and J. de Goncourt, *La Femme au XVIIIᵉ siècle*, new edn (Charpentier, 1887), p. 323.
29. P. Branca, *Women in Europe since 1750* (London, Croom Helm, 1978), p. 145, note 1.
30. *Oeuvres de Prévost* (Presses Universitaires de Grenoble, 1978), p. 425.
31. Rousseau, *O.C.*, vol. 4, p. 258.
32. *Théâtre du XVIIIᵉ siècle* (2 vols., Bibliothèque de la Pléiade, Gallimard, 1972–4), vol. 2, p. 81.
33. Compare *La Nouvelle Héloïse*, letters III, 18 and III, 20. One can note that her father is, as much as Diderot's, a master of emotional blackmail; in tears and on his knees he begs her to 'respect the white hairs of your unhappy father' (*O.C.*, vol. 2, p. 348). However, the fact that both fathers utilise it does suggest that the young were becoming more rebellious against arranged marriage; cf. G. Snyders, *La Pédagogie en France aux XVIIᵉ et XVIIIᵉ siècles* (Presses Universitaires de France, 1965), p. 325, who argues that this was in fact beginning to be the case amongst the bourgeoisie in France.
34. L. Lerner, *Love and Marriage: Literature and its Social Context* (London, Edward Arnold, 1979), p. 205 and *passim*.
35. J. L. Flandrin, *Familles: parenté, maison, sexualité dans l'ancienne société* (Hachette, 1976), p. 165. In *Les Amours paysannes* Flandrin argues that the peasantry, by comparison, was already rating affection more highly. In the French upper classes, in contrast, arranged marriages continued into the nineteenth and even the twentieth centuries. Cf. also L. Stone, *The Family, Sex and Marriage in England, 1500–1800* (London, Weidenfeld and Nicolson, 1977), p. 322.
36. Rousseau, *O.C.*, vol. 2, pp. 372–3.
37. Ibid., p. 449.
38. *Théâtre du XVIIIᵉ siècle*, vol. 2, p. 87.
39. Cf. J. L. Flandrin, *Les Amours paysannes (XVIᵉ–XIXᵉ siècles)* (Gallimard-Julliard, 1975), pp. 89–91.

40. Montaigne, *Essais* (Bibliothèque de la Pléiade, Gallimard, 1962), p. 196 (1, 30).
41. Cf. W. Roberts, *Morality and Social Class in 18th-century French literature and painting* (University of Toronto Press, 1974) for a general discussion – and also of the 'incongruities and tensions' found in novels which combined the libertine and the moralistic. Cf. also, for one example of woman as libertine, E. Thompsett, 'The theme of seduction in the eighteenth-century French novel: Barthe's *La Jolie Femme*', *Forum for Modern Language Studies*, 12 (1976), 206–16.
42. Cf. Stone, p. 55; Mercier, *L'Enfant dans la société du XVIIIe siècle*, p. 28; Flandrin, *Les Amours paysannes*, p. 60; and McManners, pp. 71–2 – who especially notes, however, that the age of first marriage often differed between classes.
43. Cited by Flandrin, *Familles*, p. 206. On the broader subject, cf. McManners, pp. 454–6 and especially the bibliography given at p. 565, note 52.

9. Town and country

1. Cf. P. Citron, *La Poésie de Paris dans la littérature française de Rousseau à Baudelaire* (2 vols., Editions de Minuit, 1961), vol. 1, books 1 and 2.
2. G. Rudé, *Europe in the Eighteenth Century* (London, Weidenfeld and Nicolson, 1972), ch. 4; cf. also J. McManners, *Death and the Enlightenment* (Oxford, Clarendon Press, 1981), p. 92.
3. R. Williams, *The Country and the City* (London, Chatto and Windus, 1973), pp. 304 and 302.
4. A. Cobban, *The Social Interpretation of the French Revolution* (Cambridge U.P., 1964), pp. 91–106.
5. C. B. A. Behrens, *The Ancien Régime* (London, Thames and Hudson, 1967), p. 44.
6. D. Meakin, *Man and Work: Literature and Culture in Industrial Society* (London, Methuen, 1976). Cf., however, K. Thomas, 'Work and leisure in pre-industrial society', *Past and Present*, 29 (1964), 50–66, for a helpful survey of the earlier period.
7. Morelly's third 'loi agraire' even requires every citizen without exception (other than for infirmity) to work at agriculture between the ages of 20 and 25; cf. *Code de la nature* (Par-Tout, Chez Le Vrai Sage, 1755), pp. 196–7. On European emigrants to America, cf. M. Holloway, *Heavens on Earth: Utopian Communities in America, 1660–1880* (London, Turnstile Press, 1951).
8. Rousseau, *O.C.*, vol. 2, pp. 611 and 603–4.
9. R. L. Meek, *The Economics of Physiocracy* (Cambridge, Mass., Harvard U.P., 1963), p. 9.
10. Rétif de la Bretonne, *La Vie de mon père* (Garnier, 1970), p. 59.
11. Rousseau, *O.C.*, vol. 2, p. 515.
12. Goethe, *Werther*, translated by B. Q. Morgan (London, John Calder, 1976), p. 41.
13. Rousseau, *O.C.*, vol. 2, p. 1105.

14. J. Barrell, *The Dark Side of the Landscape: The rural poor in English painting, 1730–1840* (Cambridge U.P., 1980), p. 77.
15. Cf. P. Maillefer, *Histoire du Canton de Vaud* and *Le Pays de Vaud au XVIIIe siècle*, cited in editor's note in Rousseau, *O.C.*, vol. 2, p. 1635.
16. The qualification may be important. P. J. Wagstaff, 'Nicolas's father: Rétif and *La Vie de mon père*', *Forum for Modern Language Studies*, 16 (1980), 358–67, interestingly argues that the novel was 'fostering some self-imposed illusions about a past life he would dearly love to recapture while realizing that the reality of that life does not measure up to his image of it'. Much of his evidence confirms my view that Rétif 'thought he was convinced', and one may doubt if his 'realizing' to the contrary was as firm or as frequent at that date.
17. M. C. Cook, *Politics in Revolutionary Fiction, St. Volt.*, 201 (1982), 237–340, shows that much the same remained true of the propaganda use made of the pastoral form during the Revolution: it criticised the present and invited the urban citizen to emulate the virtues of the country-dweller (cf. ch. 5).
18. R. Grimsley, 'Rousseau's Paris', in P. Fritz and D. Williams (eds.), *City and Society in the 18th Century* (Toronto, Hakkert, 1973), pp. 3–18.
19. For these and numerous similar quotations cf. Citron, vol. 1, pp. 113–16.
20. L. S. Mercier, *Tableau de Paris*, abridged edition (Louis-Michaud, s.d.), pp. xxiii–xxvii.
21. Saint-Pierre, *Les Etudes de la nature*, vol. 2, pp. 329–31.
22. Cf. in particular L. Crocker, 'Rousseau and the common people', in *Essays on Diderot and the Enlightenment in honor of Otis Fellows* (Geneva, Droz, 1974), p. 93.
23. Rousseau, *O.C.*, vol. 2, pp. 536 and 566–7.
24. In G. Duby and A. Wallon (eds.), *Histoire de la France rurale: L'Age classique des paysans, 1340–1789* (4 vols., Seuil, 1975–6), vol. 2, especially pp. 453, 478, 481 and 500.
25. R. Mandrou, *De la culture populaire aux XVIIe et XVIIIe siècles* (Stock, 1964); G. Bollème, *Les Almanachs populaires* (Paris and The Hague, Mouton, 1969) and *La Bibliothèque bleue* (Julliard, 1971).

10. *Unfinished business*

1. F. Braudel, *Capitalism and Material Life, 1400–1800*, translation by M. Kochan of *Civilisation matérielle et capitalisme* (Colin, 1967) (London, Weidenfeld and Nicolson, 1973), p. 32. Cf. also R. Forster and O. Ranum, *Food and Drink in History: Selections from the Annales* (Baltimore and London, Johns Hopkins U.P., 1979).
2. Cf. K. Thomas, *Man and the Natural World: Changing Attitudes in England, 1500–1800* (London, Allen Lane, 1983); H. Hastings, *Man and Beast in French Thought of the Eighteenth Century* (Baltimore, Johns Hopkins U.P., London, Oxford U.P., and Paris, 'Les Belles Lettres', 1936); G. Boas, *The Happy Beast in French Thought of the 17th Century* (Baltimore, Johns Hopkins U.P., 1933).

3. Hastings, p. 11.
4. Hastings, p. 178; Thomas, pp. 290–5.
5. Cf. J. Passmore, 'The treatment of animals', *Journal of the History of Ideas*, 36 (1975), 195–218.
6. Hastings, p. 269.
7. Rousseau, *O.C.*, vol. 4, p. 411.
8. Rousseau, *O.C.*, vol. 2, p. 453.
9. Hastings, pp. 265 and 281–2. Her view is confirmed as regards one indicator by A. Lytton Sells, *Animal Poetry in French and English Literature and the Greek Tradition* (Bloomington, Indiana U.P., 1955). He finds no 'body of real animal poetry in the eighteenth century in France' (p. 158).
10. Cited in J. Roger, *Les Sciences de la vie dans la pensée française du XVIIIe siècle* (Armand Colin, 1963), p. 406; I am indebted to his study in regard to this problem.
11. E. B. Hill, *The Role of 'le monstre' in Diderot's Thought*, St. Volt., 97 (1972), 147–261, and specifically 170 and 172.
12. A. O. Lovejoy, 'The first Gothic revival and the return to nature', in *Essays in the History of Ideas* (Baltimore, Johns Hopkins U.P., 1948), pp. 136–65.
13. A useful factual account of the *querelle* is L. Richebourg, *Contribution à l'histoire de la 'Querelle des Bouffons'* (Nizet et Bastard, 1937), with a full bibliography.
14. *Lettre sur la musique française* in *Oeuvres de J. J. Rousseau*, vol. 3, *Ecrits sur la musique* (Desenne, 1831), pp. 247ff. and specifically p. 254.
15. Cf. C. Kiernan, 'Rousseau and music in the French Enlightenment', *French Studies*, 26 (1972), 156–65.
16. Paul Van Tieghem, *Le Sentiment de la nature dans le préromantisme européen* (Nizet, 1960), p. 264.
17. M. M. Kahr, *Dutch Painting in the Seventeenth Century* (New York, Harper and Row, 1978), p. ix.
18. W. Stechow, *Dutch Landscape Painting of the Seventeenth Century*, 3rd edn (Oxford, Phaidon, 1981), p. 82.
19. Thomas, p. 303, as for the following quotation.
20. J. McManners, *Death and the Enlightenment* (Oxford, Clarendon Press, 1981), p. 462.
21. R. Dubos, *The Wooing of Earth: new perspectives on man's use of nature* (London, Athlone Press, 1980).

INDEX

Index

Index

Index

Index

Index